VOLUME 3
AUDEAMUS

FBP.
FEDERAL BUREAU OF PHYSICS

D1210928

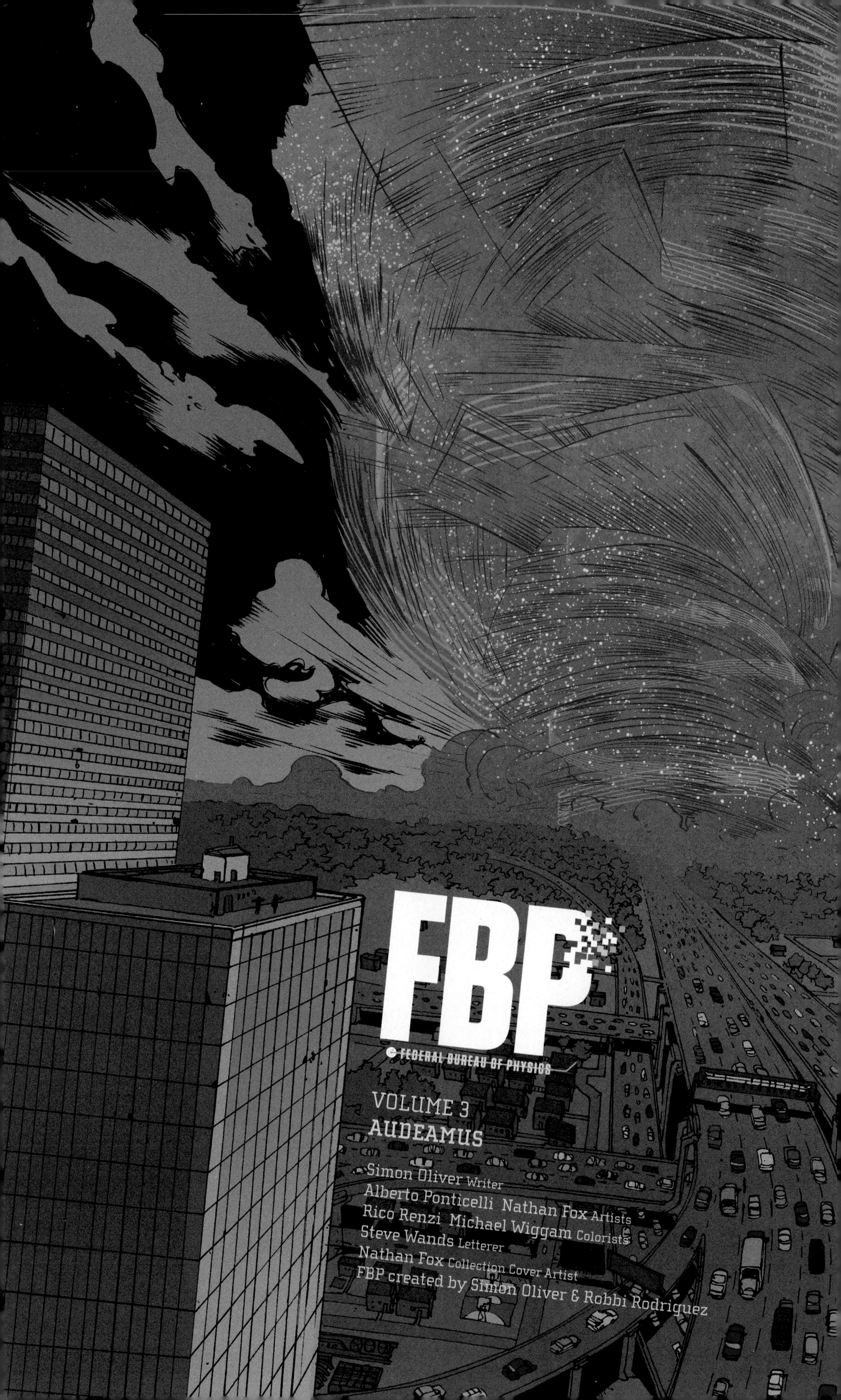

FBP

FEDERAL BUREAU OF PHYSICS

VOLUME 3

AUDEAMUS

Simon Oliver Writer
Alberto Ponticelli Nathan Fox Artists
Rico Renzi Michael Wiggam Colorists
Steve Wands Letterer
Nathan Fox Collection Cover Artist
FBP created by Simon Oliver & Robbi Rodriguez

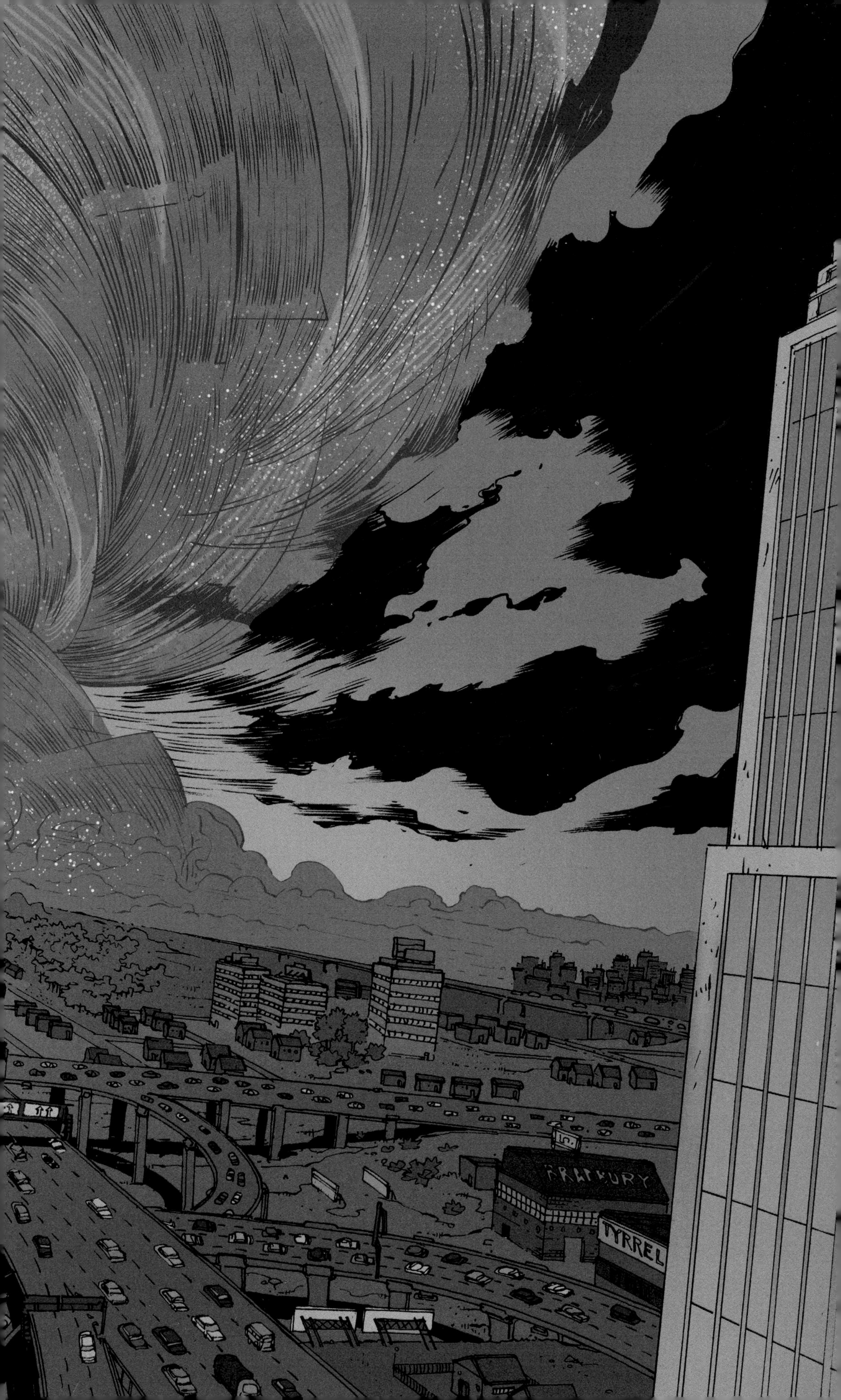
TYRREL

Greg Lockard Editor – Original Series
Sara Miller Assistant Editor – Original Series
Liz Erickson Editor
Robbin Brosterman Design Director – Books
Chris Griggs Publication Design

Shelly Bond Executive Editor - Vertigo
Hank Kanalz Senior VP – Vertigo & Integrated Publishing

Diane Nelson President
Dan DiDio and Jim Lee Co-Publishers
Geoff Johns Chief Creative Officer
Amit Desai Senior VP – Marketing & Franchise Management
Amy Genkins Senior VP – Business & Legal Affairs
Nairi Gardiner Senior VP – Finance
Jeff Boison VP – Publishing Planning
Mark Chiarello VP – Art Direction & Design
John Cunningham VP – Marketing
Terri Cunningham VP – Editorial Administration
Larry Ganem VP – Talent Relations & Services
Alison Gill Senior VP – Manufacturing & Operations
Jay Kogan VP – Business & Legal Affairs, Publishing
Jack Mahan VP – Business Affairs, Talent
Nick Napolitano VP – Manufacturing Administration
Sue Pohja VP – Book Sales
Fred Ruiz VP – Manufacturing Operations
Courtney Simmons Senior VP – Publicity
Bob Wayne Senior VP – Sales

FBP VOLUME 3: AUDEAMUS

Published by DC Comics. Copyright © 2015 Simon Oliver and Robbi Rodriguez.
All Rights Reserved.

Originally published in single magazine form in FBP: FEDERAL BUREAU OF
PHYSICS 14-19 © 2014, 2015 Simon Oliver and Robbi Rodriguez. All Rights
Reserved. All characters, their distinctive likenesses and related elements
featured in this publication are trademarks of DC Comics. VERTIGO is a
trademark of DC Comics. The stories, characters and incidents featured in
this publication are entirely fictional. DC Comics does not read or accept
unsolicited ideas, stories or artwork.

DC Comics, 4000 Warner Blvd., Burbank, CA 91522
A Warner Bros. Entertainment Company.
Printed by RR Donnelley, Owensville, MO, USA. 4/17/15. First Printing.
ISBN: 978-1-4012-5434-6

SUSTAINABLE FORESTRY INITIATIVE

Certified Chain of Custody
20% Certified Forest Content,
80% Certified Sourcing
www.sfiprogram.org
SFI-01042
APPLIES TO TEXT STOCK ONLY

Library of Congress Cataloging-in-Publication Data

Oliver, Simon.
FBP : Federal Bureau of Physics. Vol. 3 / Simon Oliver ; [illustrated
by] Alberto Ponticelli.
pages cm
ISBN 978-1-4012-5434-6 (pbk.)
1. Graphic novels. I. Title. II. Title:
PN6727.O5F37 2014
741.5'973—dc23
2013045685

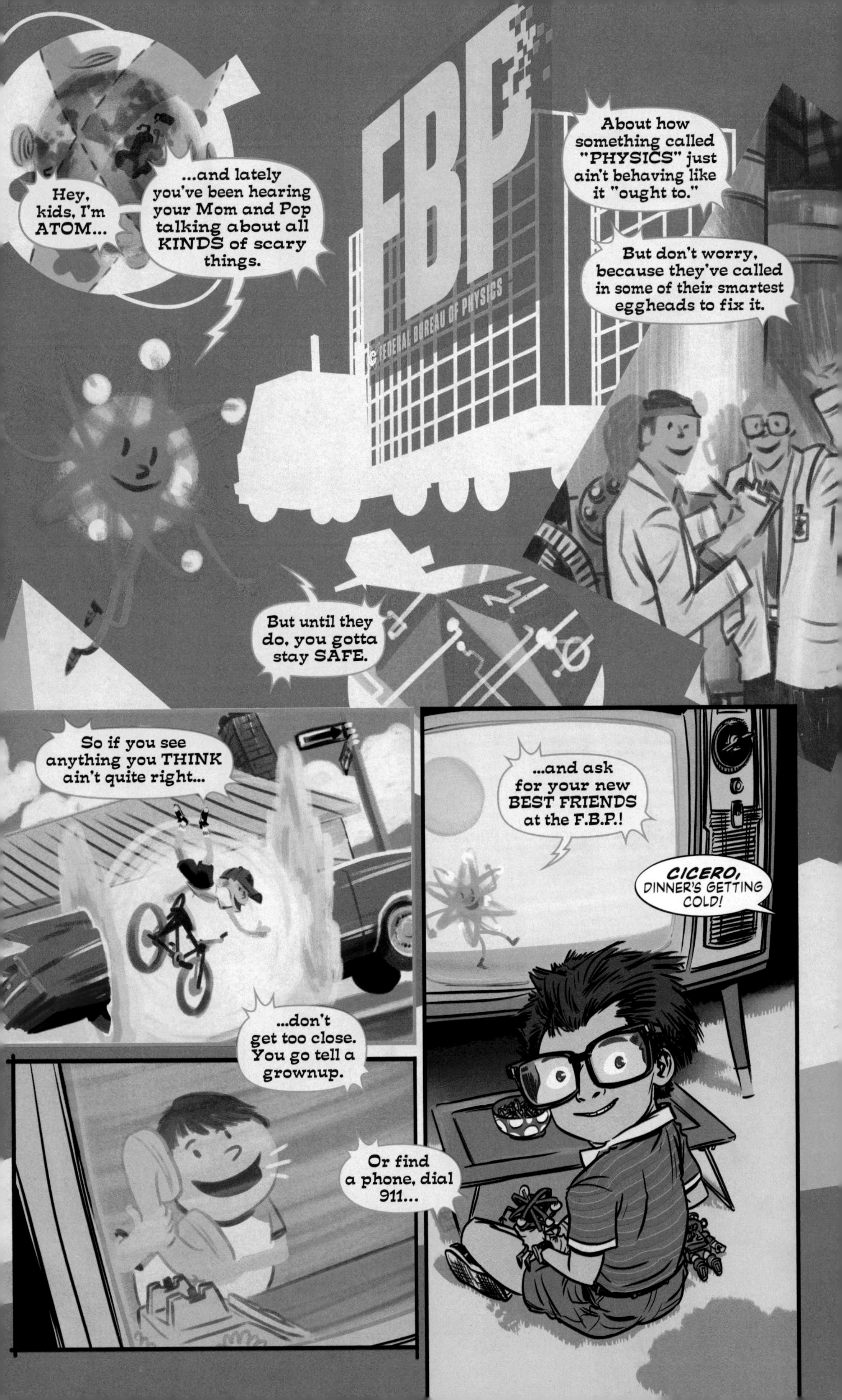
Hey, kids, I'm ATOM...
...and lately you've been hearing your Mom and Pop talking about all KINDS of scary things.
FBP
FEDERAL BUREAU OF PHYSICS
About how something called "PHYSICS" just ain't behaving like it "ought to."
But don't worry, because they've called in some of their smartest eggheads to fix it.
But until they do, you gotta stay SAFE.
So if you see anything you THINK ain't quite right...
...don't get too close. You go tell a grownup.
Or find a phone, dial 911...
...and ask for your new BEST FRIENDS at the F.B.P.!
CICERO, DINNER'S GETTING COLD!

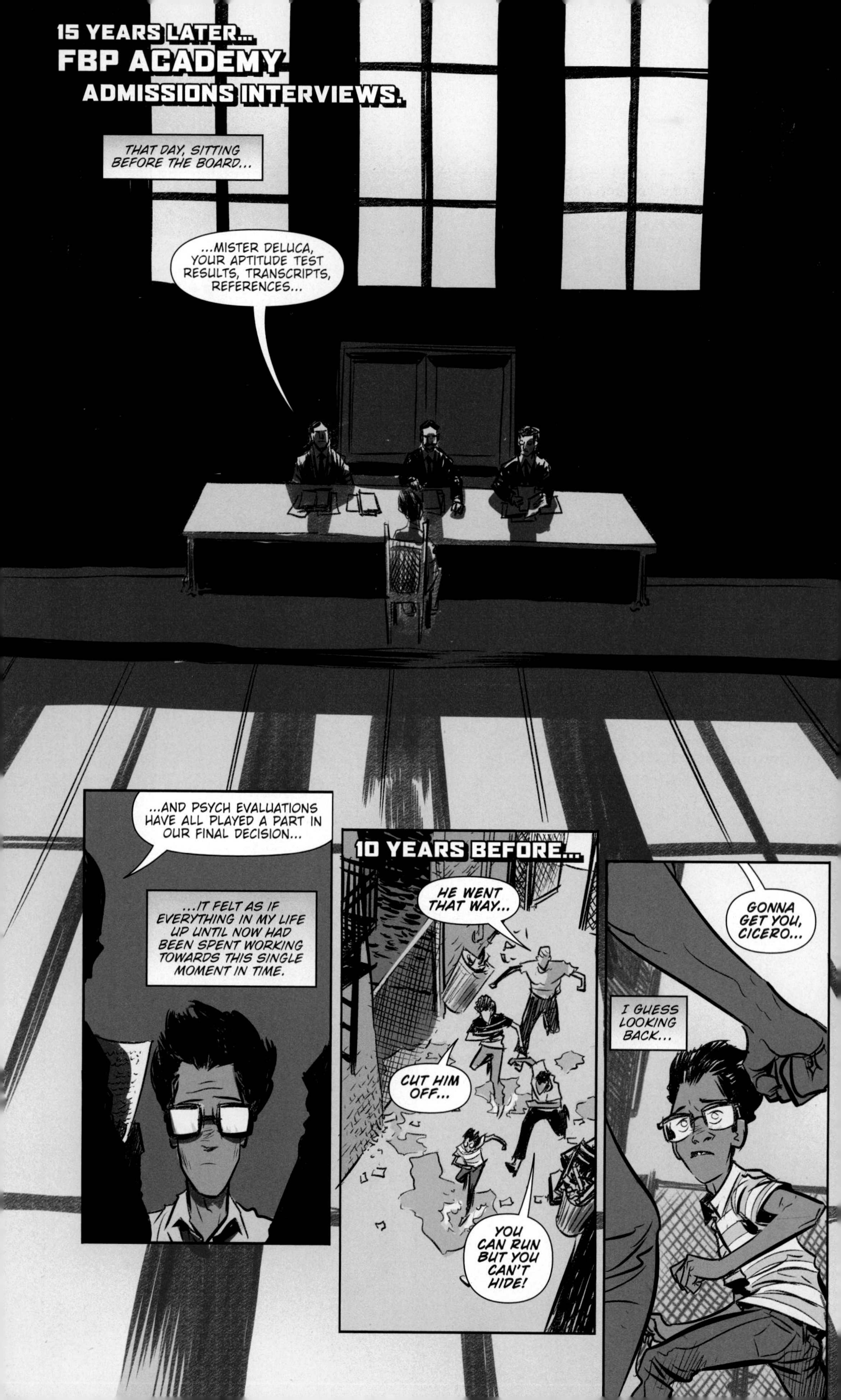
15 YEARS LATER...
FBP ACADEMY
ADMISSIONS INTERVIEWS.
THAT DAY, SITTING BEFORE THE BOARD...
...MISTER DELUCA, YOUR APTITUDE TEST RESULTS, TRANSCRIPTS, REFERENCES...
...AND PSYCH EVALUATIONS HAVE ALL PLAYED A PART IN OUR FINAL DECISION...
...IT FELT AS IF EVERYTHING IN MY LIFE UP UNTIL NOW HAD BEEN SPENT WORKING TOWARDS THIS SINGLE MOMENT IN TIME.
10 YEARS BEFORE...
HE WENT THAT WAY...
CUT HIM OFF...
YOU CAN RUN BUT YOU CAN'T HIDE!
GONNA GET YOU, CICERO...
I GUESS LOOKING BACK...

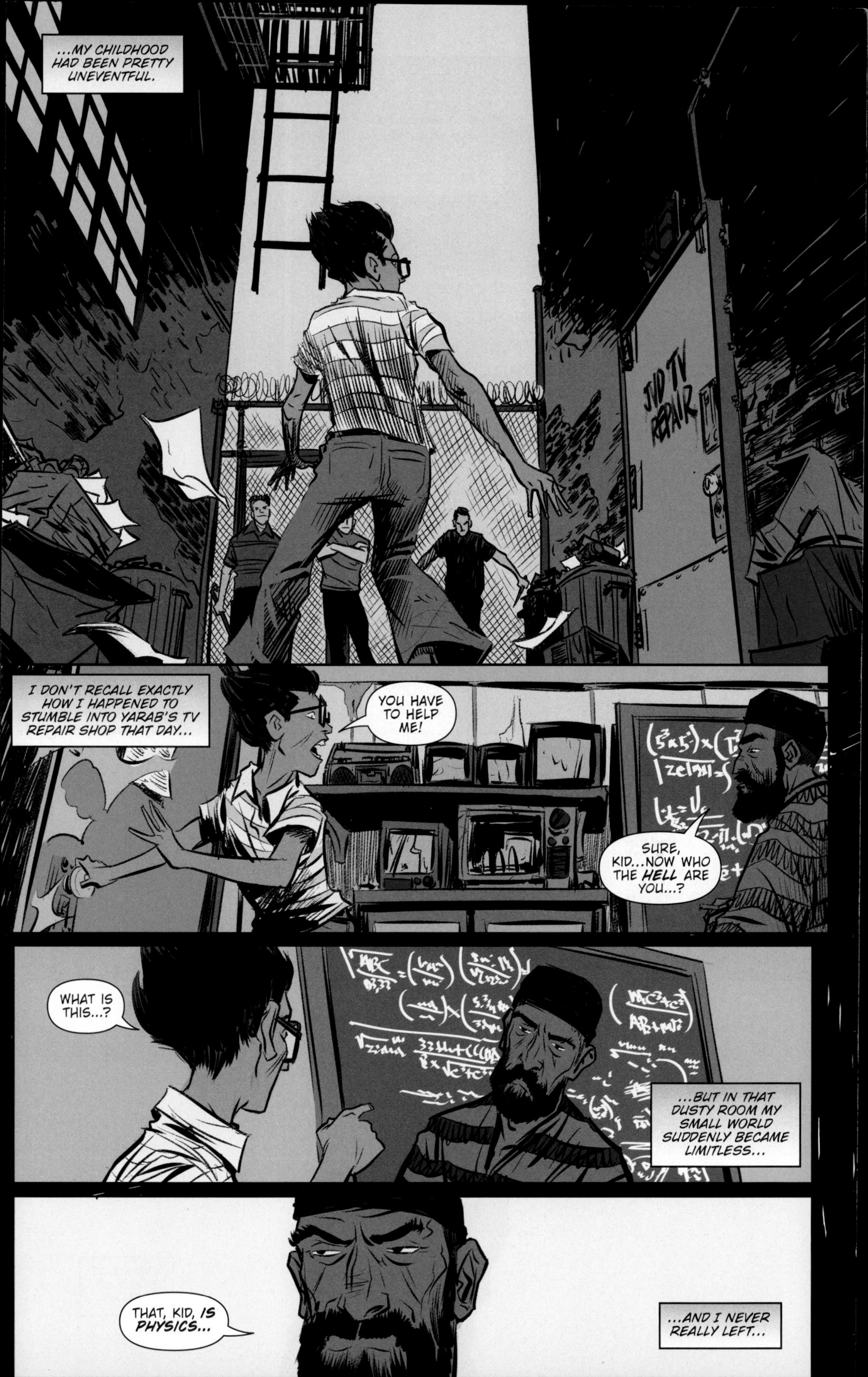
...MY CHILDHOOD HAD BEEN PRETTY UNEVENTFUL.
JVD TV REPAIR
I DON'T RECALL EXACTLY HOW I HAPPENED TO STUMBLE INTO YARAB'S TV REPAIR SHOP THAT DAY...
YOU HAVE TO HELP ME!
SURE, KID...NOW WHO THE HELL ARE YOU...?
WHAT IS THIS...?
...BUT IN THAT DUSTY ROOM MY SMALL WORLD SUDDENLY BECAME LIMITLESS...
THAT, KID, IS PHYSICS...
...AND I NEVER REALLY LEFT...

YARAB PATIENTLY TUTORED ME IN EVERYTHING MY PUBLIC SCHOOL EDUCATION HAD DEEMED TOO "ADVANCED," AND IN RETURN I FIXED THE BROKEN TVs...

...AND IT WASN'T LONG BEFORE THE UNIVERSE BEGAN TO WHISPER ITS SECRETS TO ME...

$E=MC^2$

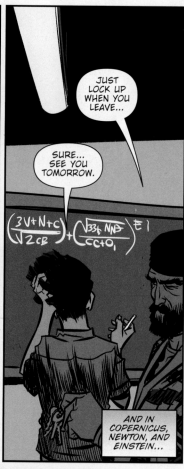

JUST LOCK UP WHEN YOU LEAVE...

SURE... SEE YOU TOMORROW.

AND IN COPERNICUS, NEWTON, AND EINSTEIN...

I'D FINALLY FOUND THE HEROES I'D BEEN LOOKING FOR ALL MY LIFE...

...SO? THEY WANT YOUR SORRY BUTT IN THEIR FANCY ACADEMY OR NOT???

I GOT IN...

AND I WAS GIVEN MY CHANCE...

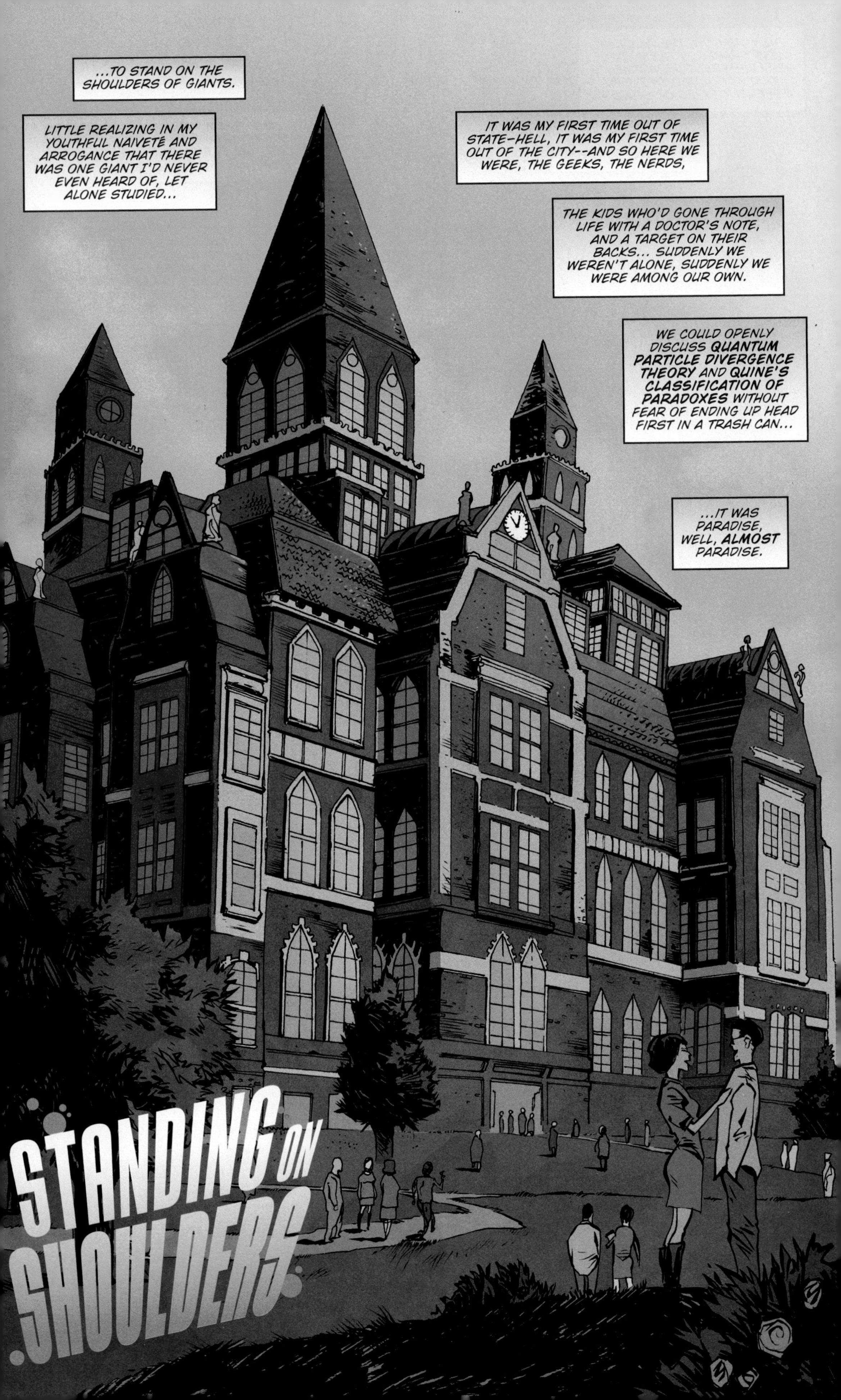
...TO STAND ON THE SHOULDERS OF GIANTS.
LITTLE REALIZING IN MY YOUTHFUL NAIVETÉ AND ARROGANCE THAT THERE WAS ONE GIANT I'D NEVER EVEN HEARD OF, LET ALONE STUDIED...
IT WAS MY FIRST TIME OUT OF STATE--HELL, IT WAS MY FIRST TIME OUT OF THE CITY--AND SO HERE WE WERE, THE GEEKS, THE NERDS,
THE KIDS WHO'D GONE THROUGH LIFE WITH A DOCTOR'S NOTE, AND A TARGET ON THEIR BACKS... SUDDENLY WE WEREN'T ALONE, SUDDENLY WE WERE AMONG OUR OWN.
WE COULD OPENLY DISCUSS **QUANTUM PARTICLE DIVERGENCE THEORY** AND **QUINE'S CLASSIFICATION OF PARADOXES** WITHOUT FEAR OF ENDING UP HEAD FIRST IN A TRASH CAN...
...IT WAS PARADISE, WELL, **ALMOST** PARADISE.
STANDING ON SHOULDERS

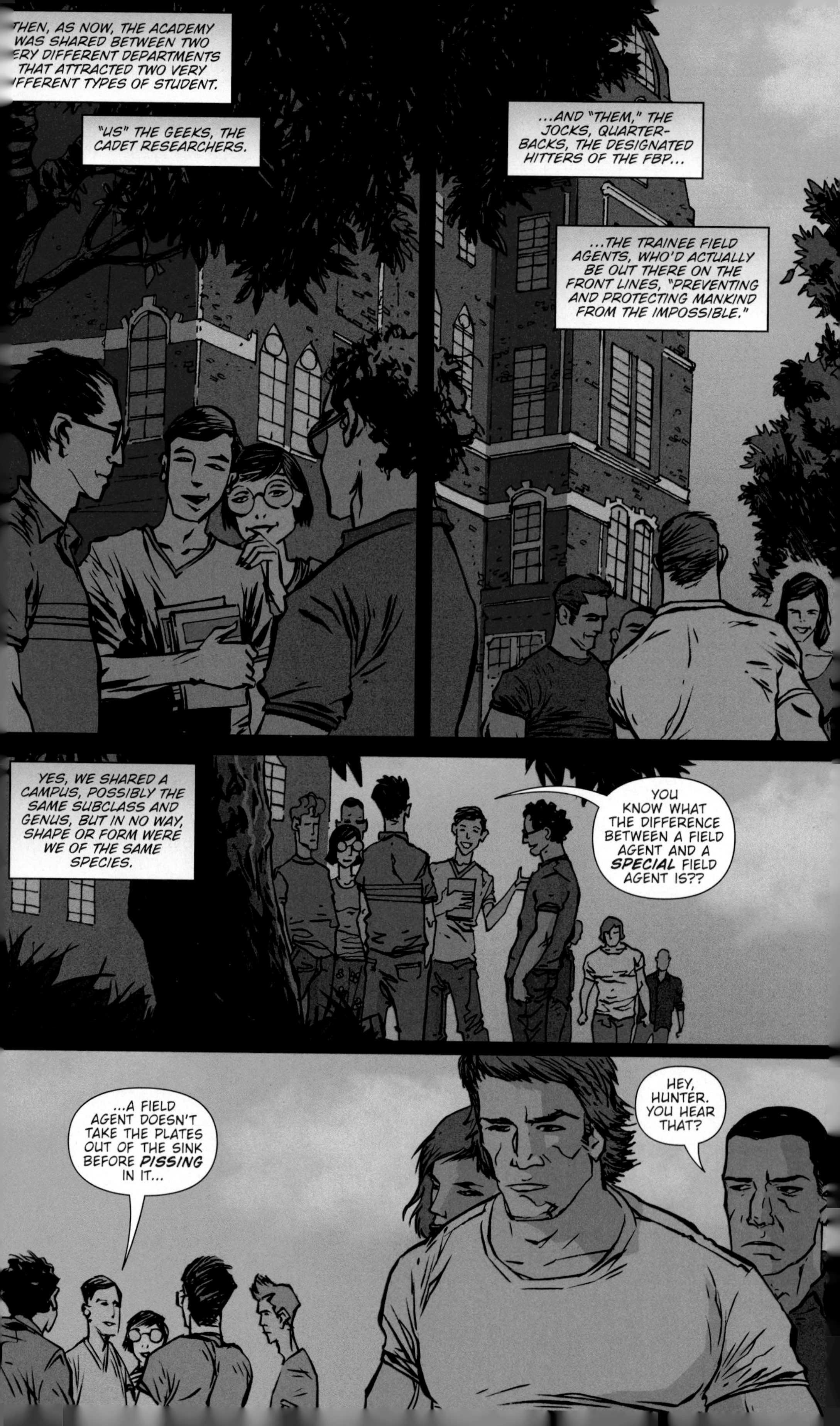
THEN, AS NOW, THE ACADEMY WAS SHARED BETWEEN TWO VERY DIFFERENT DEPARTMENTS THAT ATTRACTED TWO VERY DIFFERENT TYPES OF STUDENT.
"US" THE GEEKS, THE CADET RESEARCHERS.
...AND "THEM," THE JOCKS, QUARTER-BACKS, THE DESIGNATED HITTERS OF THE FBP...
...THE TRAINEE FIELD AGENTS, WHO'D ACTUALLY BE OUT THERE ON THE FRONT LINES, "PREVENTING AND PROTECTING MANKIND FROM THE IMPOSSIBLE."
YES, WE SHARED A CAMPUS, POSSIBLY THE SAME SUBCLASS AND GENUS, BUT IN NO WAY, SHAPE OR FORM WERE WE OF THE SAME SPECIES.
YOU KNOW WHAT THE DIFFERENCE BETWEEN A FIELD AGENT AND A SPECIAL FIELD AGENT IS??
...A FIELD AGENT DOESN'T TAKE THE PLATES OUT OF THE SINK BEFORE PISSING IN IT...
HEY, HUNTER. YOU HEAR THAT?

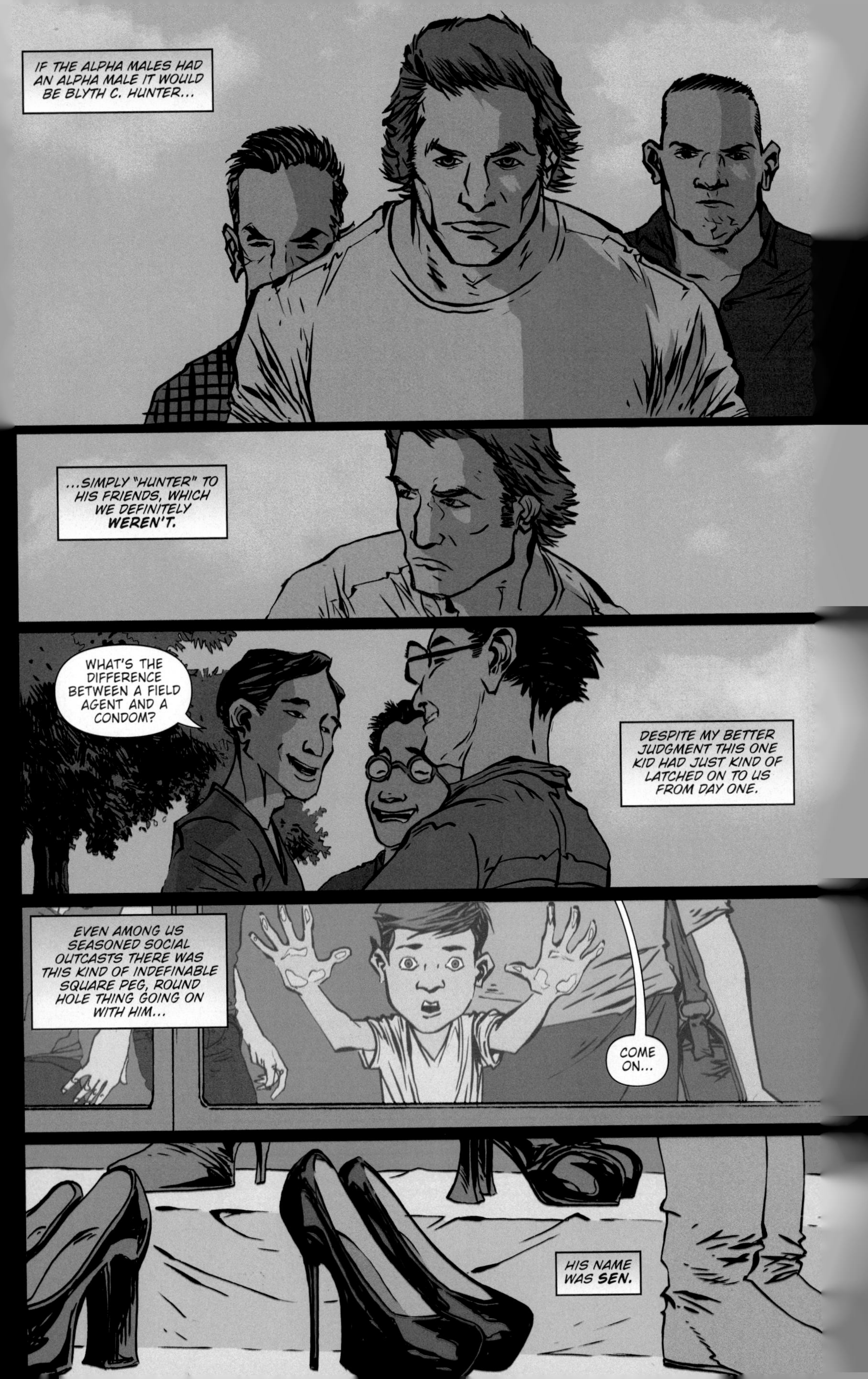
IF THE ALPHA MALES HAD AN ALPHA MALE IT WOULD BE BLYTH C. HUNTER...
...SIMPLY "HUNTER" TO HIS FRIENDS, WHICH WE DEFINITELY WEREN'T.
WHAT'S THE DIFFERENCE BETWEEN A FIELD AGENT AND A CONDOM?
DESPITE MY BETTER JUDGMENT THIS ONE KID HAD JUST KIND OF LATCHED ON TO US FROM DAY ONE.
EVEN AMONG US SEASONED SOCIAL OUTCASTS THERE WAS THIS KIND OF INDEFINABLE SQUARE PEG, ROUND HOLE THING GOING ON WITH HIM...
COME ON...
HIS NAME WAS SEN.

...OTHING WAS OFF LIMITS 'N OUR NEW SCIENTIFIC SHANGRI-LA...

...SO TO EXERT CONTROL OVER A SINGLE OBJECT IN THIS MANNER, AND UNDER LABORATORY CONDITIONS I WOULD...?

...ANYONE?

MISTER DELUCA...?

...AND UPON GRADUATION WE WOULD BE EXPECTED TO PICK A SINGLE METAPHORICAL CORNER OF THE PHYSICS UNIVERSE TO CREATE A RESEARCH CAREER FROM...

...CREATE A LOCALIZED GRAVITY FIELD.

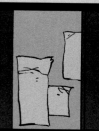

VERY GOOD...

BUT NO MATTER HOW SIMPLE-MINDED WE VIEWED THE FIELD AGENT TRAINING, THERE WAS ONE MANDATORY REQUIREMENT NONE OF US ENVIED THEM FOR...

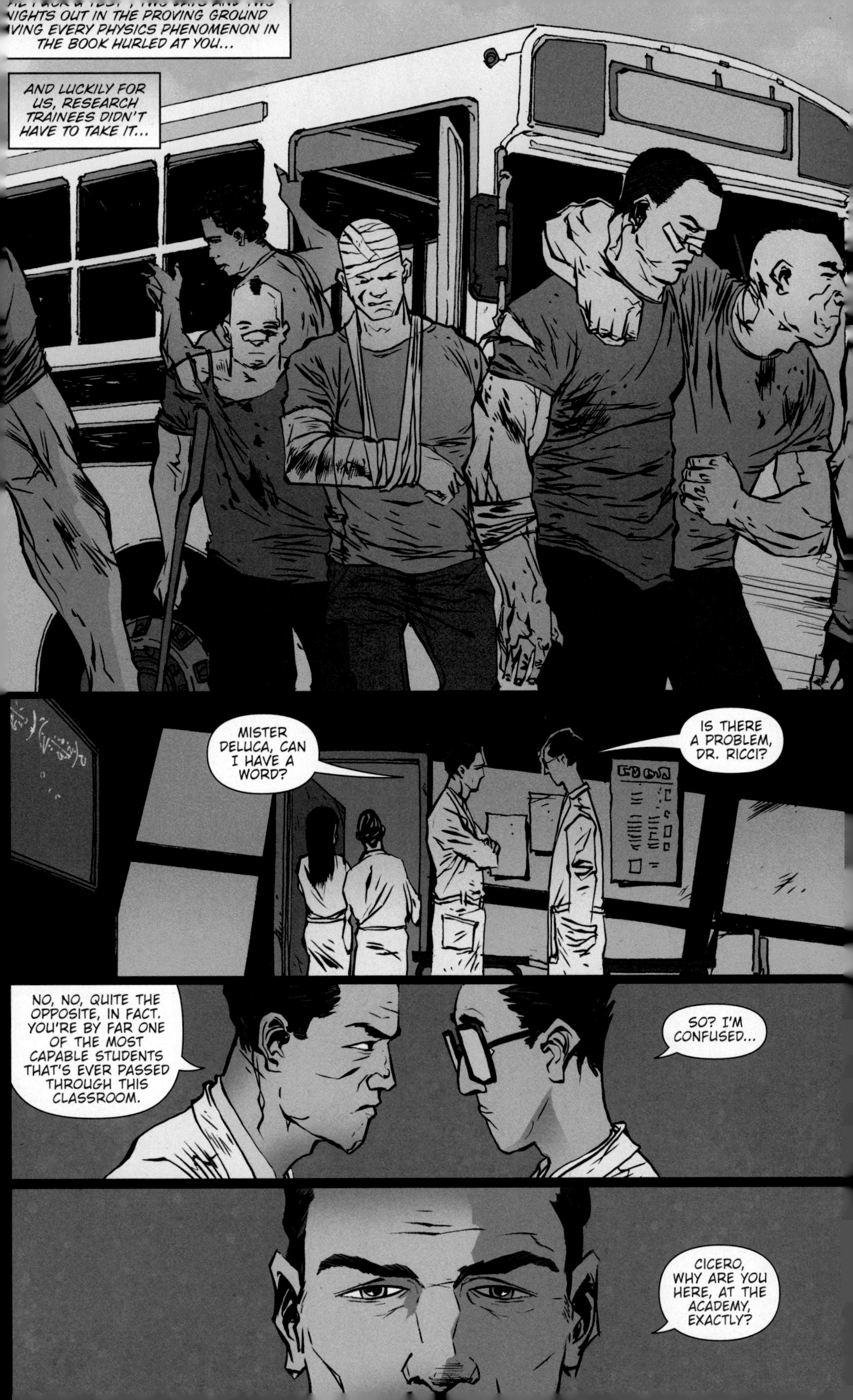

NIGHTS OUT IN THE PROVING GROUND
VING EVERY PHYSICS PHENOMENON IN THE BOOK HURLED AT YOU...
AND LUCKILY FOR US, RESEARCH TRAINEES DIDN'T HAVE TO TAKE IT...
MISTER DELUCA, CAN I HAVE A WORD?
IS THERE A PROBLEM, DR. RICCI?
NO, NO, QUITE THE OPPOSITE, IN FACT. YOU'RE BY FAR ONE OF THE MOST CAPABLE STUDENTS THAT'S EVER PASSED THROUGH THIS CLASSROOM.
SO? I'M CONFUSED...
CICERO, WHY ARE YOU HERE, AT THE ACADEMY, EXACTLY?

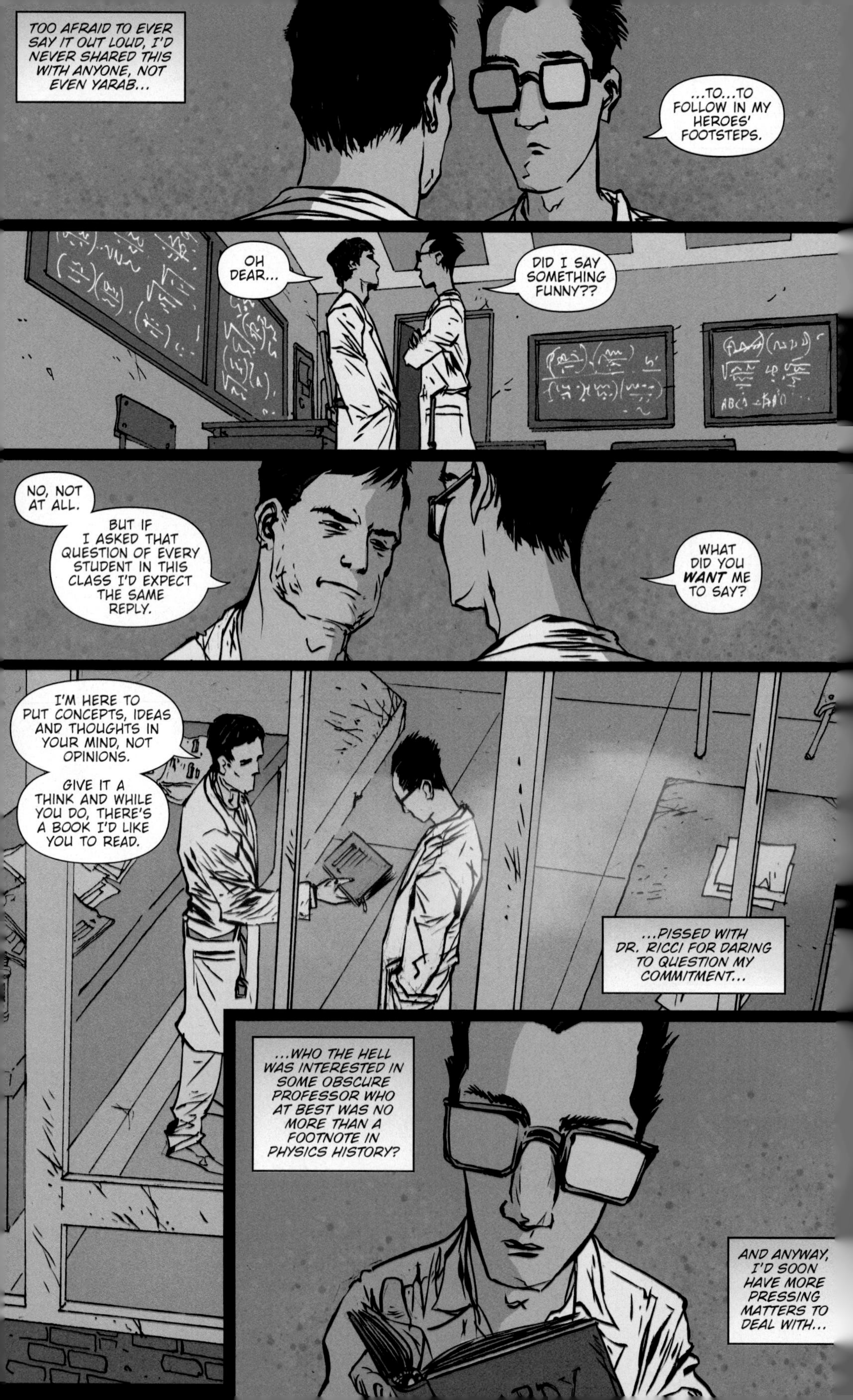
TOO AFRAID TO EVER SAY IT OUT LOUD, I'D NEVER SHARED THIS WITH ANYONE, NOT EVEN YARAB...
...TO...TO FOLLOW IN MY HEROES' FOOTSTEPS.
OH DEAR...
DID I SAY SOMETHING FUNNY??
NO, NOT AT ALL.
BUT IF I ASKED THAT QUESTION OF EVERY STUDENT IN THIS CLASS I'D EXPECT THE SAME REPLY.
WHAT DID YOU WANT ME TO SAY?
I'M HERE TO PUT CONCEPTS, IDEAS AND THOUGHTS IN YOUR MIND, NOT OPINIONS.
GIVE IT A THINK AND WHILE YOU DO, THERE'S A BOOK I'D LIKE YOU TO READ.
...PISSED WITH DR. RICCI FOR DARING TO QUESTION MY COMMITMENT...
...WHO THE HELL WAS INTERESTED IN SOME OBSCURE PROFESSOR WHO AT BEST WAS NO MORE THAN A FOOTNOTE IN PHYSICS HISTORY?
AND ANYWAY, I'D SOON HAVE MORE PRESSING MATTERS TO DEAL WITH...

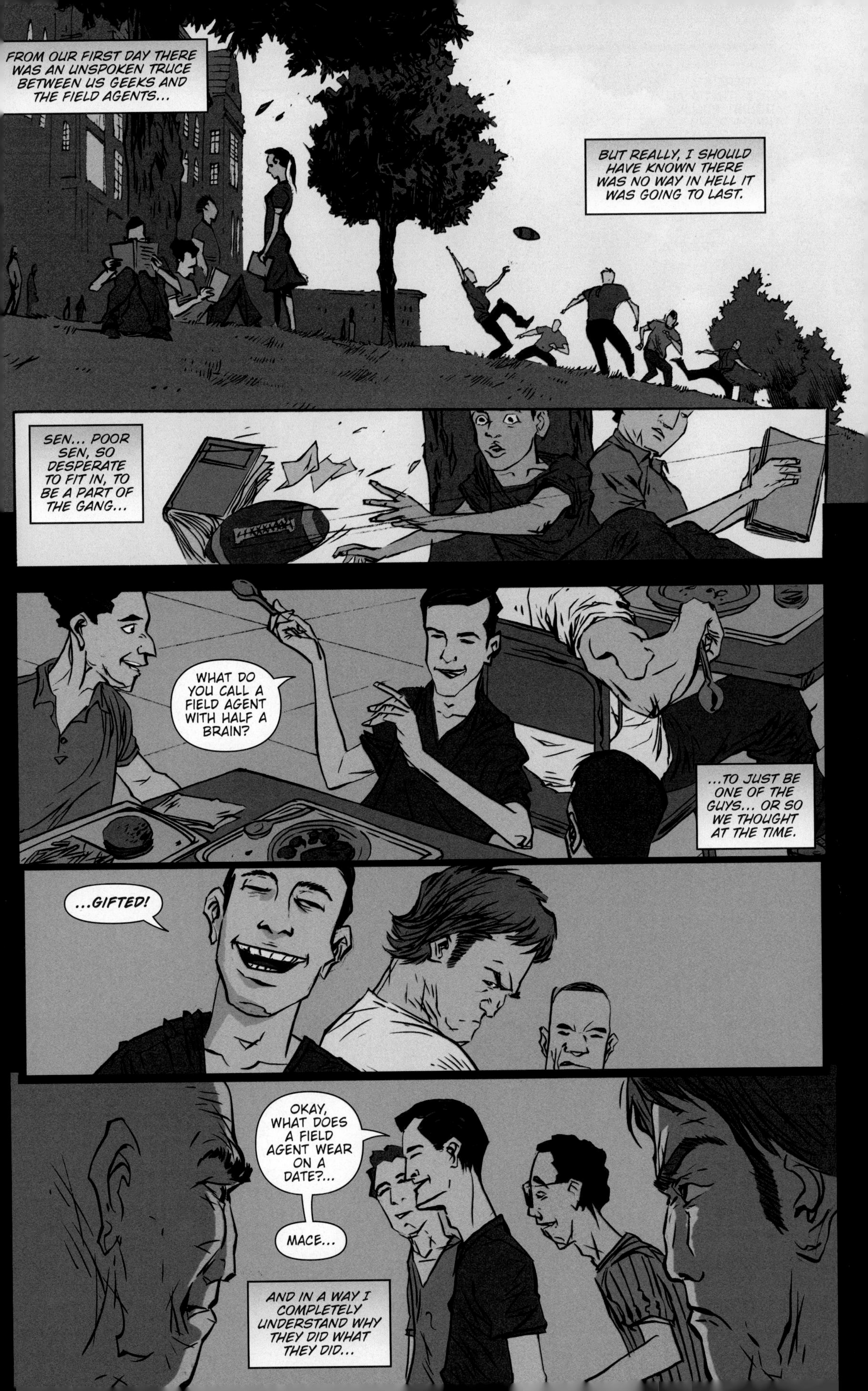
FROM OUR FIRST DAY THERE WAS AN UNSPOKEN TRUCE BETWEEN US GEEKS AND THE FIELD AGENTS...
BUT REALLY, I SHOULD HAVE KNOWN THERE WAS NO WAY IN HELL IT WAS GOING TO LAST.
SEN... POOR SEN, SO DESPERATE TO FIT IN, TO BE A PART OF THE GANG...
WHAT DO YOU CALL A FIELD AGENT WITH HALF A BRAIN?
...TO JUST BE ONE OF THE GUYS... OR SO WE THOUGHT AT THE TIME.
...GIFTED!
OKAY, WHAT DOES A FIELD AGENT WEAR ON A DATE?...
MACE...
AND IN A WAY I COMPLETELY UNDERSTAND WHY THEY DID WHAT THEY DID...

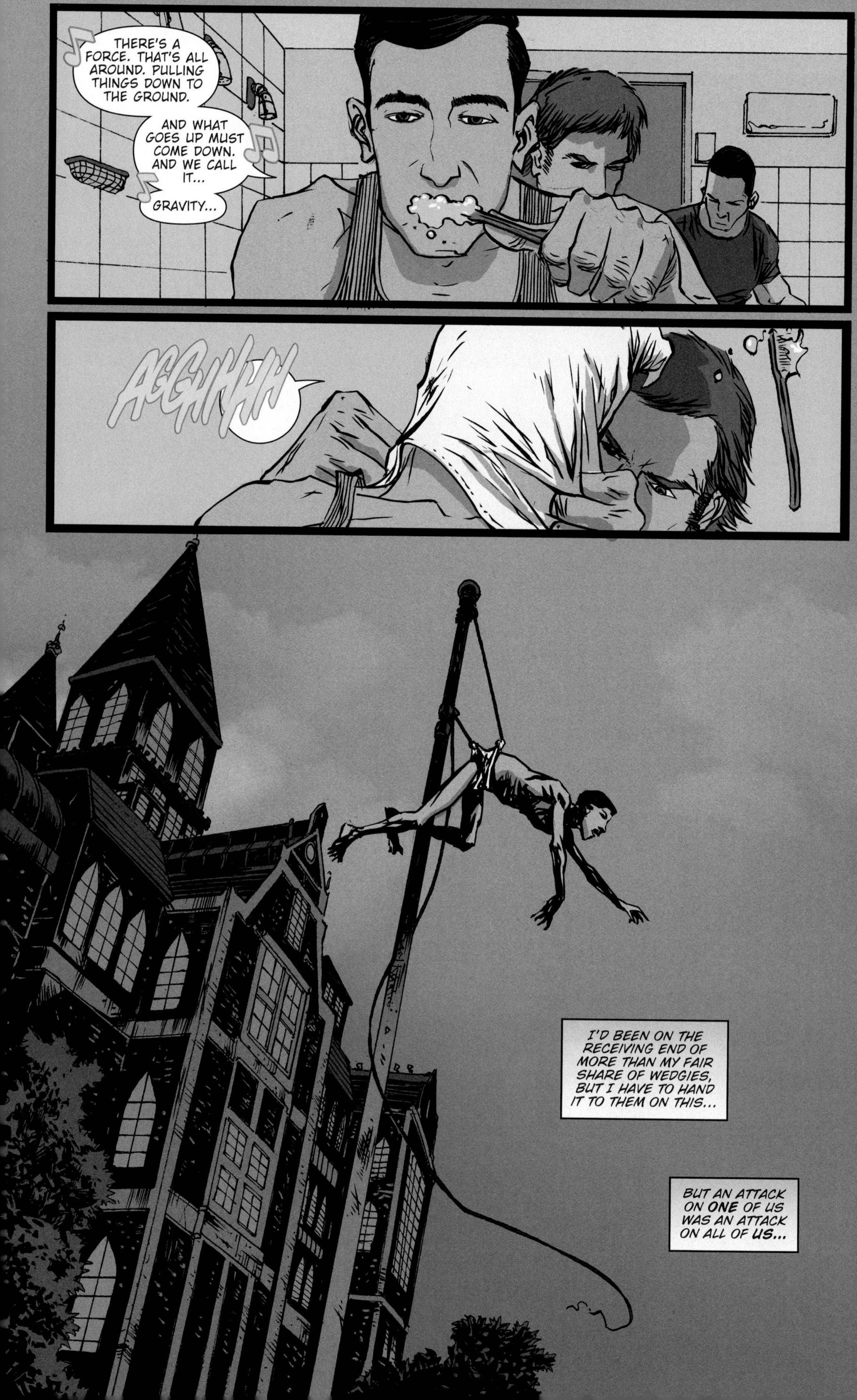
THERE'S A FORCE. THAT'S ALL AROUND. PULLING THINGS DOWN TO THE GROUND.
AND WHAT GOES UP MUST COME DOWN. AND WE CALL IT...
GRAVITY...
AGGHHHH
I'D BEEN ON THE RECEIVING END OF MORE THAN MY FAIR SHARE OF WEDGIES, BUT I HAVE TO HAND IT TO THEM ON THIS...
BUT AN ATTACK ON ONE OF US WAS AN ATTACK ON ALL OF US...

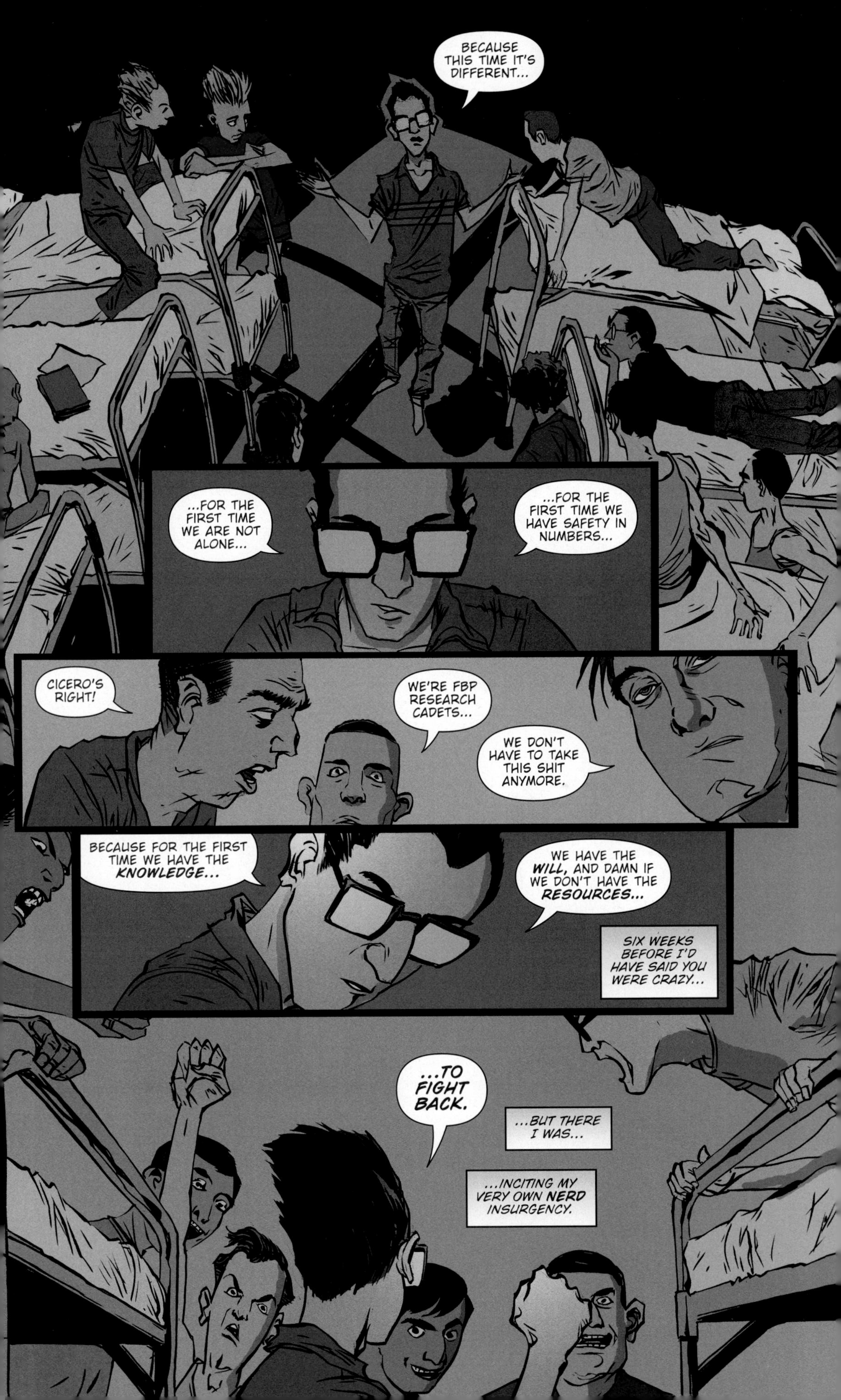

BECAUSE THIS TIME IT'S DIFFERENT...
...FOR THE FIRST TIME WE ARE NOT ALONE...
...FOR THE FIRST TIME WE HAVE SAFETY IN NUMBERS...
CICERO'S RIGHT!
WE'RE FBP RESEARCH CADETS...
WE DON'T HAVE TO TAKE THIS SHIT ANYMORE.
BECAUSE FOR THE FIRST TIME WE HAVE THE KNOWLEDGE...
WE HAVE THE WILL, AND DAMN IF WE DON'T HAVE THE RESOURCES...
SIX WEEKS BEFORE I'D HAVE SAID YOU WERE CRAZY...
...TO FIGHT BACK.
...BUT THERE I WAS...
...INCITING MY VERY OWN NERD INSURGENCY.

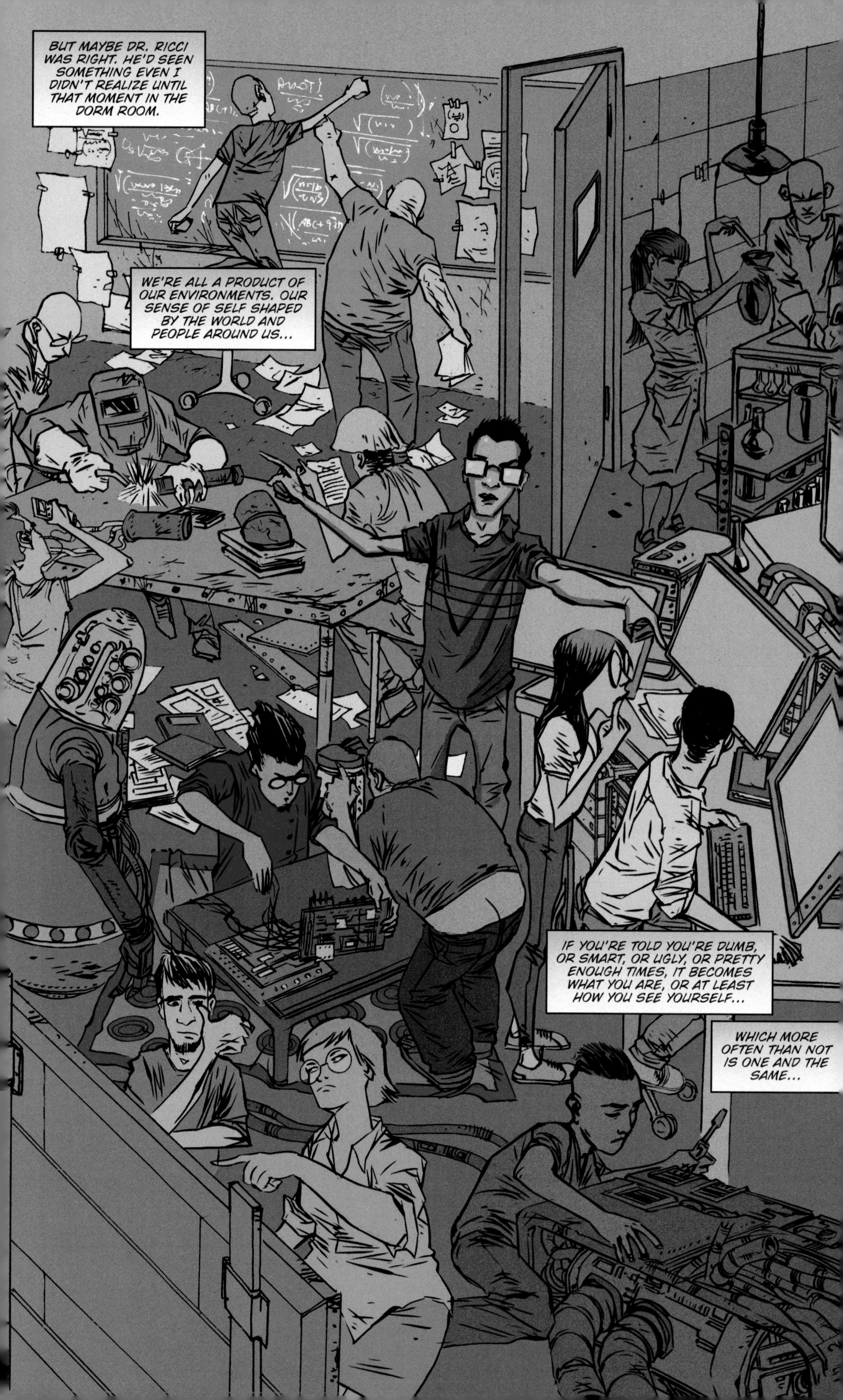
BUT MAYBE DR. RICCI WAS RIGHT. HE'D SEEN SOMETHING EVEN I DIDN'T REALIZE UNTIL THAT MOMENT IN THE DORM ROOM.
WE'RE ALL A PRODUCT OF OUR ENVIRONMENTS. OUR SENSE OF SELF SHAPED BY THE WORLD AND PEOPLE AROUND US...
IF YOU'RE TOLD YOU'RE DUMB, OR SMART, OR UGLY, OR PRETTY ENOUGH TIMES, IT BECOMES WHAT YOU ARE, OR AT LEAST HOW YOU SEE YOURSELF...
WHICH MORE OFTEN THAN NOT IS ONE AND THE SAME...

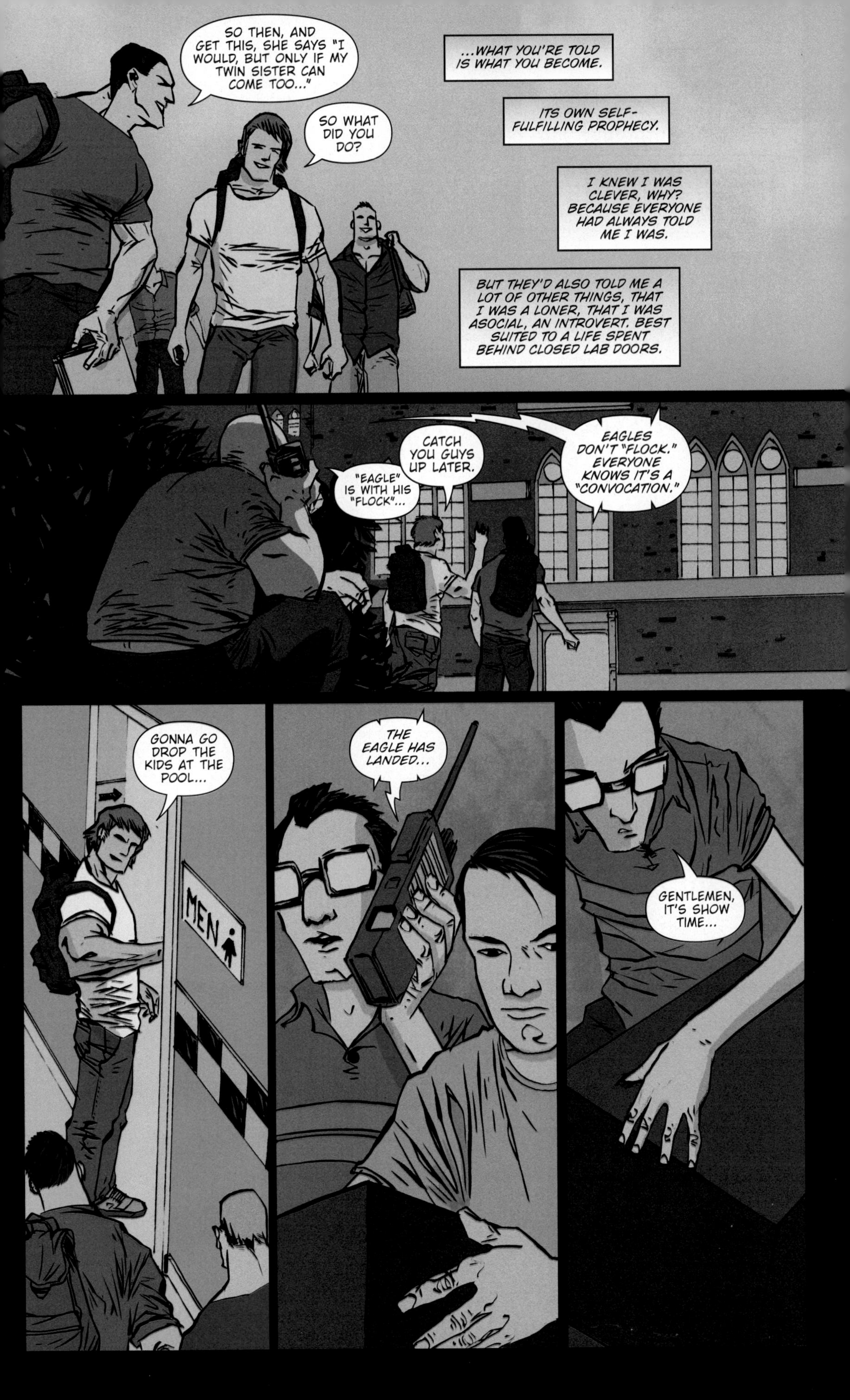
SO THEN, AND GET THIS, SHE SAYS "I WOULD, BUT ONLY IF MY TWIN SISTER CAN COME TOO..."
SO WHAT DID YOU DO?
...WHAT YOU'RE TOLD IS WHAT YOU BECOME.
ITS OWN SELF-FULFILLING PROPHECY.
I KNEW I WAS CLEVER, WHY? BECAUSE EVERYONE HAD ALWAYS TOLD ME I WAS.
BUT THEY'D ALSO TOLD ME A LOT OF OTHER THINGS, THAT I WAS A LONER, THAT I WAS ASOCIAL, AN INTROVERT. BEST SUITED TO A LIFE SPENT BEHIND CLOSED LAB DOORS.
"EAGLE" IS WITH HIS "FLOCK"...
CATCH YOU GUYS UP LATER.
EAGLES DON'T "FLOCK." EVERYONE KNOWS IT'S A "CONVOCATION."
GONNA GO DROP THE KIDS AT THE POOL...
MEN
THE EAGLE HAS LANDED...
GENTLEMEN, IT'S SHOW TIME...

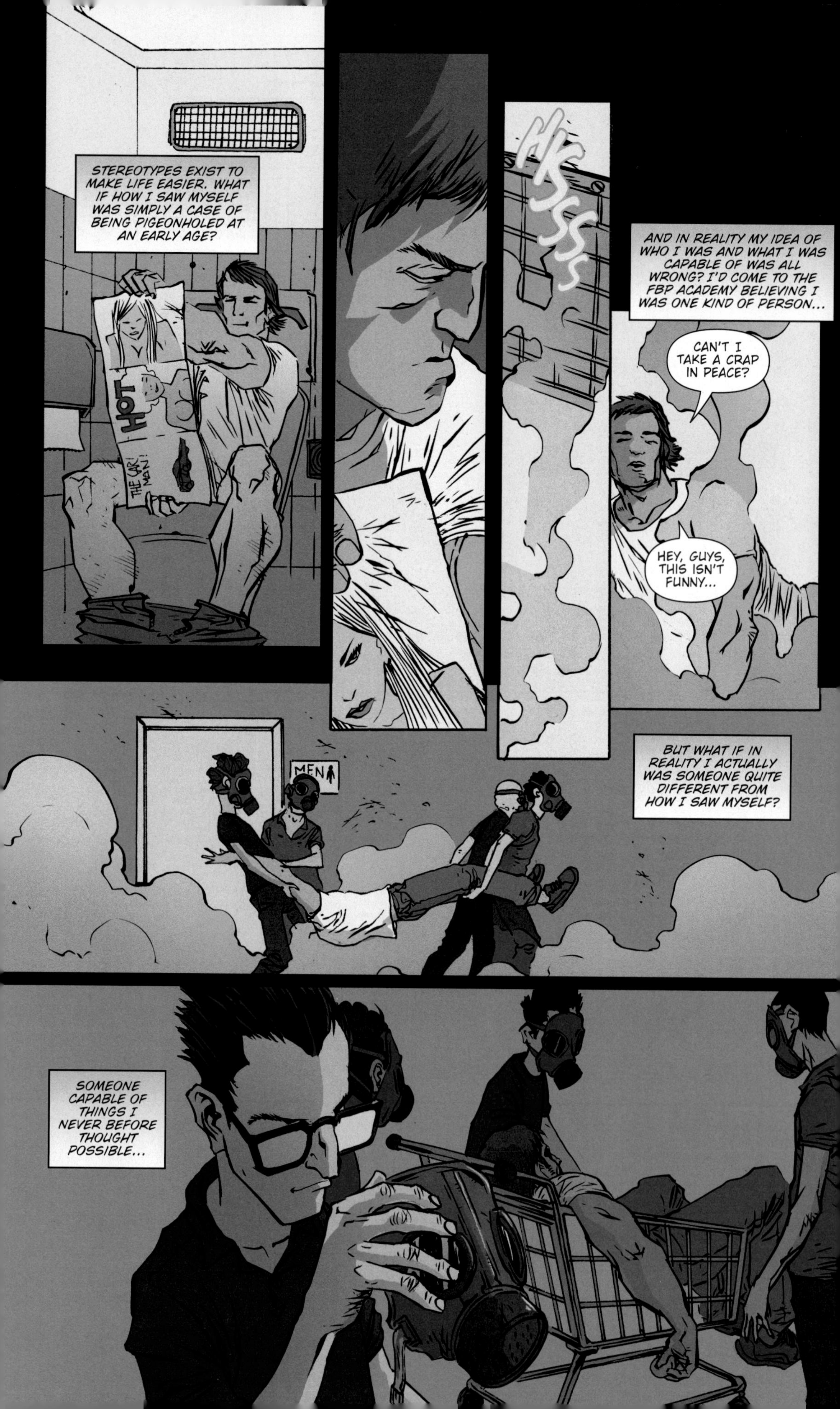
STEREOTYPES EXIST TO MAKE LIFE EASIER. WHAT IF HOW I SAW MYSELF WAS SIMPLY A CASE OF BEING PIGEONHOLED AT AN EARLY AGE?
HOT
THE CAR! MAN!
HKSSSS
AND IN REALITY MY IDEA OF WHO I WAS AND WHAT I WAS CAPABLE OF WAS ALL WRONG? I'D COME TO THE FBP ACADEMY BELIEVING I WAS ONE KIND OF PERSON...
CAN'T I TAKE A CRAP IN PEACE?
HEY, GUYS, THIS ISN'T FUNNY...
MEN
BUT WHAT IF IN REALITY I ACTUALLY WAS SOMEONE QUITE DIFFERENT FROM HOW I SAW MYSELF?
SOMEONE CAPABLE OF THINGS I NEVER BEFORE THOUGHT POSSIBLE...

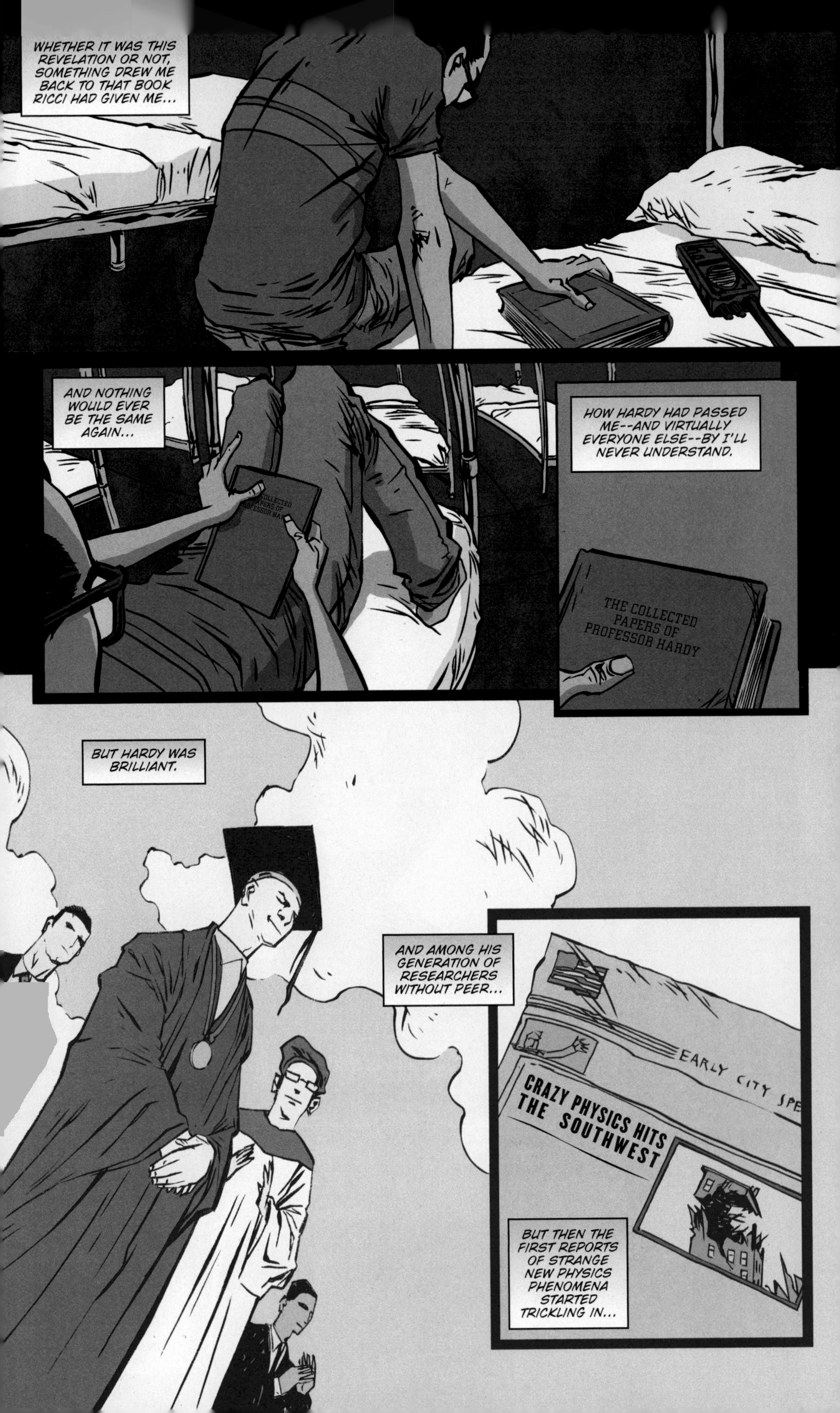
WHETHER IT WAS THIS REVELATION OR NOT, SOMETHING DREW ME BACK TO THAT BOOK RICCI HAD GIVEN ME...
AND NOTHING WOULD EVER BE THE SAME AGAIN...
HOW HARDY HAD PASSED ME--AND VIRTUALLY EVERYONE ELSE--BY I'LL NEVER UNDERSTAND.
THE COLLECTED PAPERS OF PROFESSOR HARDY
BUT HARDY WAS BRILLIANT.
AND AMONG HIS GENERATION OF RESEARCHERS WITHOUT PEER...
EARLY CITY SPE
CRAZY PHYSICS HITS THE SOUTHWEST
BUT THEN THE FIRST REPORTS OF STRANGE NEW PHYSICS PHENOMENA STARTED TRICKLING IN...

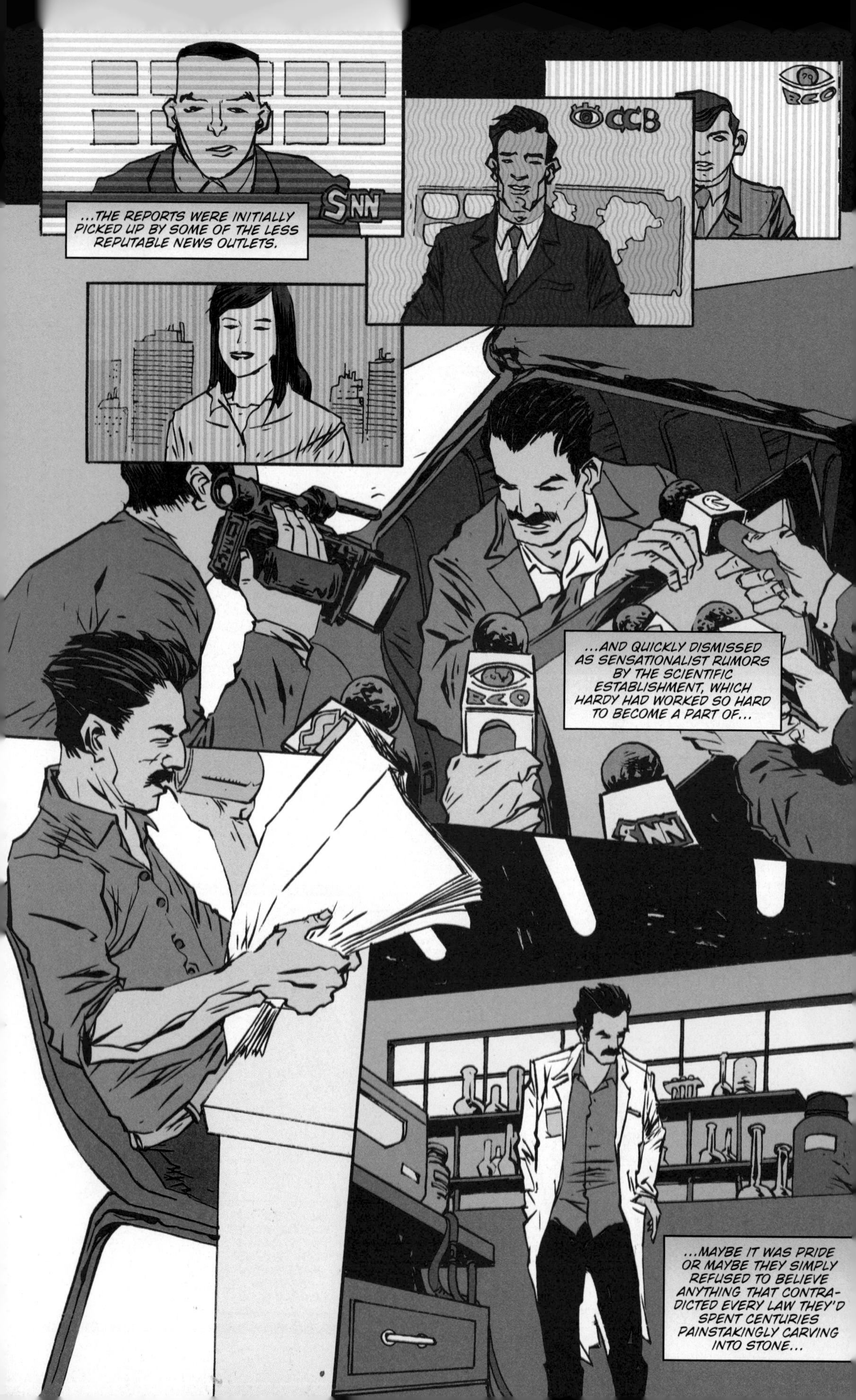
SNN
CCB
BCQ
...THE REPORTS WERE INITIALLY PICKED UP BY SOME OF THE LESS REPUTABLE NEWS OUTLETS.
...AND QUICKLY DISMISSED AS SENSATIONALIST RUMORS BY THE SCIENTIFIC ESTABLISHMENT, WHICH HARDY HAD WORKED SO HARD TO BECOME A PART OF...
...MAYBE IT WAS PRIDE OR MAYBE THEY SIMPLY REFUSED TO BELIEVE ANYTHING THAT CONTRADICTED EVERY LAW THEY'D SPENT CENTURIES PAINSTAKINGLY CARVING INTO STONE...

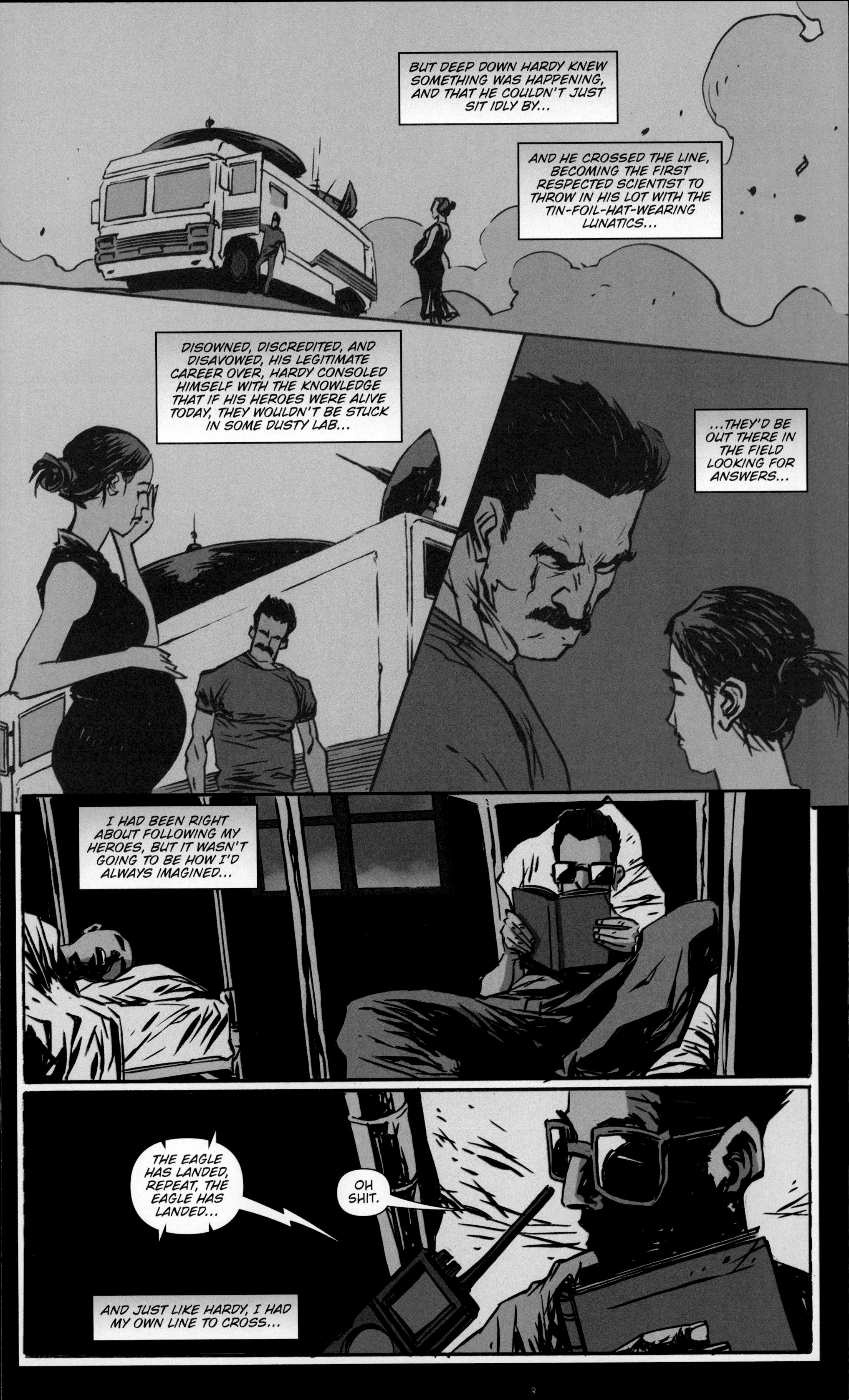
BUT DEEP DOWN HARDY KNEW SOMETHING WAS HAPPENING, AND THAT HE COULDN'T JUST SIT IDLY BY...
AND HE CROSSED THE LINE, BECOMING THE FIRST RESPECTED SCIENTIST TO THROW IN HIS LOT WITH THE TIN-FOIL-HAT-WEARING LUNATICS...
DISOWNED, DISCREDITED, AND DISAVOWED, HIS LEGITIMATE CAREER OVER, HARDY CONSOLED HIMSELF WITH THE KNOWLEDGE THAT IF HIS HEROES WERE ALIVE TODAY, THEY WOULDN'T BE STUCK IN SOME DUSTY LAB...
...THEY'D BE OUT THERE IN THE FIELD LOOKING FOR ANSWERS...
I HAD BEEN RIGHT ABOUT FOLLOWING MY HEROES, BUT IT WASN'T GOING TO BE HOW I'D ALWAYS IMAGINED...
THE EAGLE HAS LANDED, REPEAT, THE EAGLE HAS LANDED...
OH SHIT.
AND JUST LIKE HARDY, I HAD MY OWN LINE TO CROSS...

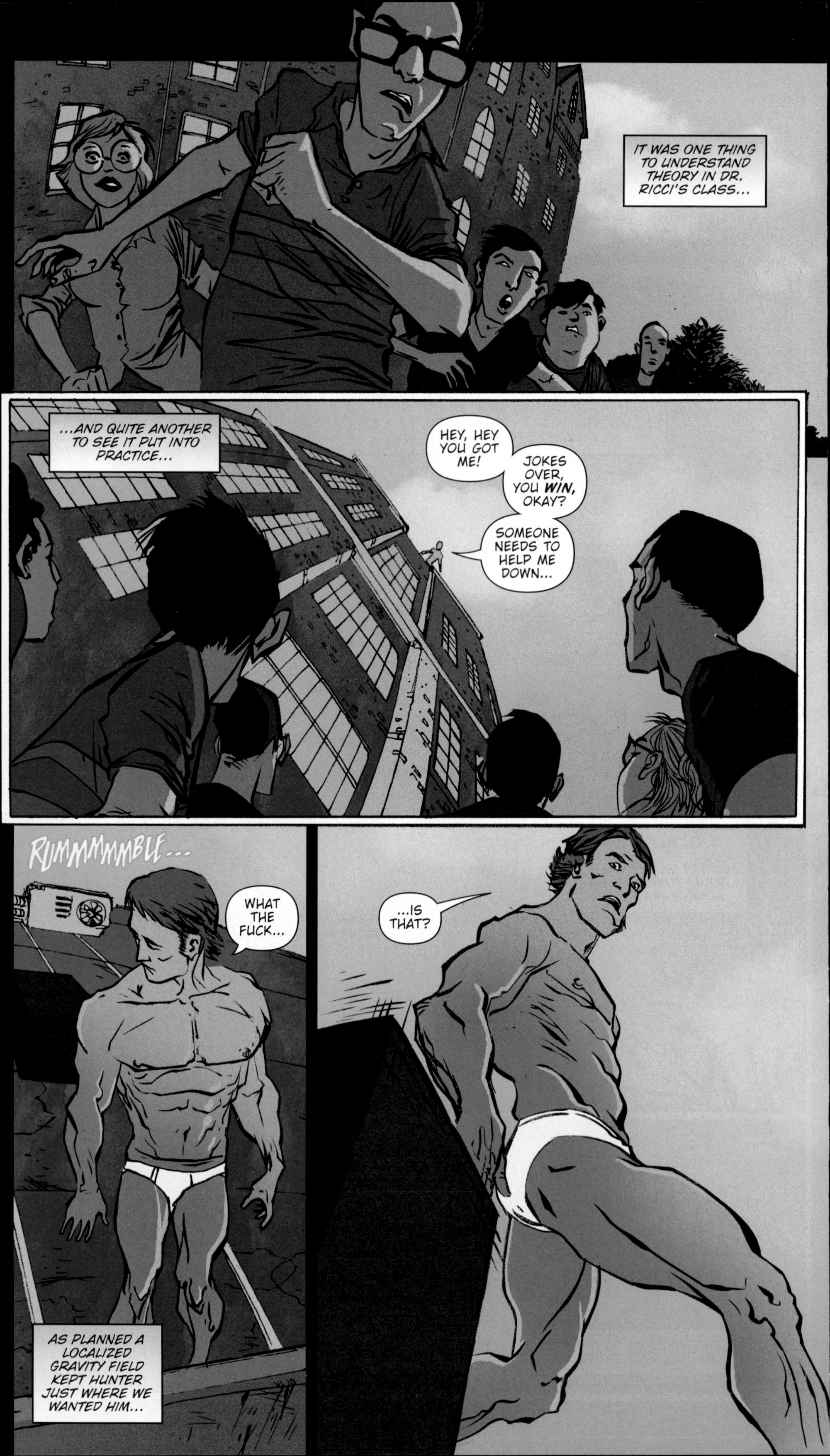
IT WAS ONE THING TO UNDERSTAND THEORY IN DR. RICCI'S CLASS...
...AND QUITE ANOTHER TO SEE IT PUT INTO PRACTICE...
HEY, HEY YOU GOT ME!
JOKES OVER, YOU WIN, OKAY?
SOMEONE NEEDS TO HELP ME DOWN...
RUMMMMMBLE...
WHAT THE FUCK...
...IS THAT?
AS PLANNED A LOCALIZED GRAVITY FIELD KEPT HUNTER JUST WHERE WE WANTED HIM...

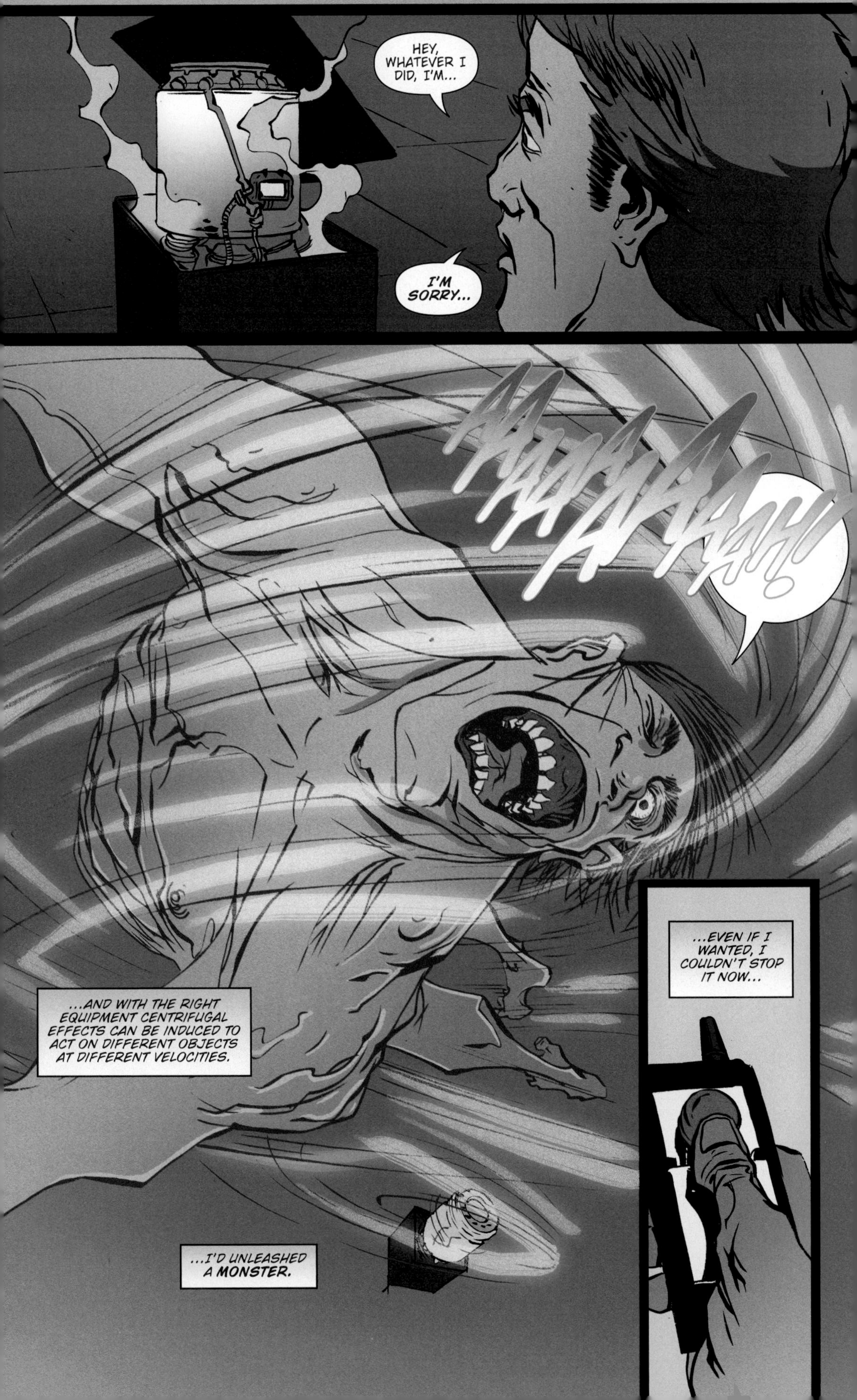
HEY, WHATEVER I DID, I'M...
I'M SORRY...
AAAAAAAAAH!
...AND WITH THE RIGHT EQUIPMENT CENTRIFUGAL EFFECTS CAN BE INDUCED TO ACT ON DIFFERENT OBJECTS AT DIFFERENT VELOCITIES.
...EVEN IF I WANTED, I COULDN'T STOP IT NOW...
...I'D UNLEASHED A MONSTER.

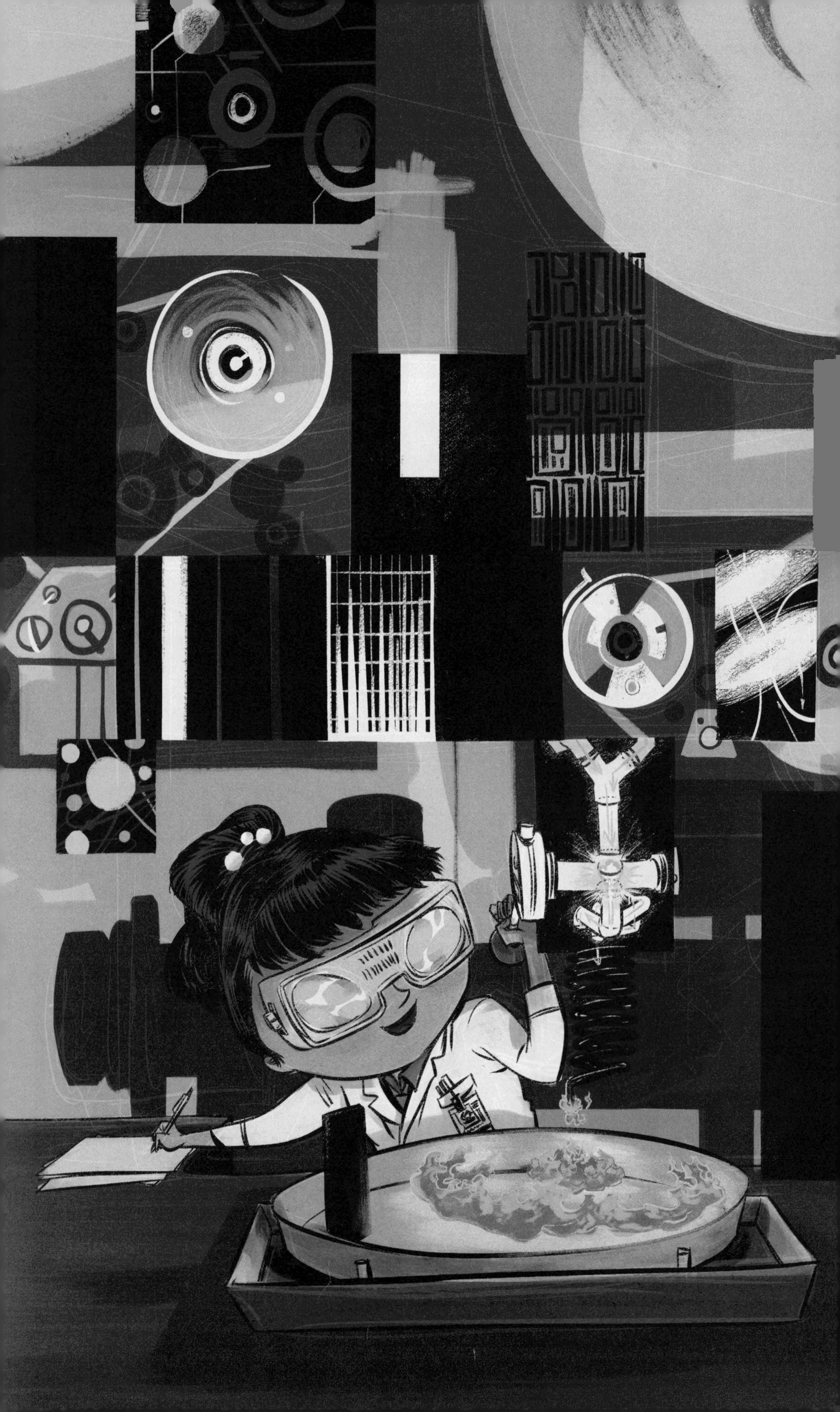

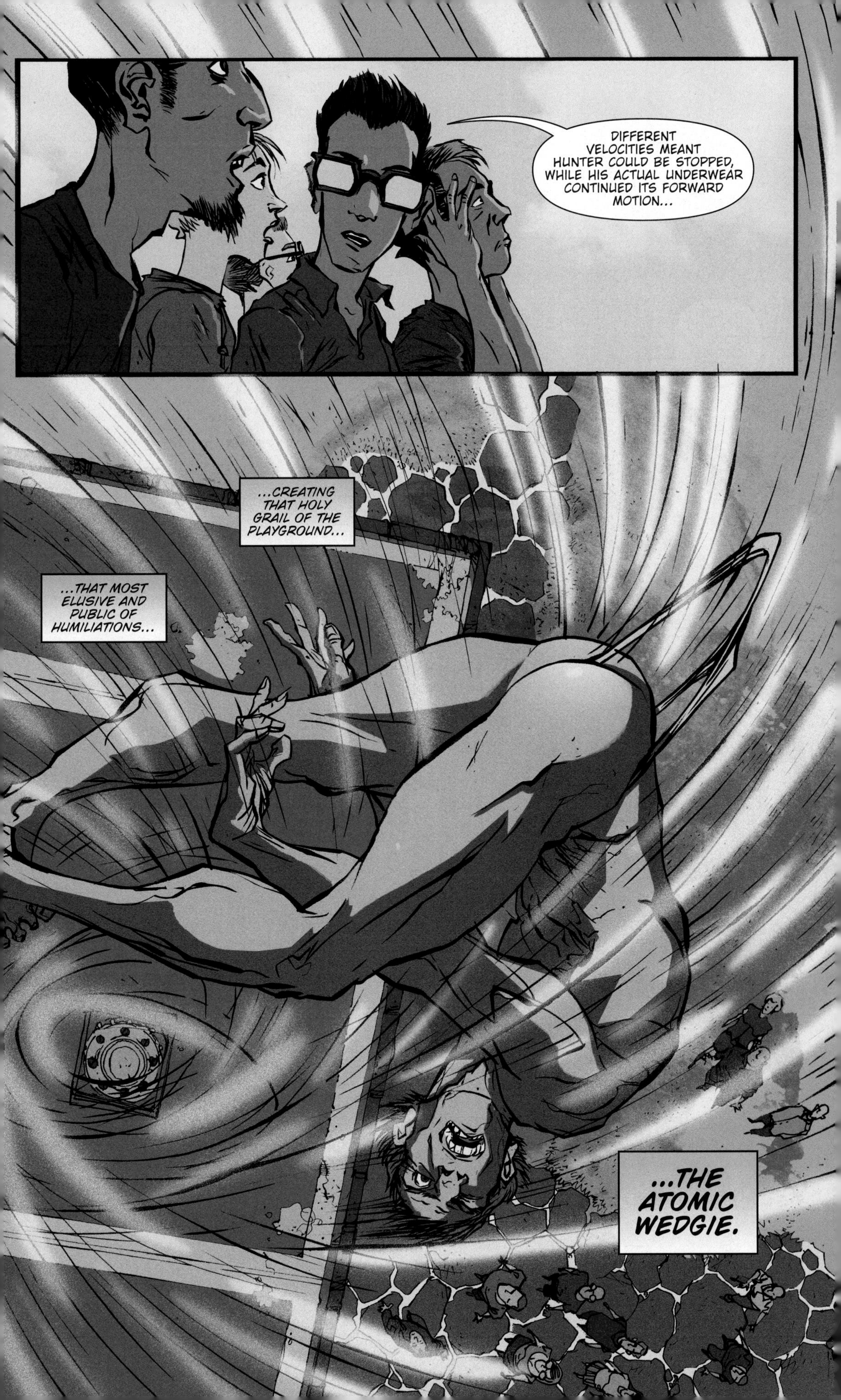
DIFFERENT VELOCITIES MEANT HUNTER COULD BE STOPPED, WHILE HIS ACTUAL UNDERWEAR CONTINUED ITS FORWARD MOTION...
...CREATING THAT HOLY GRAIL OF THE PLAYGROUND...
...THAT MOST ELUSIVE AND PUBLIC OF HUMILIATIONS...
...THE ATOMIC WEDGIE.

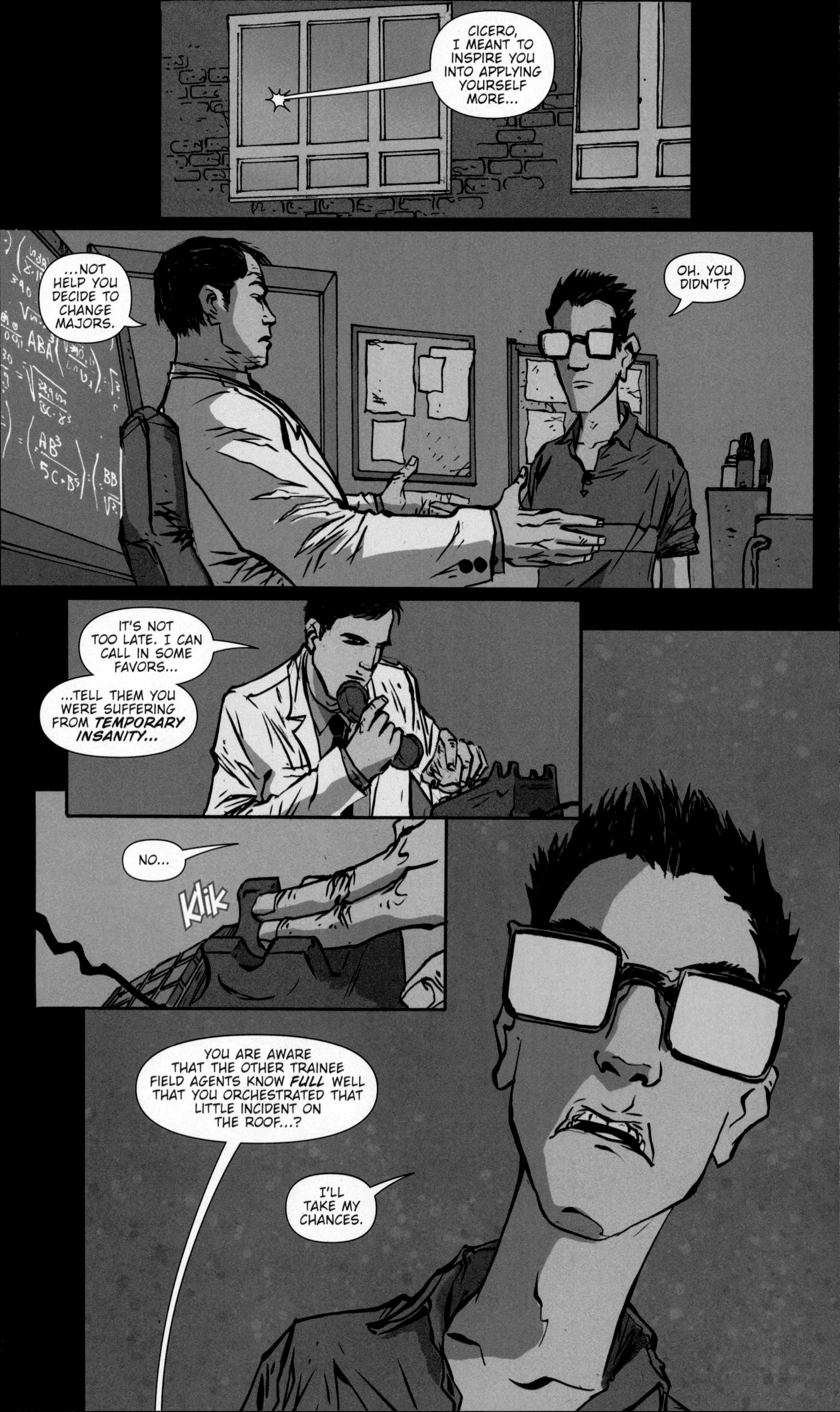
CICERO, I MEANT TO INSPIRE YOU INTO APPLYING YOURSELF MORE...
...NOT HELP YOU DECIDE TO CHANGE MAJORS.
OH. YOU DIDN'T?
IT'S NOT TOO LATE. I CAN CALL IN SOME FAVORS...
...TELL THEM YOU WERE SUFFERING FROM TEMPORARY INSANITY...
NO...
KLIK
YOU ARE AWARE THAT THE OTHER TRAINEE FIELD AGENTS KNOW FULL WELL THAT YOU ORCHESTRATED THAT LITTLE INCIDENT ON THE ROOF...?
I'LL TAKE MY CHANCES.

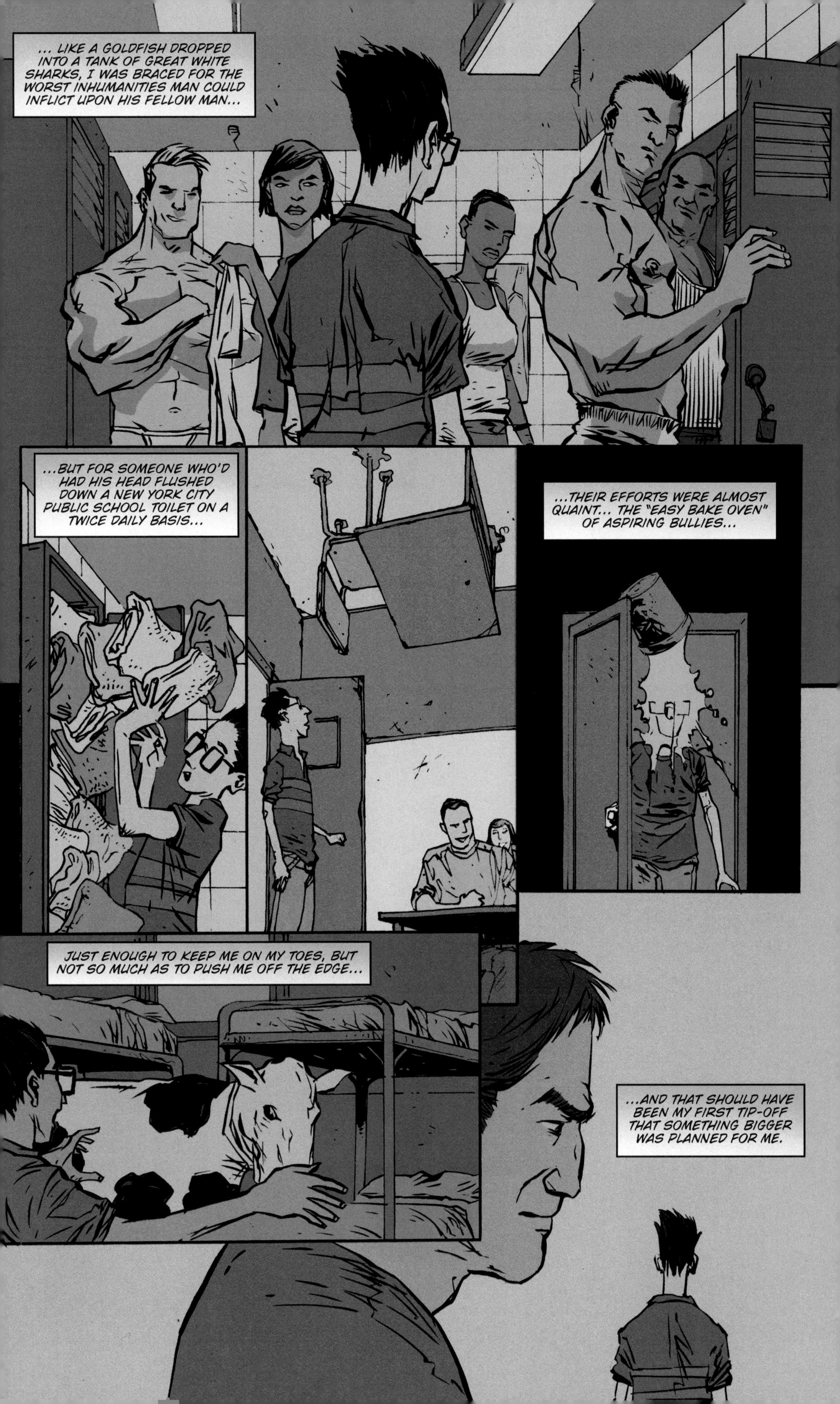
... LIKE A GOLDFISH DROPPED INTO A TANK OF GREAT WHITE SHARKS, I WAS BRACED FOR THE WORST INHUMANITIES MAN COULD INFLICT UPON HIS FELLOW MAN...
...BUT FOR SOMEONE WHO'D HAD HIS HEAD FLUSHED DOWN A NEW YORK CITY PUBLIC SCHOOL TOILET ON A TWICE DAILY BASIS...
...THEIR EFFORTS WERE ALMOST QUAINT... THE "EASY BAKE OVEN" OF ASPIRING BULLIES...
JUST ENOUGH TO KEEP ME ON MY TOES, BUT NOT SO MUCH AS TO PUSH ME OFF THE EDGE...
...AND THAT SHOULD HAVE BEEN MY FIRST TIP-OFF THAT SOMETHING BIGGER WAS PLANNED FOR ME.

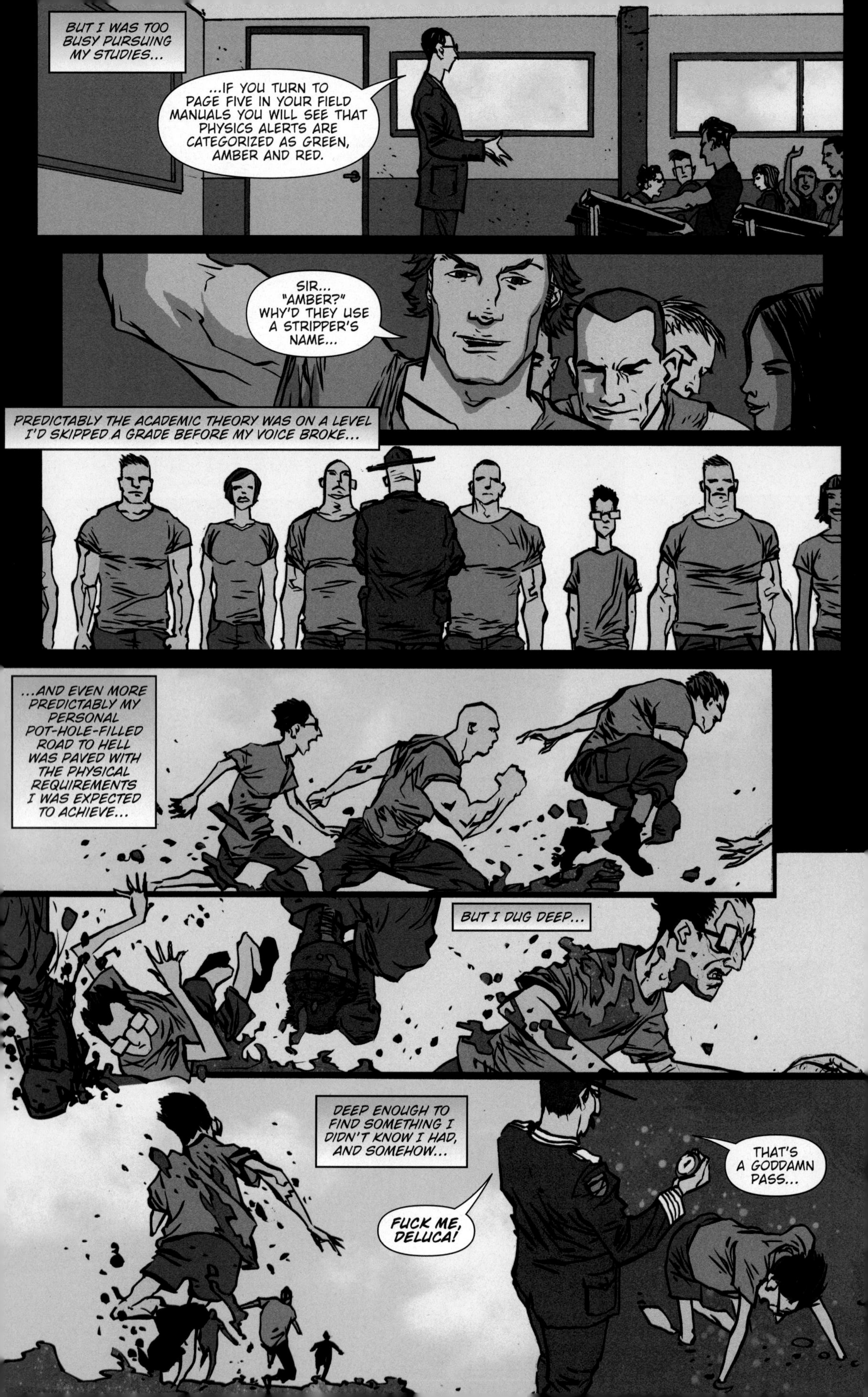
BUT I WAS TOO BUSY PURSUING MY STUDIES...
...IF YOU TURN TO PAGE FIVE IN YOUR FIELD MANUALS YOU WILL SEE THAT PHYSICS ALERTS ARE CATEGORIZED AS GREEN, AMBER AND RED.
SIR... "AMBER?" WHY'D THEY USE A STRIPPER'S NAME...
PREDICTABLY THE ACADEMIC THEORY WAS ON A LEVEL I'D SKIPPED A GRADE BEFORE MY VOICE BROKE...
...AND EVEN MORE PREDICTABLY MY PERSONAL POT-HOLE-FILLED ROAD TO HELL WAS PAVED WITH THE PHYSICAL REQUIREMENTS I WAS EXPECTED TO ACHIEVE...
BUT I DUG DEEP...
DEEP ENOUGH TO FIND SOMETHING I DIDN'T KNOW I HAD, AND SOMEHOW...
FUCK ME, DELUCA!
THAT'S A GODDAMN PASS...

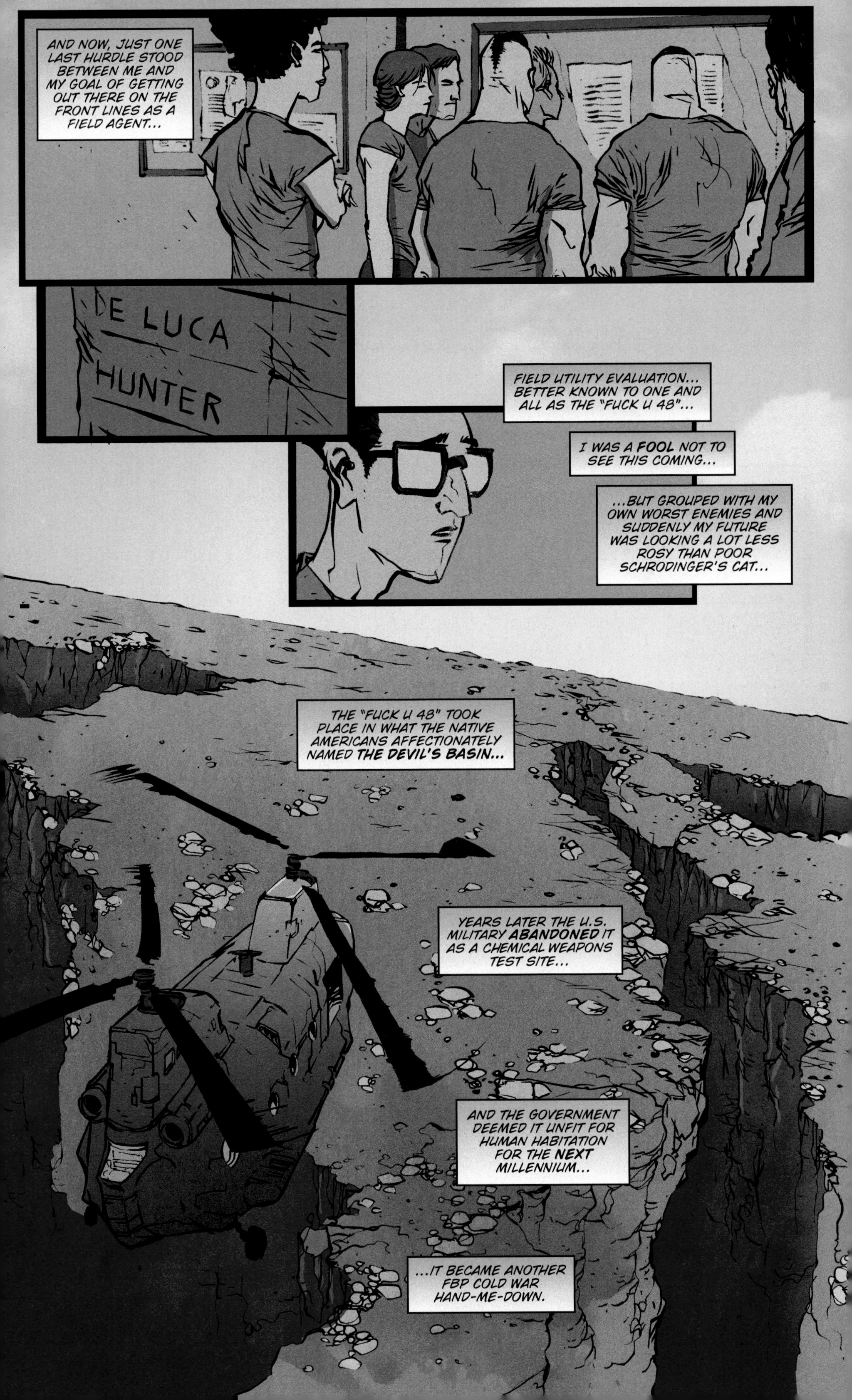
AND NOW, JUST ONE LAST HURDLE STOOD BETWEEN ME AND MY GOAL OF GETTING OUT THERE ON THE FRONT LINES AS A FIELD AGENT...
DE LUCA
HUNTER
FIELD UTILITY EVALUATION... BETTER KNOWN TO ONE AND ALL AS THE "FUCK U 48"...
I WAS A FOOL NOT TO SEE THIS COMING...
...BUT GROUPED WITH MY OWN WORST ENEMIES AND SUDDENLY MY FUTURE WAS LOOKING A LOT LESS ROSY THAN POOR SCHRODINGER'S CAT...
THE "FUCK U 48" TOOK PLACE IN WHAT THE NATIVE AMERICANS AFFECTIONATELY NAMED THE DEVIL'S BASIN...
YEARS LATER THE U.S. MILITARY ABANDONED IT AS A CHEMICAL WEAPONS TEST SITE...
AND THE GOVERNMENT DEEMED IT UNFIT FOR HUMAN HABITATION FOR THE NEXT MILLENNIUM...
...IT BECAME ANOTHER FBP COLD WAR HAND-ME-DOWN.

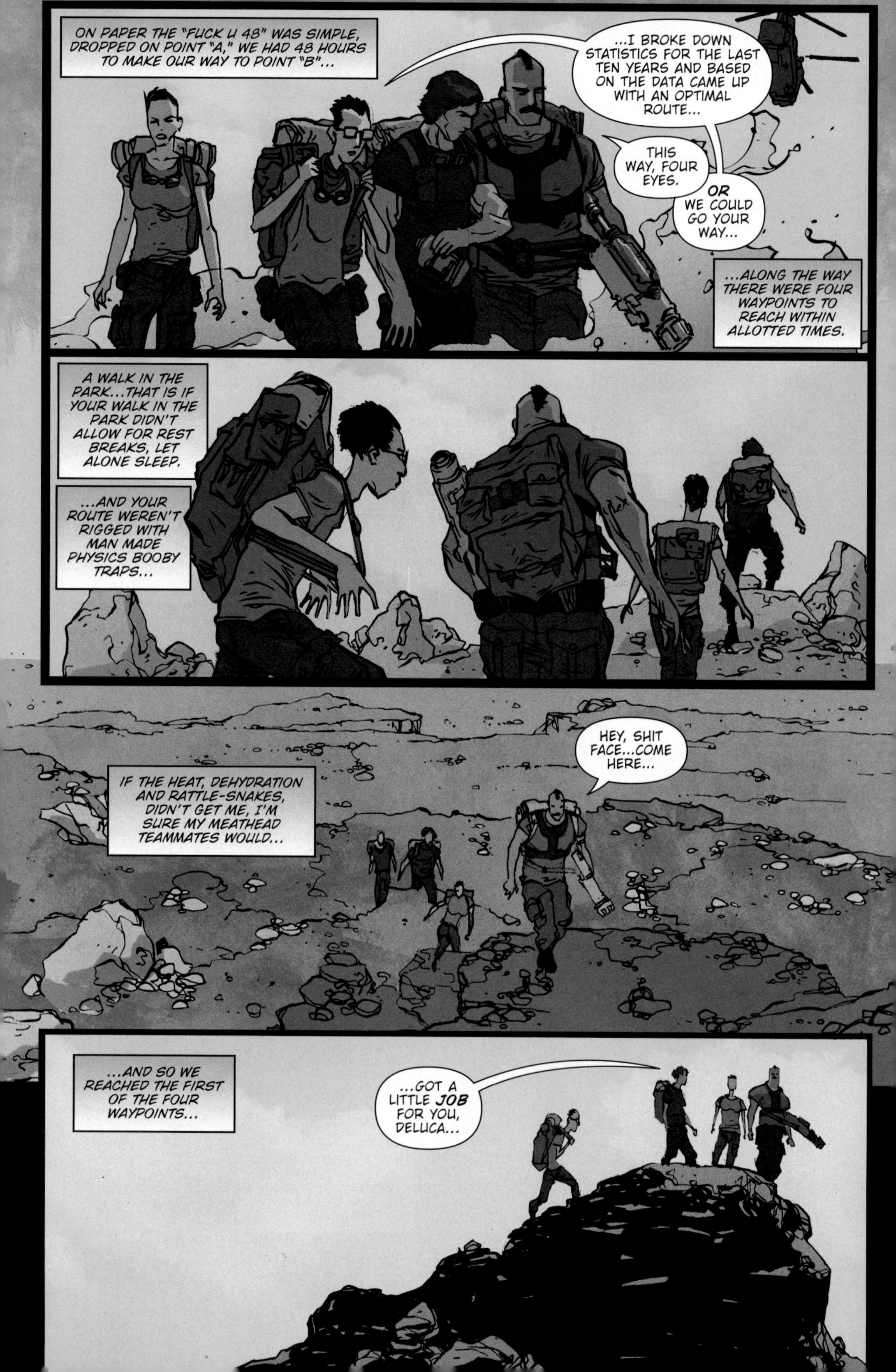
ON PAPER THE "FUCK U 48" WAS SIMPLE, DROPPED ON POINT "A," WE HAD 48 HOURS TO MAKE OUR WAY TO POINT "B"...
...I BROKE DOWN STATISTICS FOR THE LAST TEN YEARS AND BASED ON THE DATA CAME UP WITH AN OPTIMAL ROUTE...
THIS WAY, FOUR EYES.
OR WE COULD GO YOUR WAY...
...ALONG THE WAY THERE WERE FOUR WAYPOINTS TO REACH WITHIN ALLOTTED TIMES.
A WALK IN THE PARK...THAT IS IF YOUR WALK IN THE PARK DIDN'T ALLOW FOR REST BREAKS, LET ALONE SLEEP.
...AND YOUR ROUTE WEREN'T RIGGED WITH MAN MADE PHYSICS BOOBY TRAPS...
IF THE HEAT, DEHYDRATION AND RATTLE-SNAKES, DIDN'T GET ME, I'M SURE MY MEATHEAD TEAMMATES WOULD...
HEY, SHIT FACE...COME HERE...
...AND SO WE REACHED THE FIRST OF THE FOUR WAYPOINTS...
...GOT A LITTLE JOB FOR YOU, DELUCA...

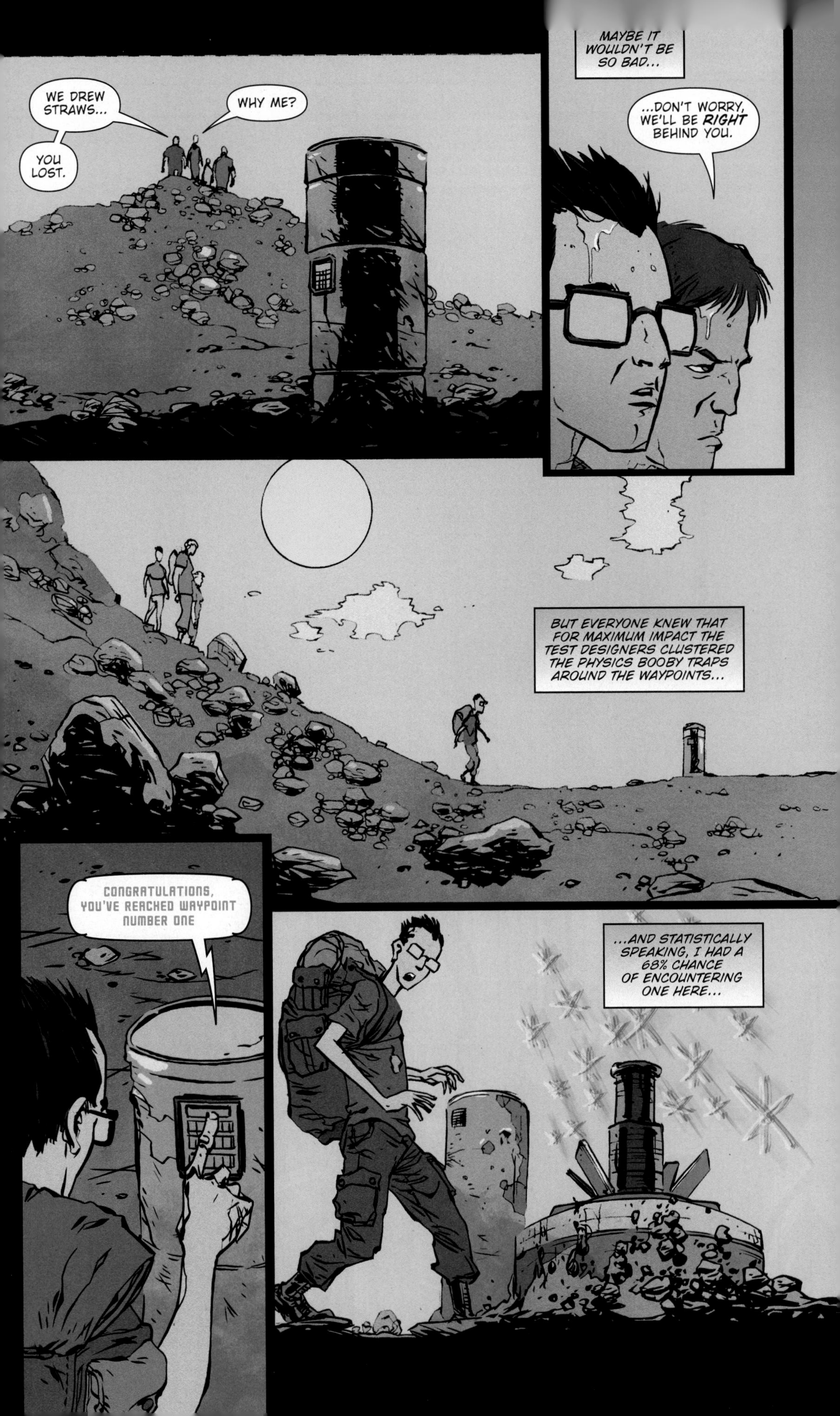
WE DREW STRAWS...
YOU LOST.
WHY ME?
MAYBE IT WOULDN'T BE SO BAD...
...DON'T WORRY, WE'LL BE RIGHT BEHIND YOU.
BUT EVERYONE KNEW THAT FOR MAXIMUM IMPACT THE TEST DESIGNERS CLUSTERED THE PHYSICS BOOBY TRAPS AROUND THE WAYPOINTS...
CONGRATULATIONS, YOU'VE REACHED WAYPOINT NUMBER ONE
...AND STATISTICALLY SPEAKING, I HAD A 68% CHANCE OF ENCOUNTERING ONE HERE...

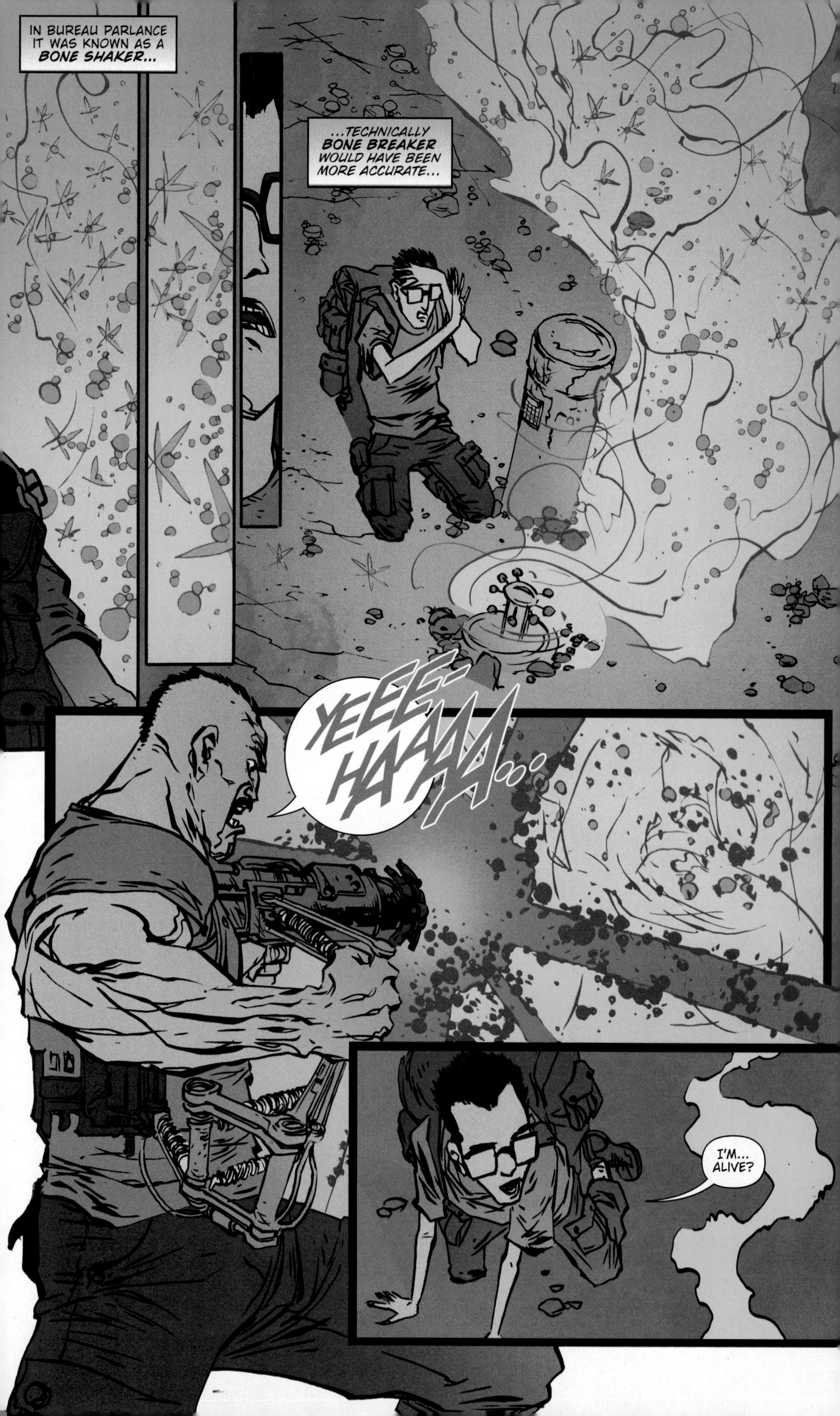
IN BUREAU PARLANCE IT WAS KNOWN AS A BONE SHAKER...
...TECHNICALLY BONE BREAKER WOULD HAVE BEEN MORE ACCURATE...
YEEEE-HAAAAA...
I'M... ALIVE?

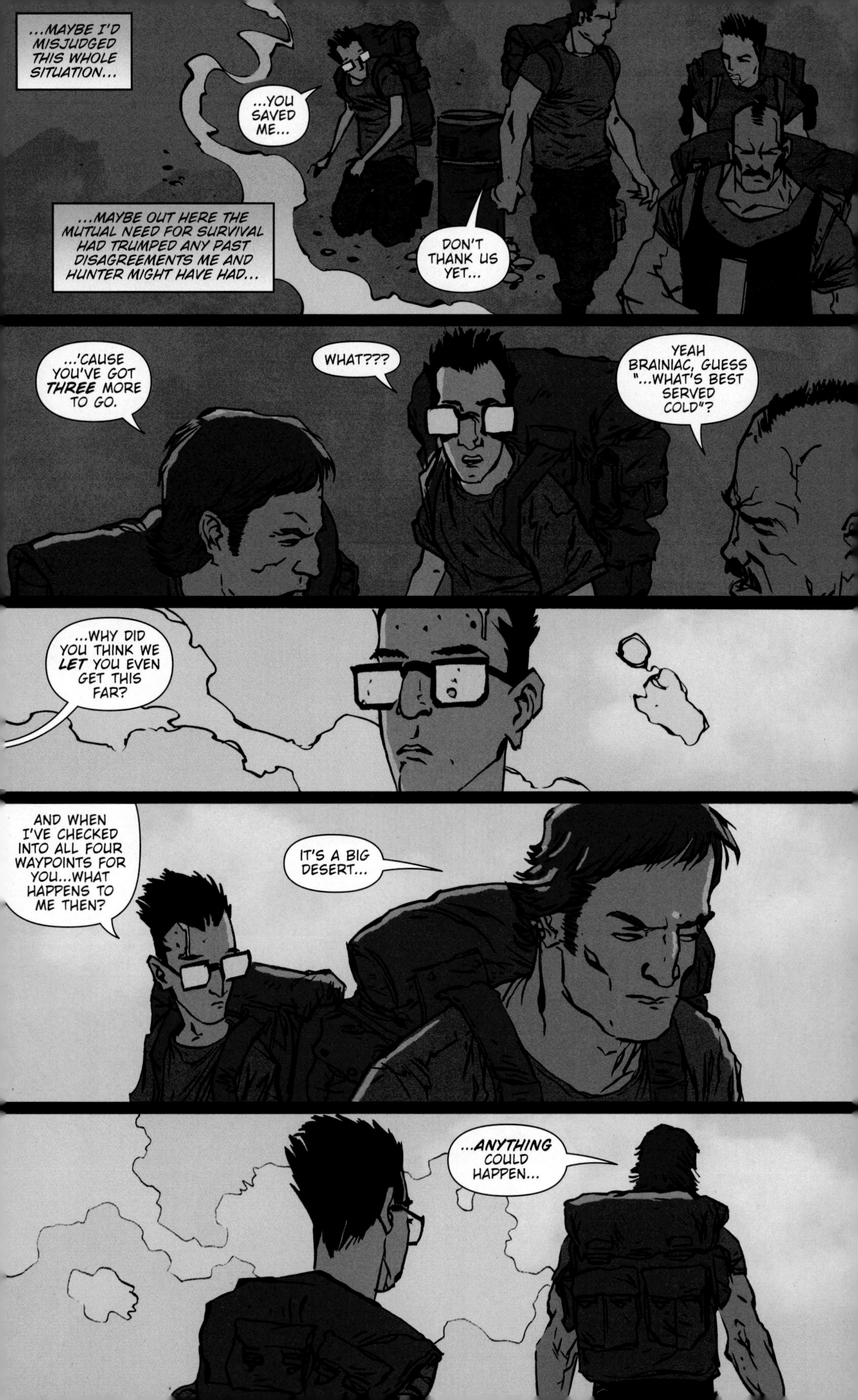
...MAYBE I'D MISJUDGED THIS WHOLE SITUATION...
...YOU SAVED ME...
...MAYBE OUT HERE THE MUTUAL NEED FOR SURVIVAL HAD TRUMPED ANY PAST DISAGREEMENTS ME AND HUNTER MIGHT HAVE HAD...
DON'T THANK US YET...
...'CAUSE YOU'VE GOT THREE MORE TO GO.
WHAT???
YEAH BRAINIAC, GUESS "...WHAT'S BEST SERVED COLD"?
...WHY DID YOU THINK WE LET YOU EVEN GET THIS FAR?
AND WHEN I'VE CHECKED INTO ALL FOUR WAYPOINTS FOR YOU...WHAT HAPPENS TO ME THEN?
IT'S A BIG DESERT...
...ANYTHING COULD HAPPEN...

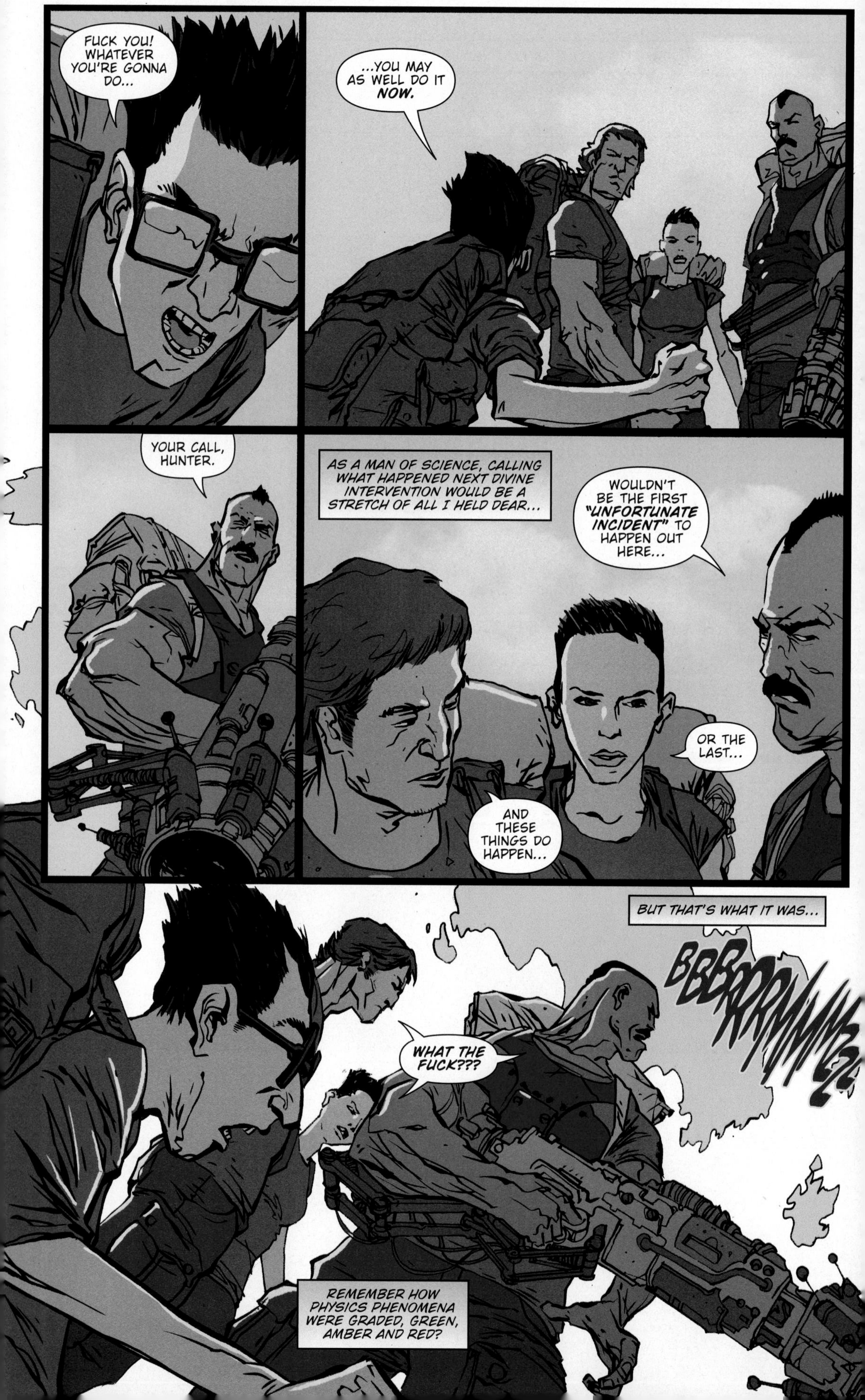
FUCK YOU! WHATEVER YOU'RE GONNA DO...
...YOU MAY AS WELL DO IT NOW.
YOUR CALL, HUNTER.
AS A MAN OF SCIENCE, CALLING WHAT HAPPENED NEXT DIVINE INTERVENTION WOULD BE A STRETCH OF ALL I HELD DEAR...
WOULDN'T BE THE FIRST "UNFORTUNATE INCIDENT" TO HAPPEN OUT HERE...
OR THE LAST...
AND THESE THINGS DO HAPPEN...
BUT THAT'S WHAT IT WAS...
BBBRRRMMMM
WHAT THE FUCK???
REMEMBER HOW PHYSICS PHENOMENA WERE GRADED, GREEN, AMBER AND RED?

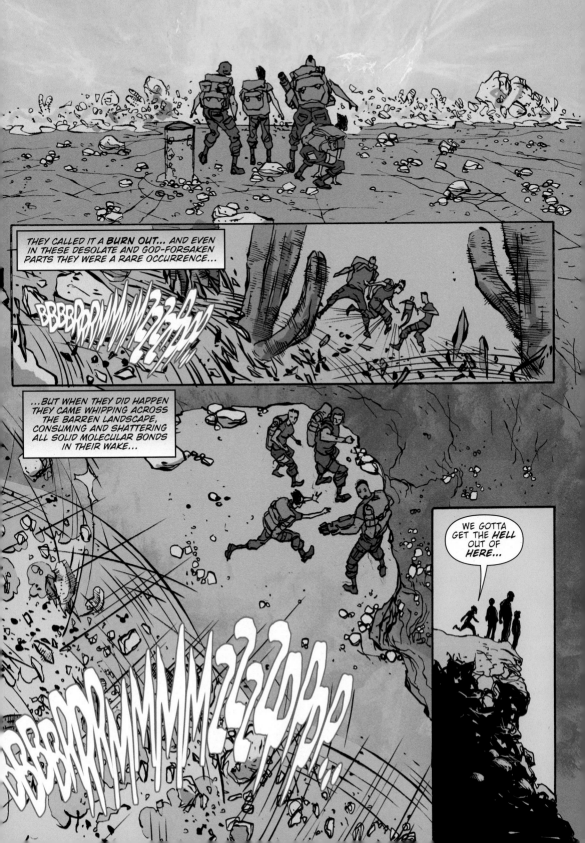

...WHAT WAS NOW BEARING DOWN ON US WITH GREAT VENGEANCE AND FURIOUS ANGER WAS A STRAIGHT-UP *DOUBLE RED*...

THEY CALLED IT A *BURN OUT*... AND EVEN IN THESE DESOLATE AND GOD-FORSAKEN PARTS THEY WERE A RARE OCCURRENCE...

BBBBRRRMMMMZZZZ...

...BUT WHEN THEY DID HAPPEN THEY CAME WHIPPING ACROSS THE BARREN LANDSCAPE, CONSUMING AND SHATTERING ALL SOLID MOLECULAR BONDS IN THEIR WAKE...

WE GOTTA GET THE *HELL* OUT OF *HERE*...

BBBBRRRMMMMZZZZZRR...

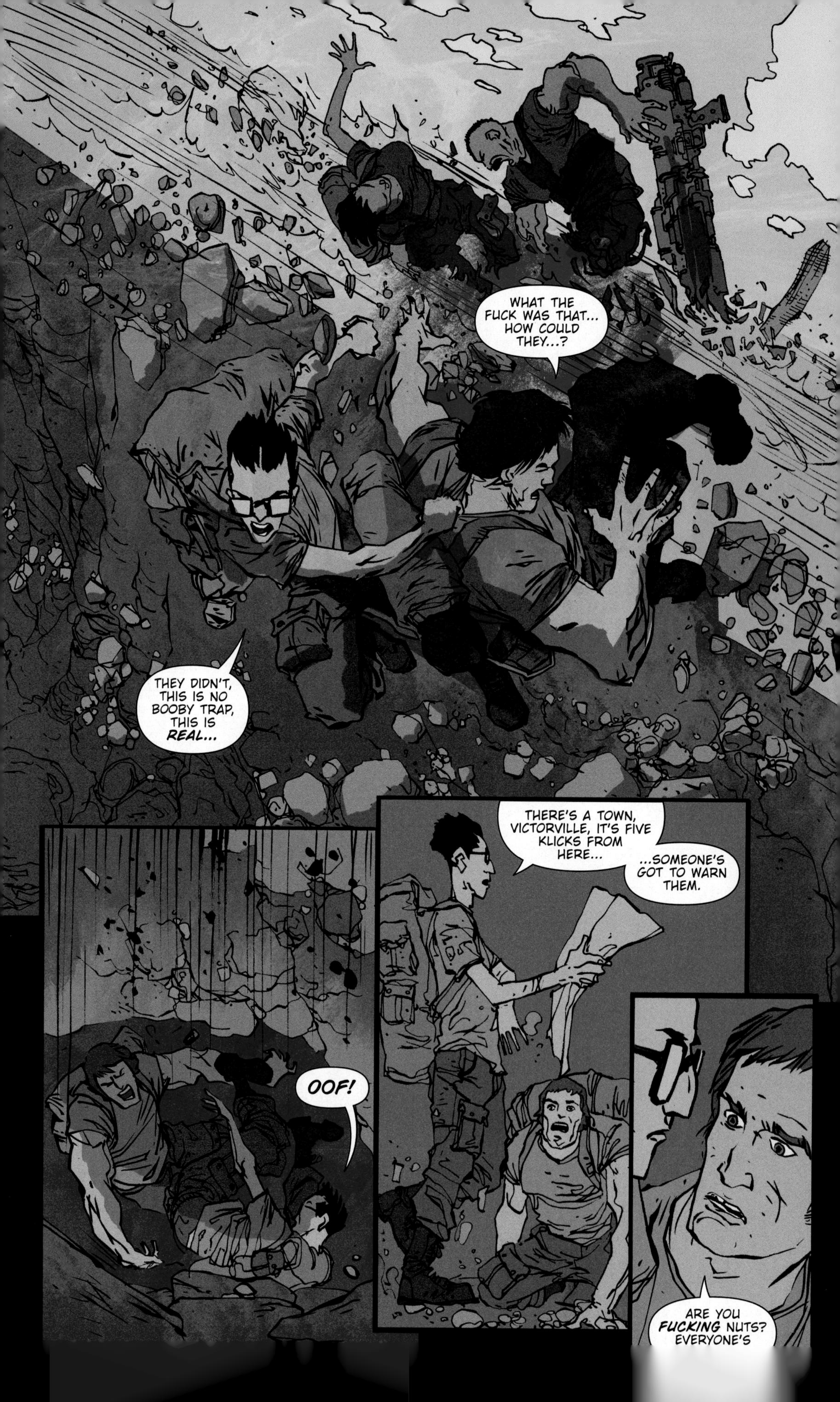
WHAT THE FUCK WAS THAT... HOW COULD THEY...?
THEY DIDN'T, THIS IS NO BOOBY TRAP, THIS IS **REAL...**
OOF!
THERE'S A TOWN, VICTORVILLE, IT'S FIVE KLICKS FROM HERE...
...SOMEONE'S GOT TO WARN THEM.
ARE YOU **FUCKING** NUTS? EVERYONE'S

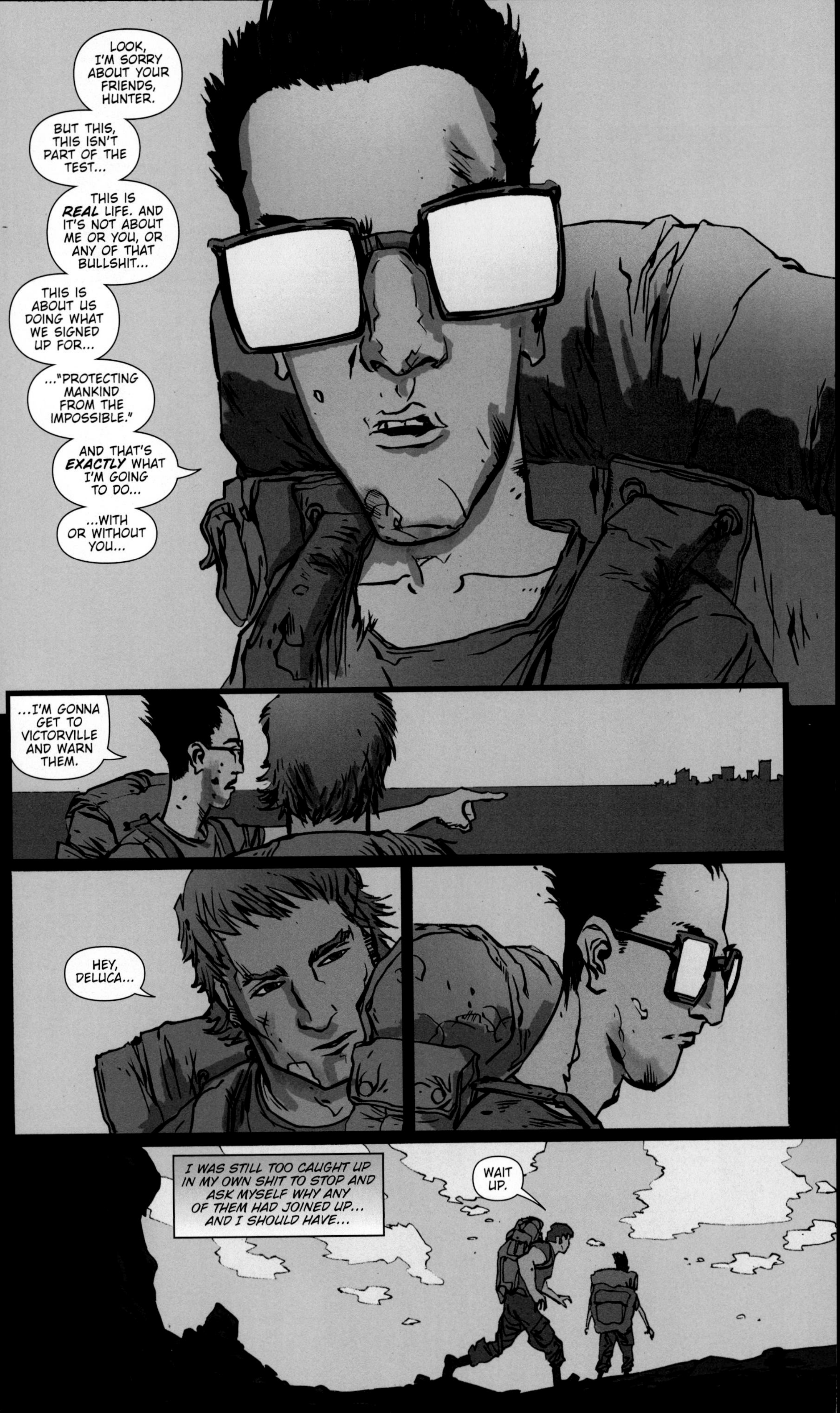
LOOK, I'M SORRY ABOUT YOUR FRIENDS, HUNTER.
BUT THIS, THIS ISN'T PART OF THE TEST...
THIS IS REAL LIFE. AND IT'S NOT ABOUT ME OR YOU, OR ANY OF THAT BULLSHIT...
THIS IS ABOUT US DOING WHAT WE SIGNED UP FOR...
..."PROTECTING MANKIND FROM THE IMPOSSIBLE."
AND THAT'S EXACTLY WHAT I'M GOING TO DO...
...WITH OR WITHOUT YOU...
...I'M GONNA GET TO VICTORVILLE AND WARN THEM.
HEY, DELUCA...
I WAS STILL TOO CAUGHT UP IN MY OWN SHIT TO STOP AND ASK MYSELF WHY ANY OF THEM HAD JOINED UP... AND I SHOULD HAVE...
WAIT UP.

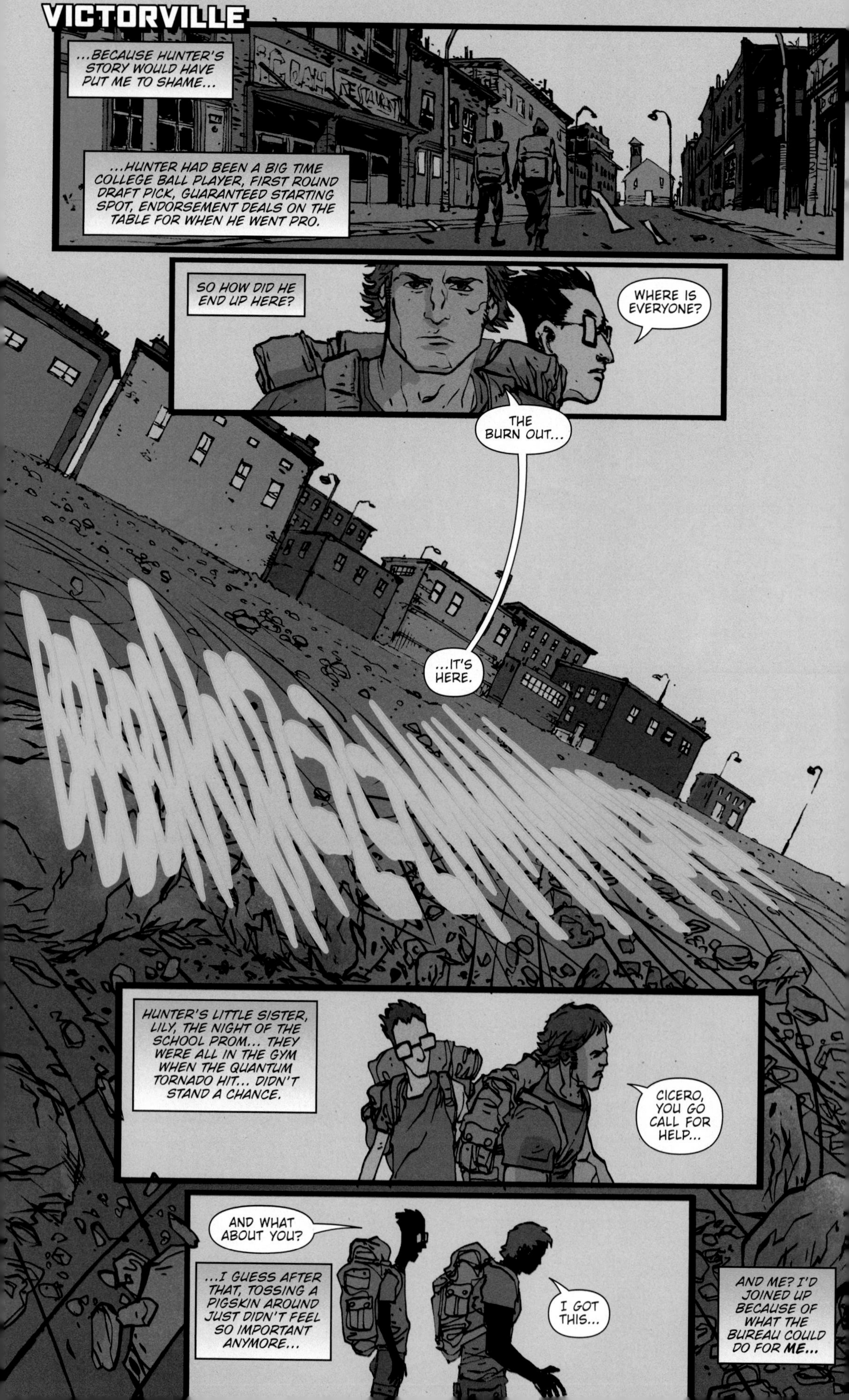
VICTORVILLE
...BECAUSE HUNTER'S STORY WOULD HAVE PUT ME TO SHAME...
...HUNTER HAD BEEN A BIG TIME COLLEGE BALL PLAYER, FIRST ROUND DRAFT PICK, GUARANTEED STARTING SPOT, ENDORSEMENT DEALS ON THE TABLE FOR WHEN HE WENT PRO.
SO HOW DID HE END UP HERE?
WHERE IS EVERYONE?
THE BURN OUT...
...IT'S HERE.
HUNTER'S LITTLE SISTER, LILY, THE NIGHT OF THE SCHOOL PROM... THEY WERE ALL IN THE GYM WHEN THE QUANTUM TORNADO HIT... DIDN'T STAND A CHANCE.
CICERO, YOU GO CALL FOR HELP...
AND WHAT ABOUT YOU?
...I GUESS AFTER THAT, TOSSING A PIGSKIN AROUND JUST DIDN'T FEEL SO IMPORTANT ANYMORE...
I GOT THIS...
AND ME? I'D JOINED UP BECAUSE OF WHAT THE BUREAU COULD DO FOR **ME...**

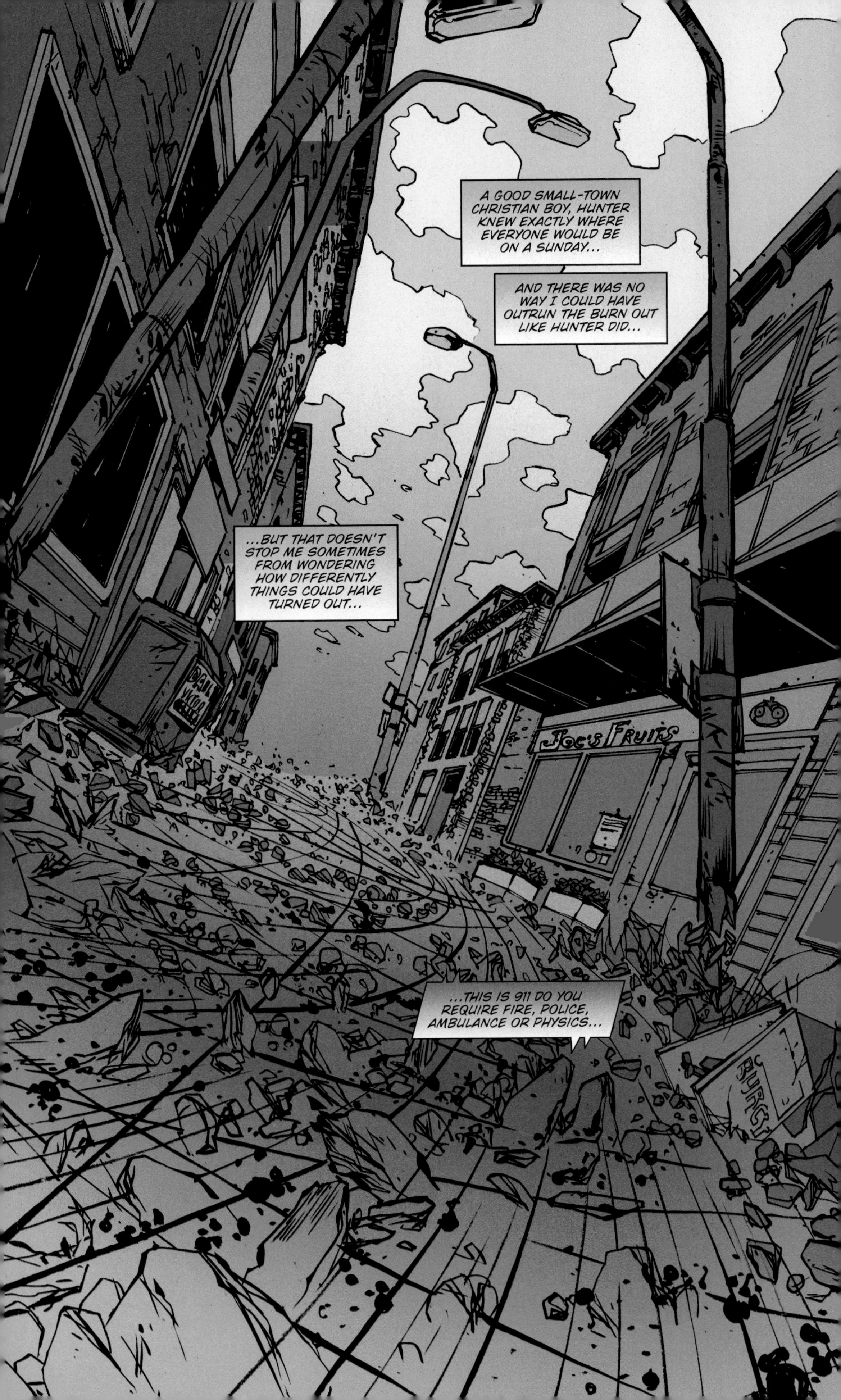
A GOOD SMALL-TOWN CHRISTIAN BOY, HUNTER KNEW EXACTLY WHERE EVERYONE WOULD BE ON A SUNDAY...
AND THERE WAS NO WAY I COULD HAVE OUTRUN THE BURN OUT LIKE HUNTER DID...
...BUT THAT DOESN'T STOP ME SOMETIMES FROM WONDERING HOW DIFFERENTLY THINGS COULD HAVE TURNED OUT...
JOE'S FRUITS
...THIS IS 911 DO YOU REQUIRE FIRE, POLICE, AMBULANCE OR PHYSICS...

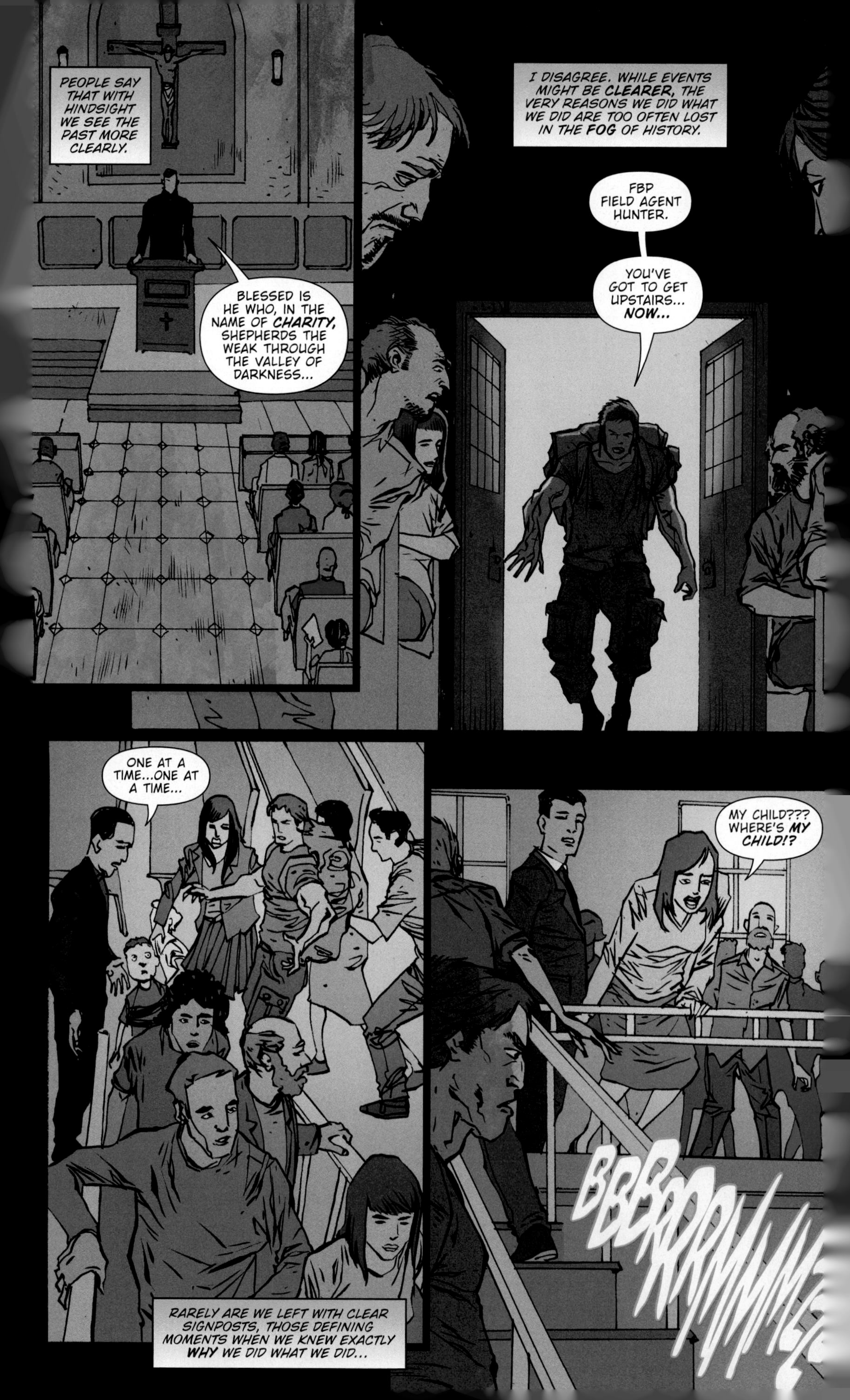
PEOPLE SAY THAT WITH HINDSIGHT WE SEE THE PAST MORE CLEARLY.
BLESSED IS HE WHO, IN THE NAME OF CHARITY, SHEPHERDS THE WEAK THROUGH THE VALLEY OF DARKNESS...
I DISAGREE. WHILE EVENTS MIGHT BE CLEARER, THE VERY REASONS WE DID WHAT WE DID ARE TOO OFTEN LOST IN THE FOG OF HISTORY.
FBP FIELD AGENT HUNTER.
YOU'VE GOT TO GET UPSTAIRS... NOW...
ONE AT A TIME...ONE AT A TIME...
RARELY ARE WE LEFT WITH CLEAR SIGNPOSTS, THOSE DEFINING MOMENTS WHEN WE KNEW EXACTLY WHY WE DID WHAT WE DID...
MY CHILD??? WHERE'S MY CHILD!?
BBBRRRMMMMM

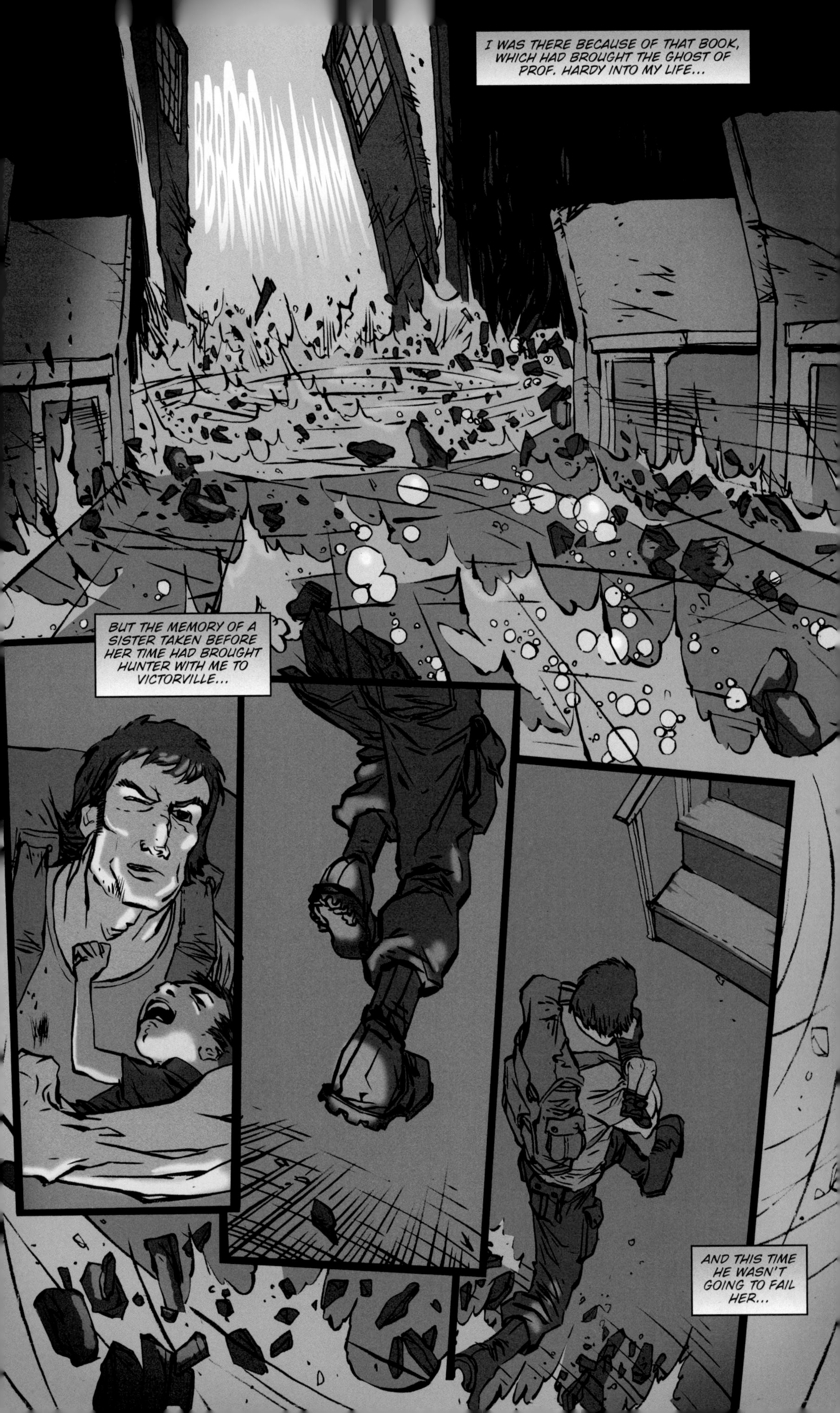
I WAS THERE BECAUSE OF THAT BOOK, WHICH HAD BROUGHT THE GHOST OF PROF. HARDY INTO MY LIFE...
BBBRRRRMMMMMM
BUT THE MEMORY OF A SISTER TAKEN BEFORE HER TIME HAD BROUGHT HUNTER WITH ME TO VICTORVILLE...
AND THIS TIME HE WASN'T GOING TO FAIL HER...

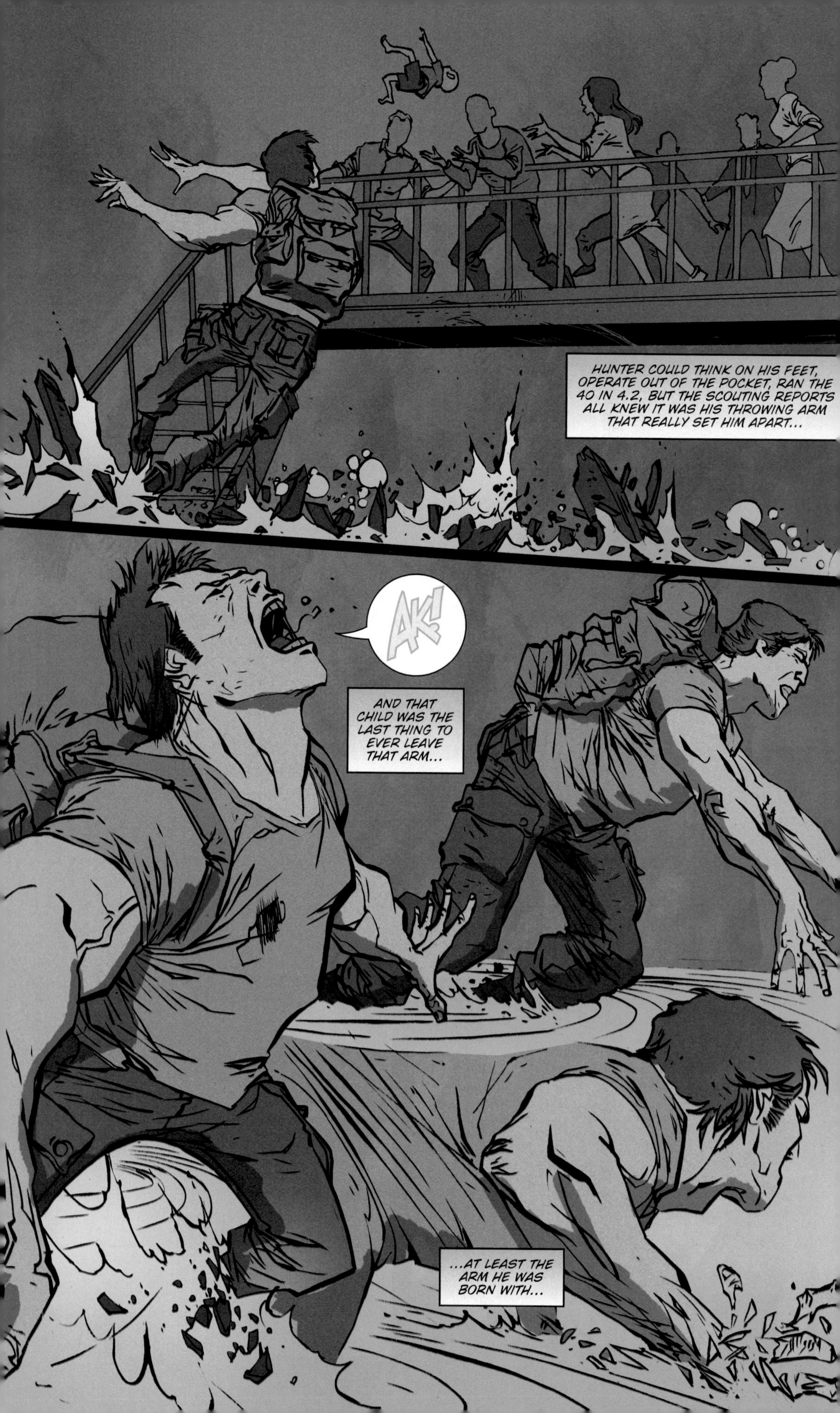
HUNTER COULD THINK ON HIS FEET, OPERATE OUT OF THE POCKET, RAN THE 40 IN 4.2, BUT THE SCOUTING REPORTS ALL KNEW IT WAS HIS THROWING ARM THAT REALLY SET HIM APART...
AK!
AND THAT CHILD WAS THE LAST THING TO EVER LEAVE THAT ARM...
...AT LEAST THE ARM HE WAS BORN WITH...

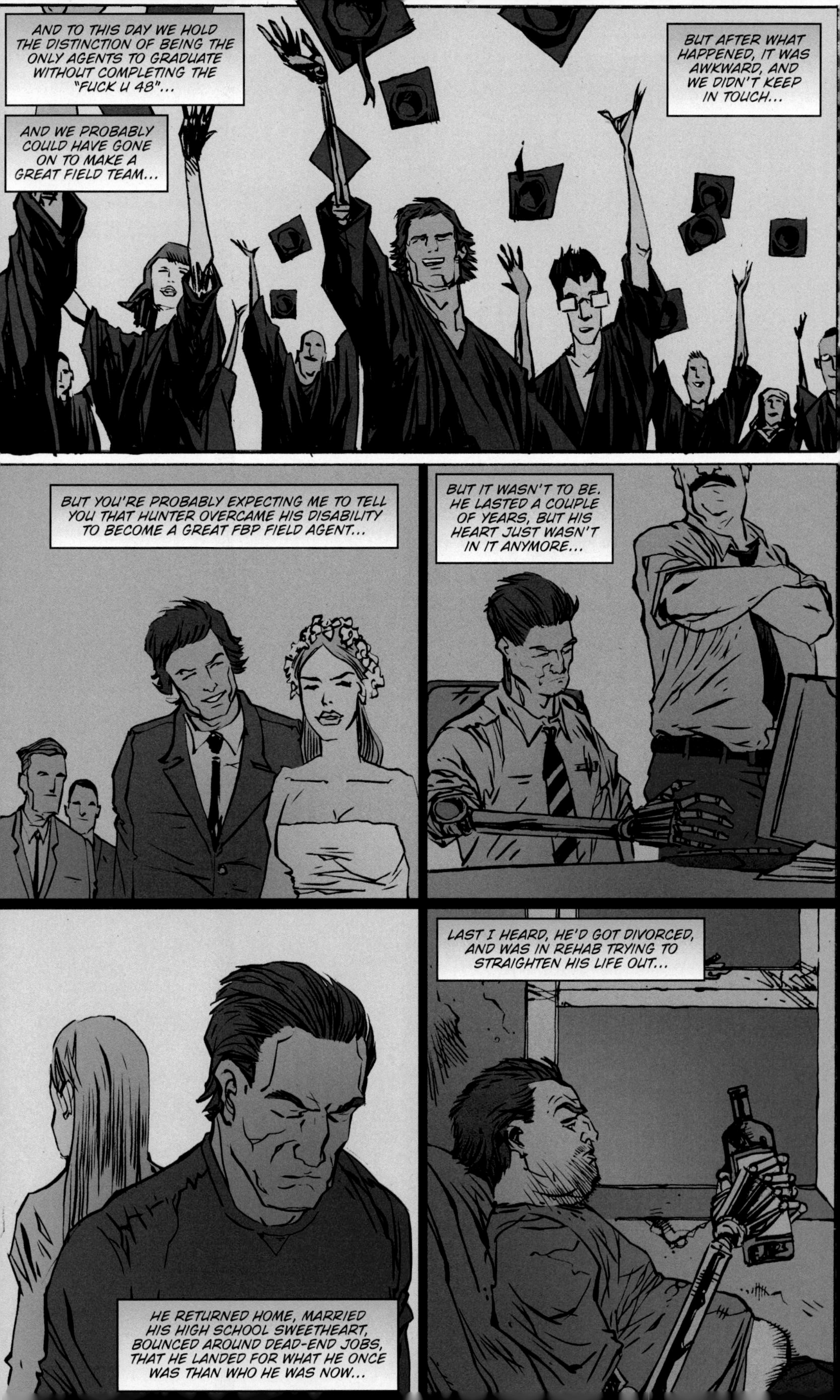
AND TO THIS DAY WE HOLD THE DISTINCTION OF BEING THE ONLY AGENTS TO GRADUATE WITHOUT COMPLETING THE "FUCK U 48"...
AND WE PROBABLY COULD HAVE GONE ON TO MAKE A GREAT FIELD TEAM...
BUT AFTER WHAT HAPPENED, IT WAS AWKWARD, AND WE DIDN'T KEEP IN TOUCH...
BUT YOU'RE PROBABLY EXPECTING ME TO TELL YOU THAT HUNTER OVERCAME HIS DISABILITY TO BECOME A GREAT FBP FIELD AGENT...
BUT IT WASN'T TO BE. HE LASTED A COUPLE OF YEARS, BUT HIS HEART JUST WASN'T IN IT ANYMORE...
HE RETURNED HOME, MARRIED HIS HIGH SCHOOL SWEETHEART, BOUNCED AROUND DEAD-END JOBS, THAT HE LANDED FOR WHAT HE ONCE WAS THAN WHO HE WAS NOW...
LAST I HEARD, HE'D GOT DIVORCED, AND WAS IN REHAB TRYING TO STRAIGHTEN HIS LIFE OUT...

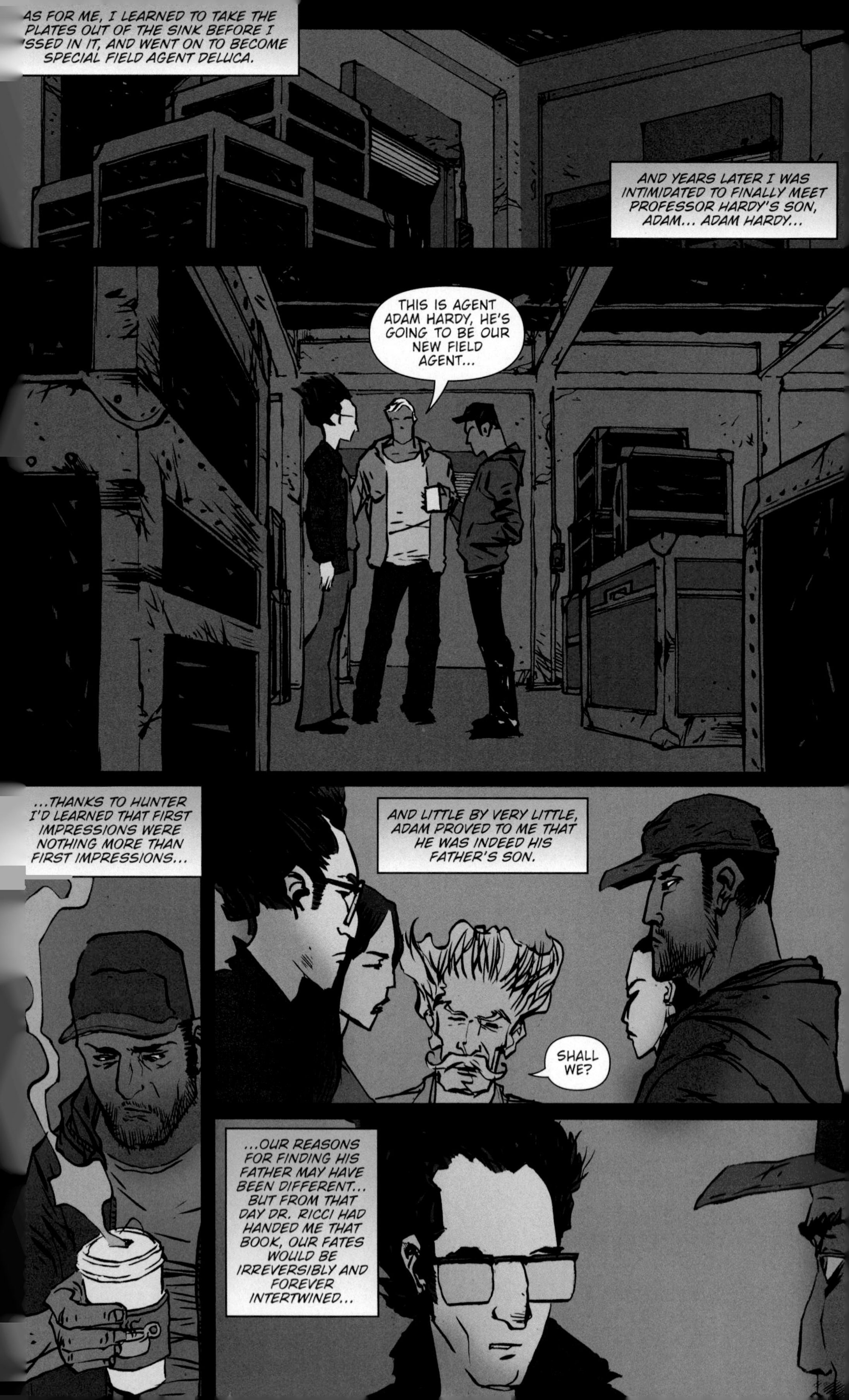
AS FOR ME, I LEARNED TO TAKE THE PLATES OUT OF THE SINK BEFORE I SSED IN IT, AND WENT ON TO BECOME SPECIAL FIELD AGENT DELUCA.
AND YEARS LATER I WAS INTIMIDATED TO FINALLY MEET PROFESSOR HARDY'S SON, ADAM... ADAM HARDY...
THIS IS AGENT ADAM HARDY, HE'S GOING TO BE OUR NEW FIELD AGENT...
...THANKS TO HUNTER I'D LEARNED THAT FIRST IMPRESSIONS WERE NOTHING MORE THAN FIRST IMPRESSIONS...
AND LITTLE BY VERY LITTLE, ADAM PROVED TO ME THAT HE WAS INDEED HIS FATHER'S SON.
SHALL WE?
...OUR REASONS FOR FINDING HIS FATHER MAY HAVE BEEN DIFFERENT... BUT FROM THAT DAY DR. RICCI HAD HANDED ME THAT BOOK, OUR FATES WOULD BE IRREVERSIBLY AND FOREVER INTERTWINED...

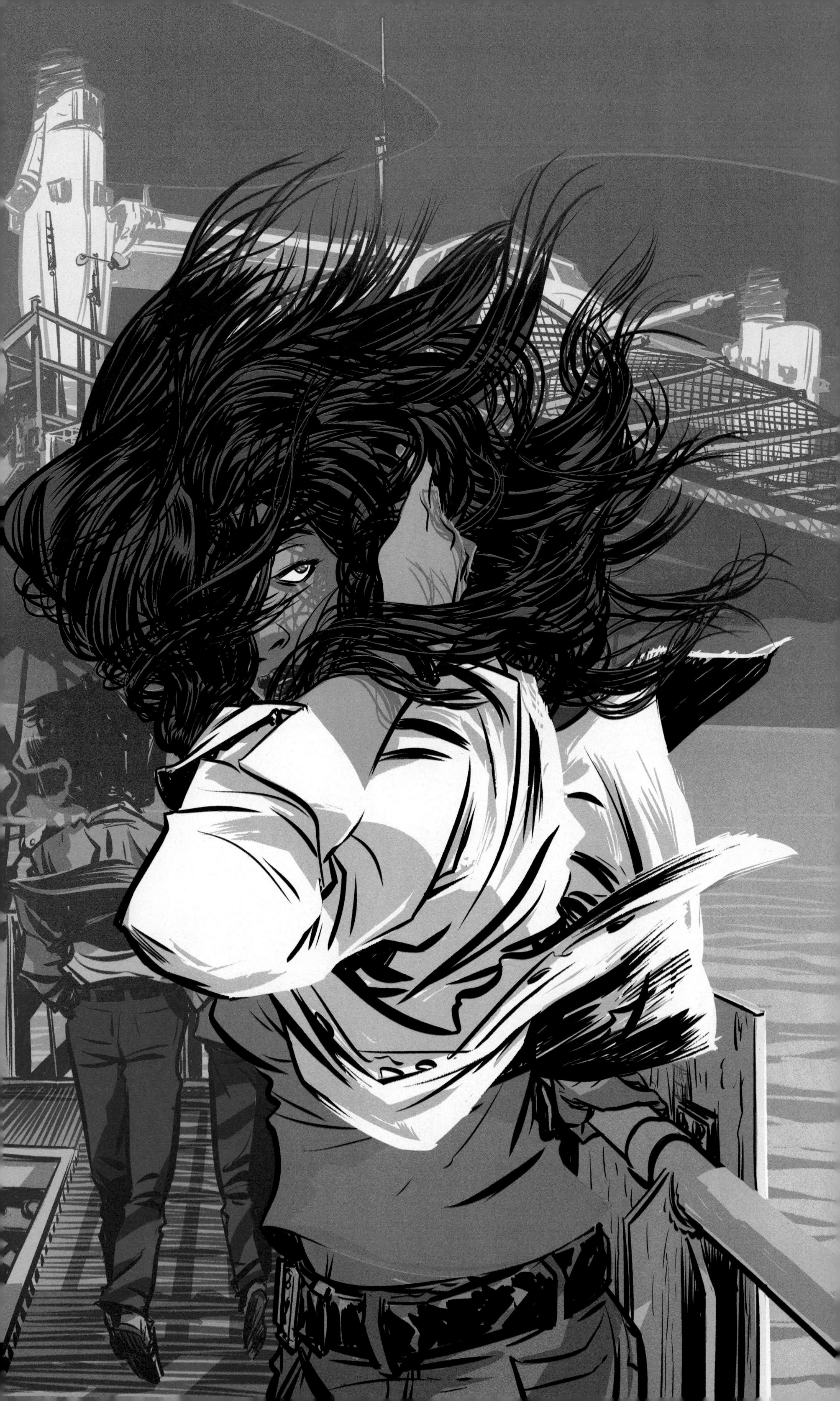

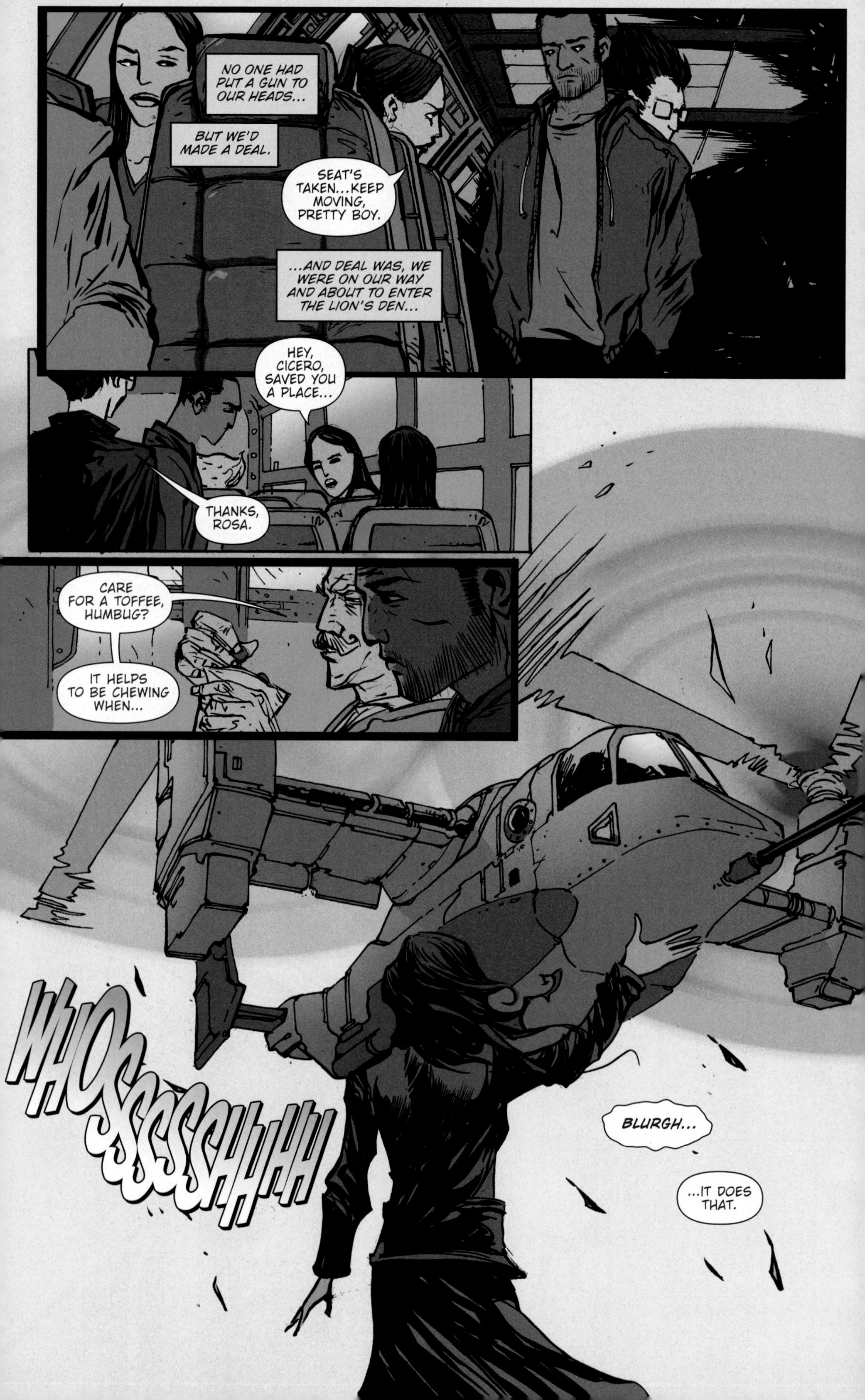

NO ONE HAD PUT A GUN TO OUR HEADS...
BUT WE'D MADE A DEAL.
SEAT'S TAKEN...KEEP MOVING, PRETTY BOY.
...AND DEAL WAS, WE WERE ON OUR WAY AND ABOUT TO ENTER THE LION'S DEN...
HEY, CICERO, SAVED YOU A PLACE...
THANKS, ROSA.
CARE FOR A TOFFEE, HUMBUG?
IT HELPS TO BE CHEWING WHEN...
WHOSSSSCHHHH
BLURGH...
...IT DOES THAT.

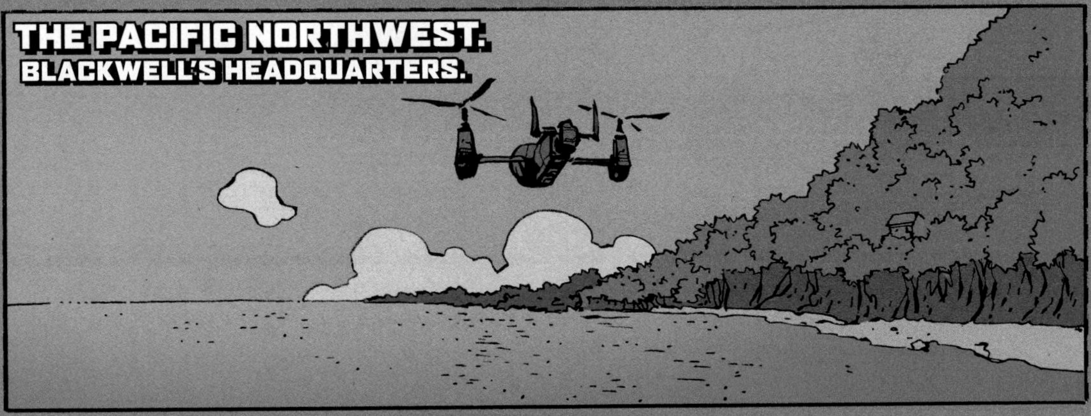
THE PACIFIC NORTHWEST.
BLACKWELL'S HEADQUARTERS.

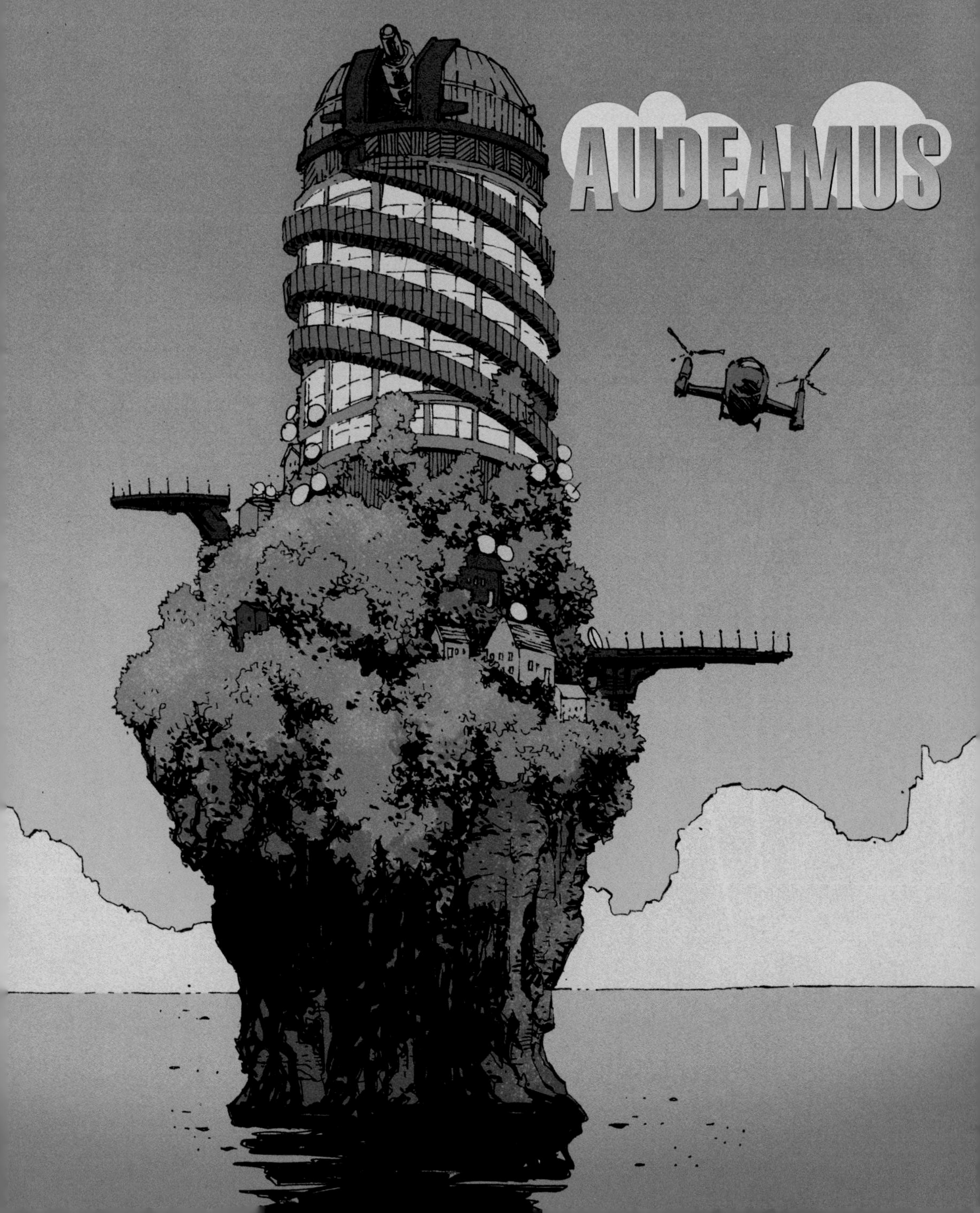
AUDEAMUS

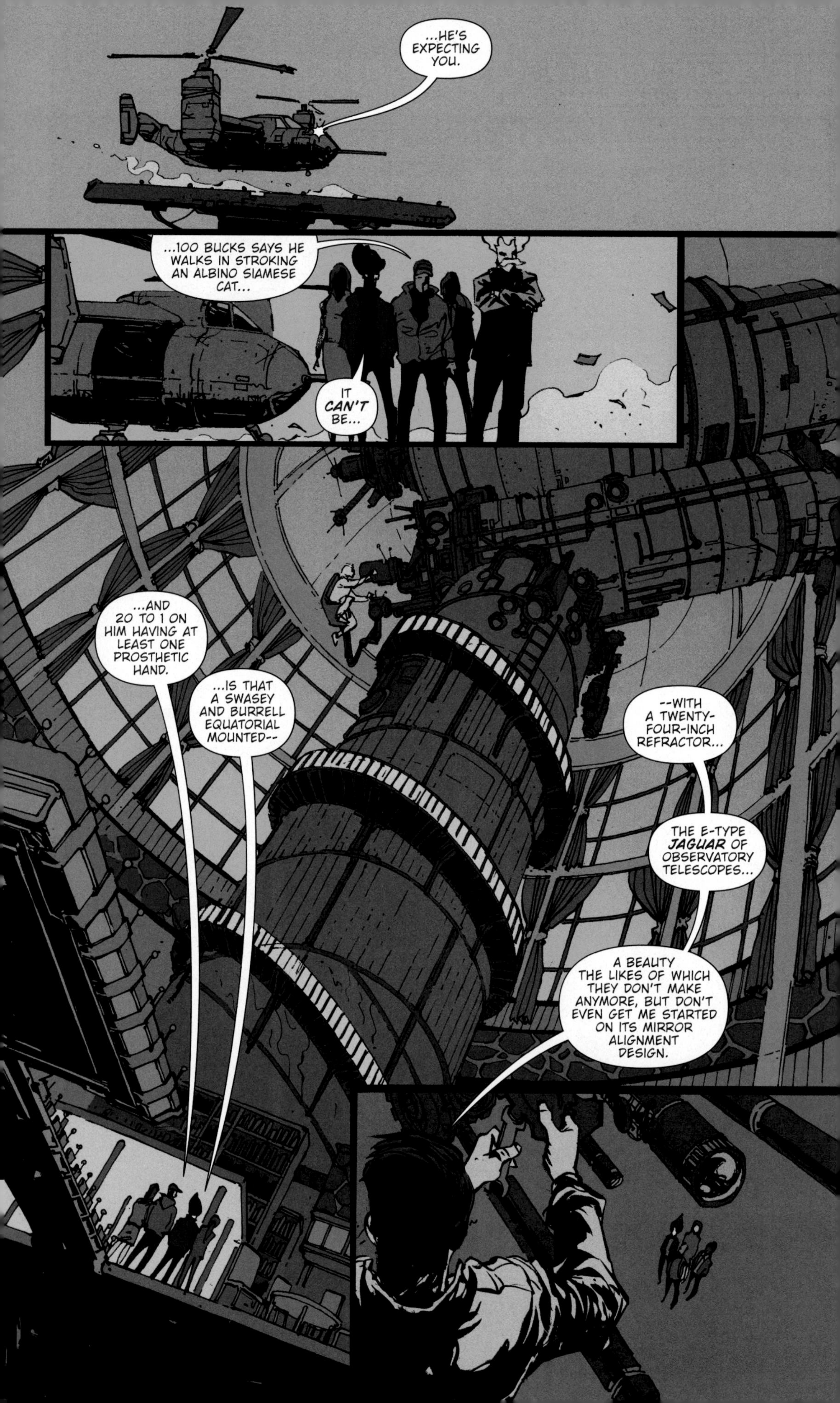

...HE'S EXPECTING YOU.
...100 BUCKS SAYS HE WALKS IN STROKING AN ALBINO SIAMESE CAT...
IT *CAN'T* BE...
...AND 20 TO 1 ON HIM HAVING AT LEAST ONE PROSTHETIC HAND.
...IS THAT A SWASEY AND BURRELL EQUATORIAL MOUNTED--
--WITH A TWENTY-FOUR-INCH REFRACTOR...
THE E-TYPE ***JAGUAR*** OF OBSERVATORY TELESCOPES...
A BEAUTY THE LIKES OF WHICH THEY DON'T MAKE ANYMORE, BUT DON'T EVEN GET ME STARTED ON ITS MIRROR ALIGNMENT DESIGN.

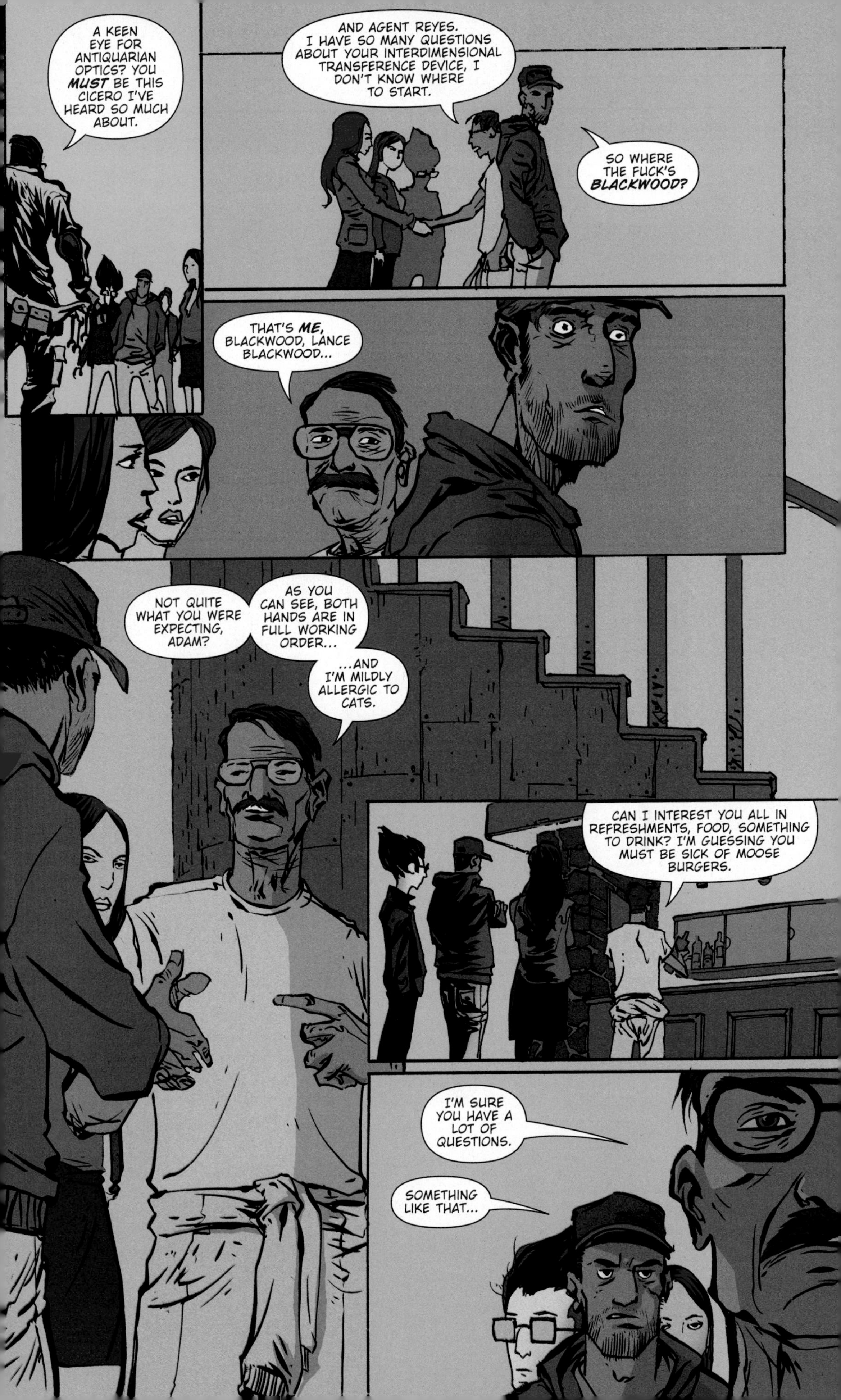
A KEEN EYE FOR ANTIQUARIAN OPTICS? YOU *MUST* BE THIS CICERO I'VE HEARD SO MUCH ABOUT.
AND AGENT REYES. I HAVE SO MANY QUESTIONS ABOUT YOUR INTERDIMENSIONAL TRANSFERENCE DEVICE, I DON'T KNOW WHERE TO START.
SO WHERE THE FUCK'S ***BLACKWOOD?***
THAT'S *ME,* BLACKWOOD, LANCE BLACKWOOD...
NOT QUITE WHAT YOU WERE EXPECTING, ADAM?
AS YOU CAN SEE, BOTH HANDS ARE IN FULL WORKING ORDER...
...AND I'M MILDLY ALLERGIC TO CATS.
CAN I INTEREST YOU ALL IN REFRESHMENTS, FOOD, SOMETHING TO DRINK? I'M GUESSING YOU MUST BE SICK OF MOOSE BURGERS.
I'M SURE YOU HAVE A LOT OF QUESTIONS.
SOMETHING LIKE THAT...

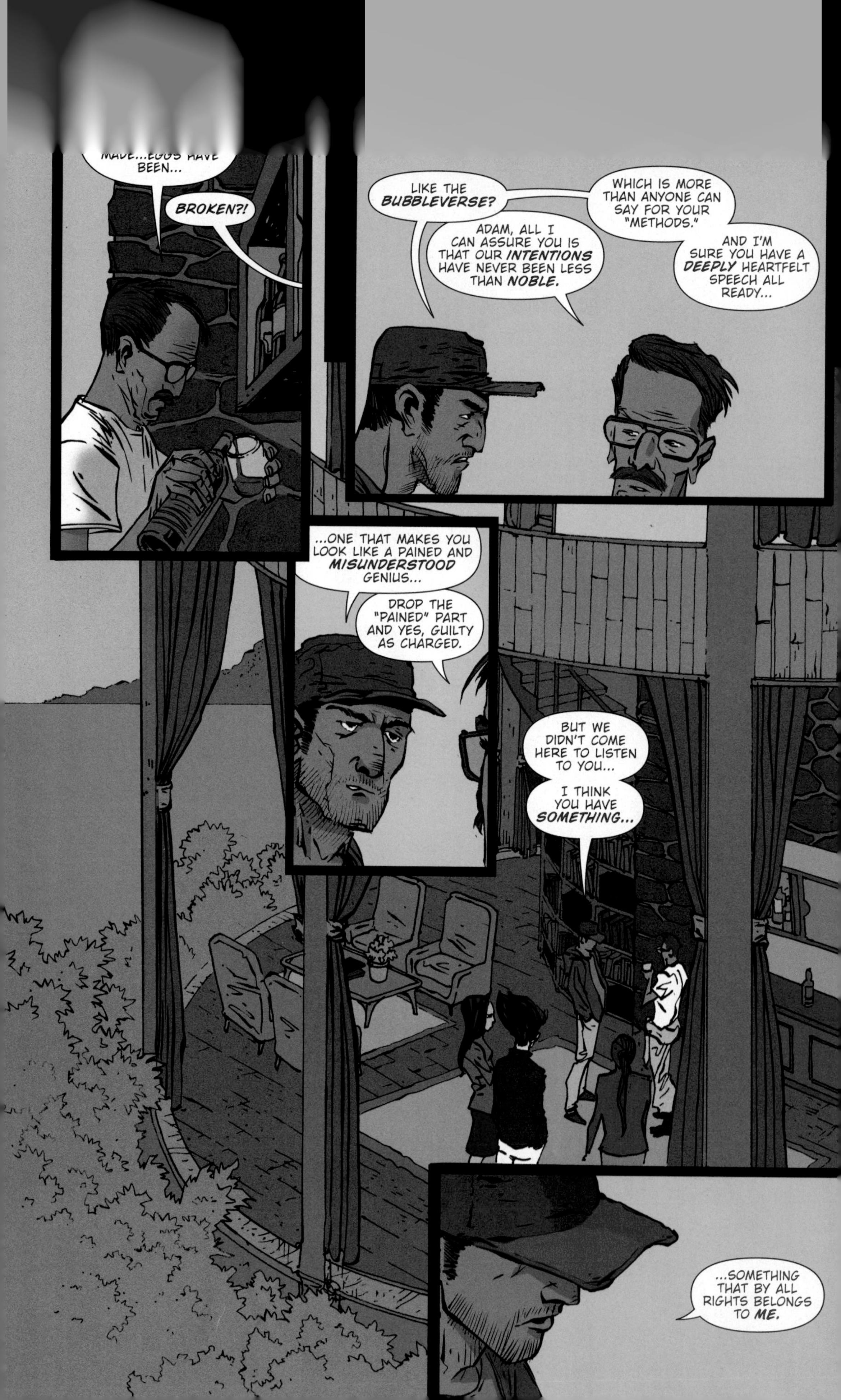

MADE...EGGS HAVE BEEN...
BROKEN?!
LIKE THE BUBBLEVERSE?
ADAM, ALL I CAN ASSURE YOU IS THAT OUR INTENTIONS HAVE NEVER BEEN LESS THAN NOBLE.
WHICH IS MORE THAN ANYONE CAN SAY FOR YOUR "METHODS."
AND I'M SURE YOU HAVE A DEEPLY HEARTFELT SPEECH ALL READY...
...ONE THAT MAKES YOU LOOK LIKE A PAINED AND MISUNDERSTOOD GENIUS...
DROP THE "PAINED" PART AND YES, GUILTY AS CHARGED.
BUT WE DIDN'T COME HERE TO LISTEN TO YOU...
I THINK YOU HAVE SOMETHING...
...SOMETHING THAT BY ALL RIGHTS BELONGS TO ME.

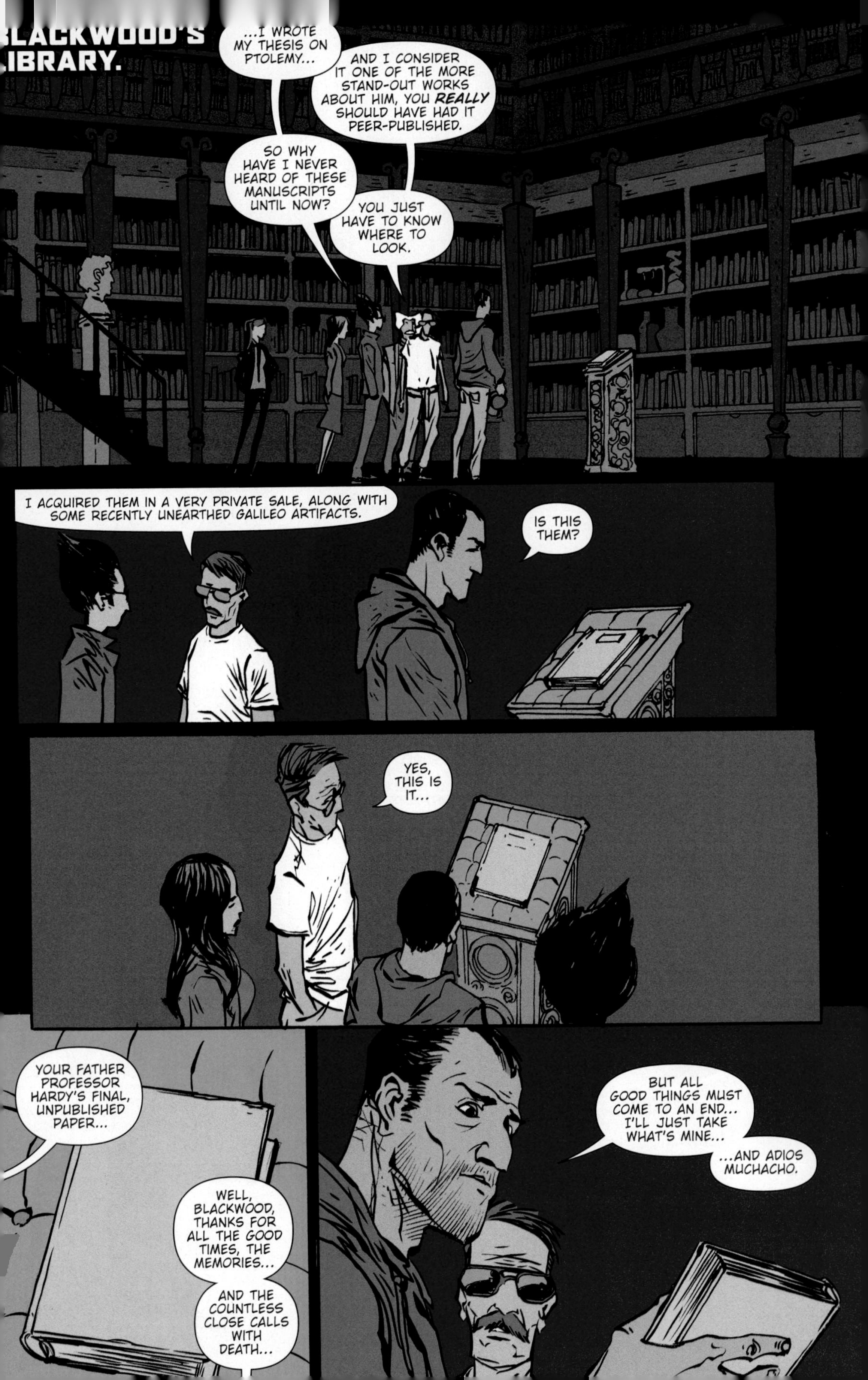
BLACKWOOD'S LIBRARY.
...I WROTE MY THESIS ON PTOLEMY...
AND I CONSIDER IT ONE OF THE MORE STAND-OUT WORKS ABOUT HIM, YOU REALLY SHOULD HAVE HAD IT PEER-PUBLISHED.
SO WHY HAVE I NEVER HEARD OF THESE MANUSCRIPTS UNTIL NOW?
YOU JUST HAVE TO KNOW WHERE TO LOOK.
I ACQUIRED THEM IN A VERY PRIVATE SALE, ALONG WITH SOME RECENTLY UNEARTHED GALILEO ARTIFACTS.
IS THIS THEM?
YES, THIS IS IT...
YOUR FATHER PROFESSOR HARDY'S FINAL, UNPUBLISHED PAPER...
WELL, BLACKWOOD, THANKS FOR ALL THE GOOD TIMES, THE MEMORIES...
AND THE COUNTLESS CLOSE CALLS WITH DEATH...
BUT ALL GOOD THINGS MUST COME TO AN END... I'LL JUST TAKE WHAT'S MINE...
...AND ADIOS MUCHACHO.

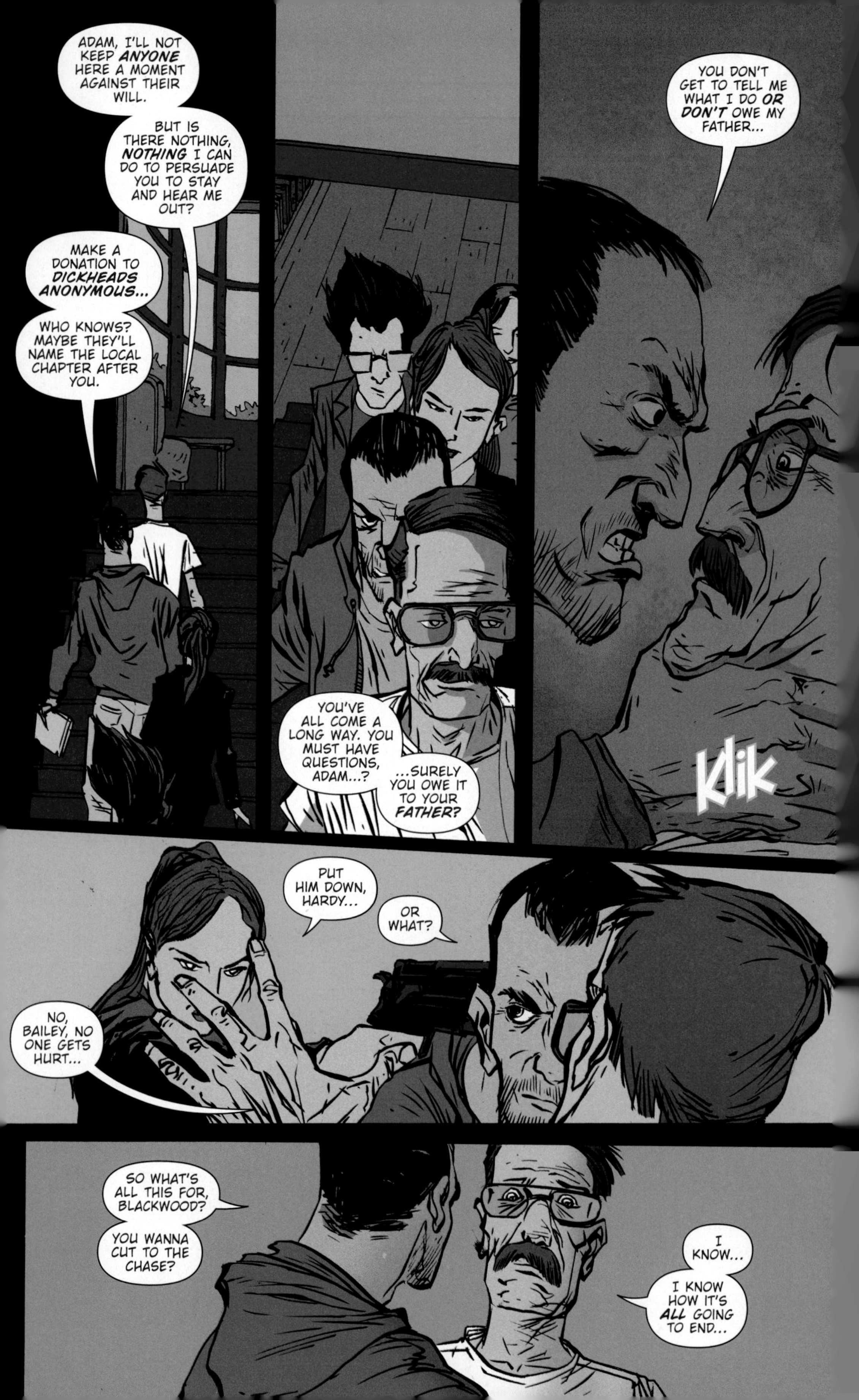
ADAM, I'LL NOT KEEP ANYONE HERE A MOMENT AGAINST THEIR WILL.
BUT IS THERE NOTHING, NOTHING I CAN DO TO PERSUADE YOU TO STAY AND HEAR ME OUT?
MAKE A DONATION TO DICKHEADS ANONYMOUS...
WHO KNOWS? MAYBE THEY'LL NAME THE LOCAL CHAPTER AFTER YOU.
YOU'VE ALL COME A LONG WAY. YOU MUST HAVE QUESTIONS, ADAM...?
...SURELY YOU OWE IT TO YOUR FATHER?
YOU DON'T GET TO TELL ME WHAT I DO OR DON'T OWE MY FATHER...
KLIK
PUT HIM DOWN, HARDY...
OR WHAT?
NO, BAILEY, NO ONE GETS HURT...
SO WHAT'S ALL THIS FOR, BLACKWOOD?
YOU WANNA CUT TO THE CHASE?
I KNOW...
I KNOW HOW IT'S ALL GOING TO END...

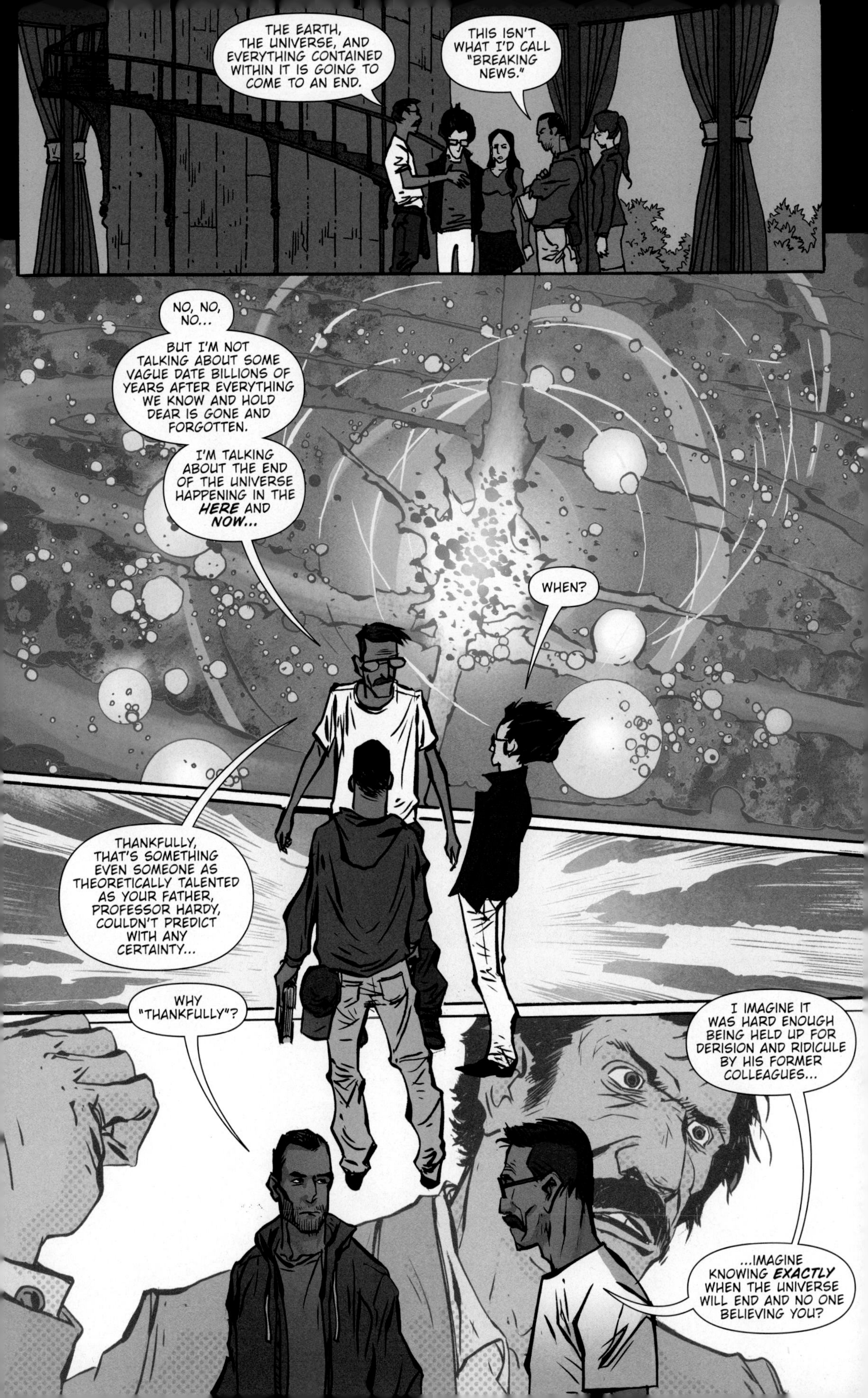
THE EARTH, THE UNIVERSE, AND EVERYTHING CONTAINED WITHIN IT IS GOING TO COME TO AN END.
THIS ISN'T WHAT I'D CALL "BREAKING NEWS."
NO, NO, NO...
BUT I'M NOT TALKING ABOUT SOME VAGUE DATE BILLIONS OF YEARS AFTER EVERYTHING WE KNOW AND HOLD DEAR IS GONE AND FORGOTTEN.
I'M TALKING ABOUT THE END OF THE UNIVERSE HAPPENING IN THE HERE AND NOW...
WHEN?
THANKFULLY, THAT'S SOMETHING EVEN SOMEONE AS THEORETICALLY TALENTED AS YOUR FATHER, PROFESSOR HARDY, COULDN'T PREDICT WITH ANY CERTAINTY...
WHY "THANKFULLY"?
I IMAGINE IT WAS HARD ENOUGH BEING HELD UP FOR DERISION AND RIDICULE BY HIS FORMER COLLEAGUES...
...IMAGINE KNOWING EXACTLY WHEN THE UNIVERSE WILL END AND NO ONE BELIEVING YOU?

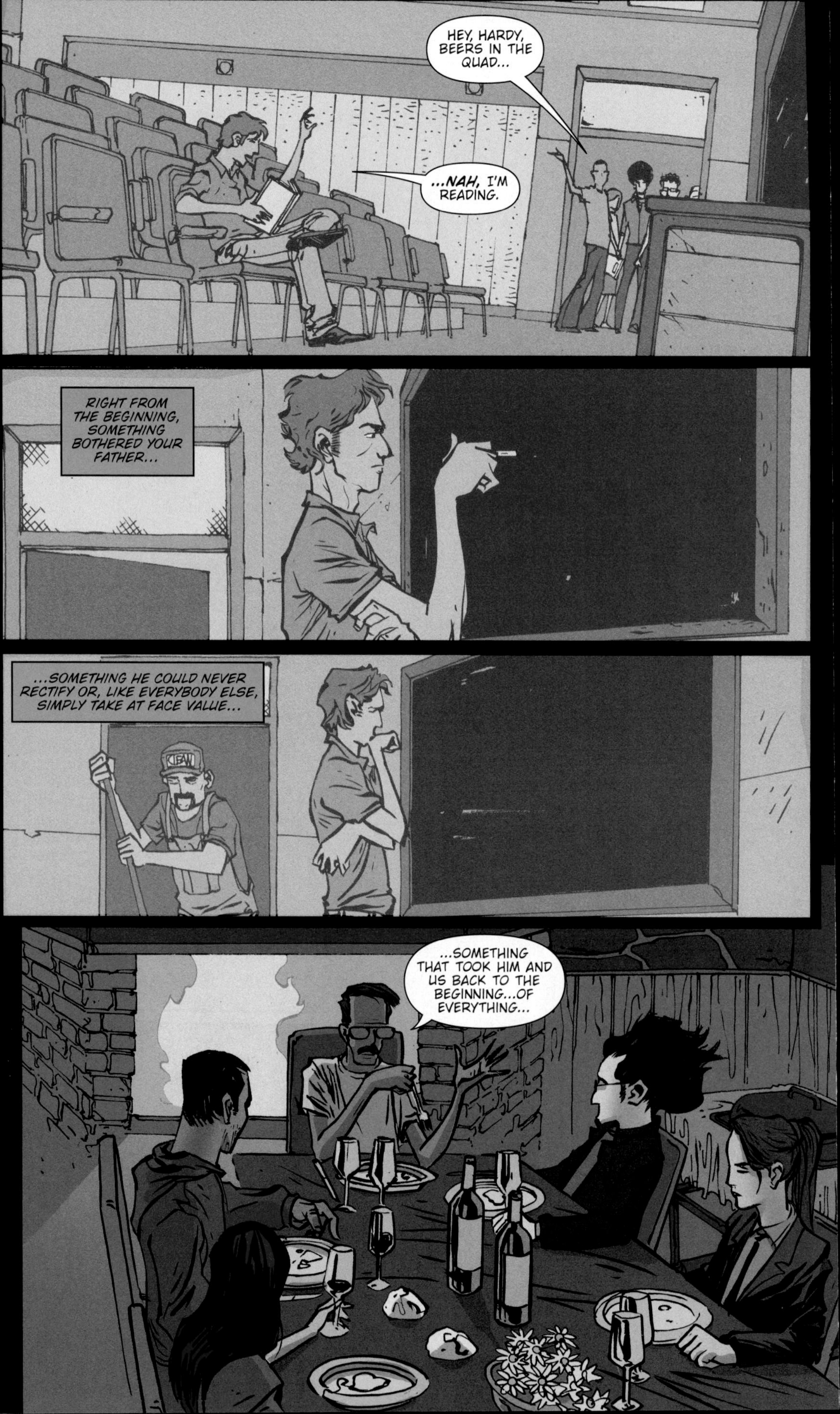
HEY, HARDY, BEERS IN THE QUAD...
...NAH, I'M READING.
RIGHT FROM THE BEGINNING, SOMETHING BOTHERED YOUR FATHER...
...SOMETHING HE COULD NEVER RECTIFY OR, LIKE EVERYBODY ELSE, SIMPLY TAKE AT FACE VALUE...
CLEAN
...SOMETHING THAT TOOK HIM AND US BACK TO THE BEGINNING...OF EVERYTHING...

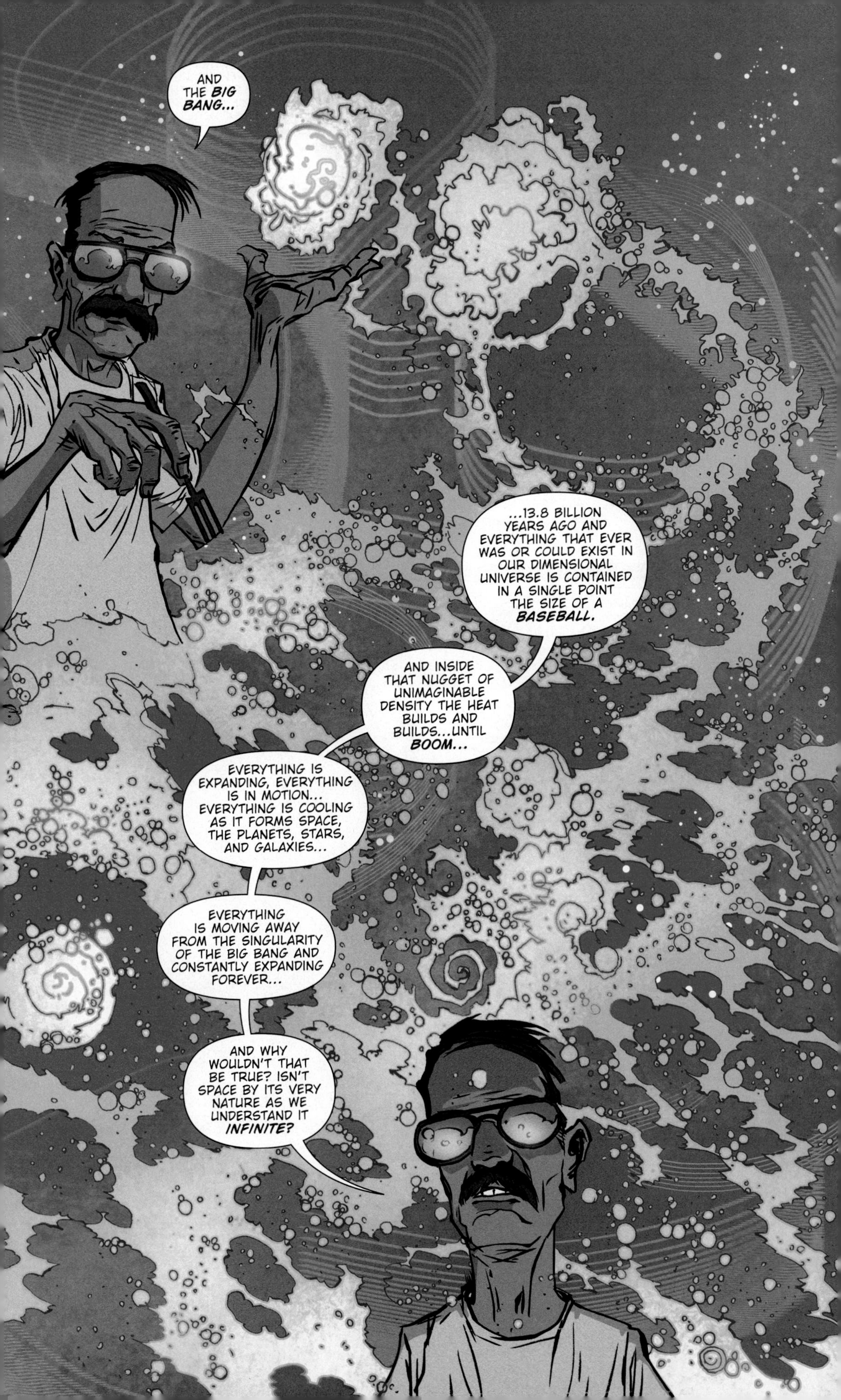
AND THE BIG BANG...
...13.8 BILLION YEARS AGO AND EVERYTHING THAT EVER WAS OR COULD EXIST IN OUR DIMENSIONAL UNIVERSE IS CONTAINED IN A SINGLE POINT THE SIZE OF A BASEBALL.
AND INSIDE THAT NUGGET OF UNIMAGINABLE DENSITY THE HEAT BUILDS AND BUILDS...UNTIL BOOM...
EVERYTHING IS EXPANDING, EVERYTHING IS IN MOTION... EVERYTHING IS COOLING AS IT FORMS SPACE, THE PLANETS, STARS, AND GALAXIES...
EVERYTHING IS MOVING AWAY FROM THE SINGULARITY OF THE BIG BANG AND CONSTANTLY EXPANDING FOREVER...
AND WHY WOULDN'T THAT BE TRUE? ISN'T SPACE BY ITS VERY NATURE AS WE UNDERSTAND IT INFINITE?

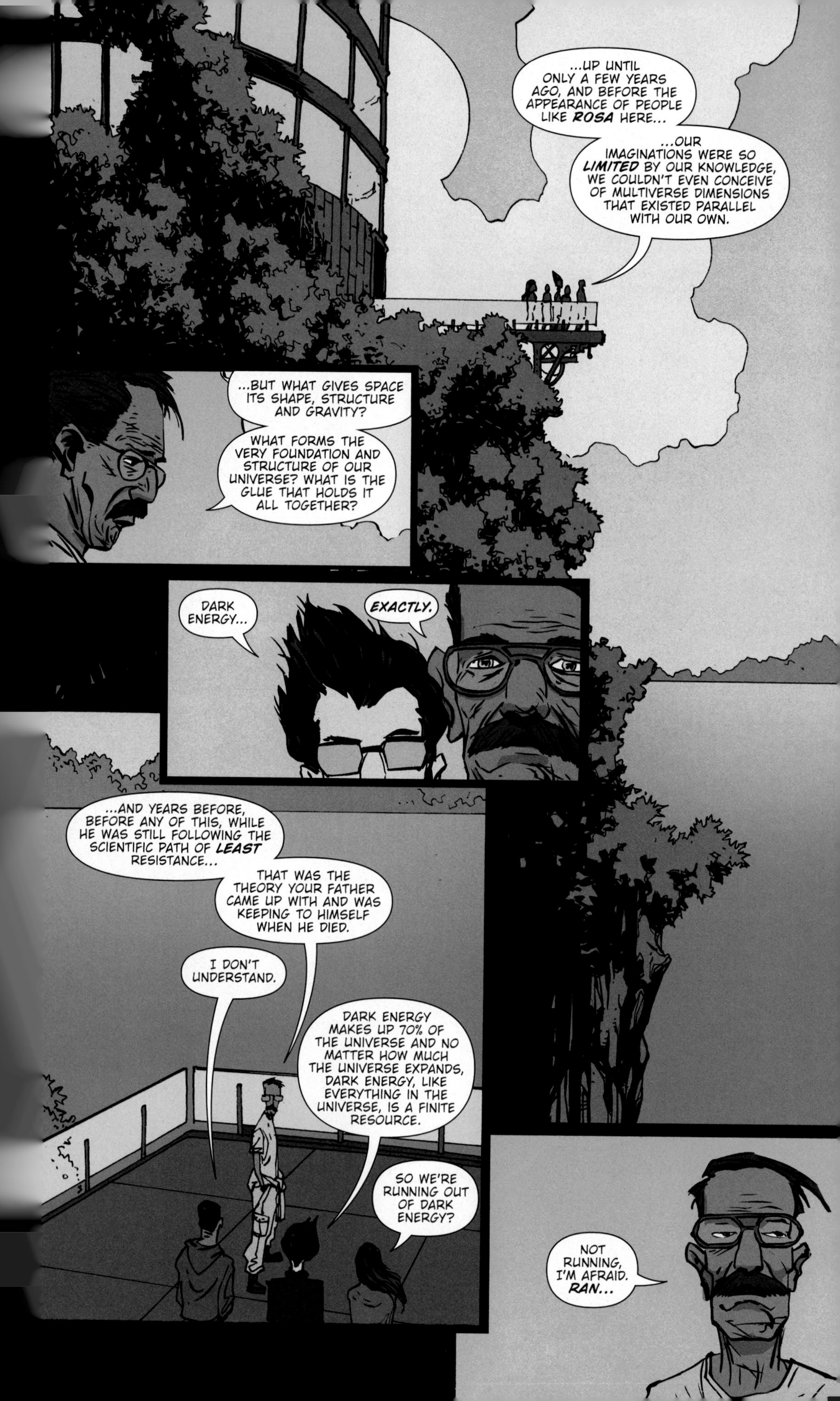
...UP UNTIL ONLY A FEW YEARS AGO, AND BEFORE THE APPEARANCE OF PEOPLE LIKE ROSA HERE...
...OUR IMAGINATIONS WERE SO LIMITED BY OUR KNOWLEDGE, WE COULDN'T EVEN CONCEIVE OF MULTIVERSE DIMENSIONS THAT EXISTED PARALLEL WITH OUR OWN.
...BUT WHAT GIVES SPACE ITS SHAPE, STRUCTURE AND GRAVITY?
WHAT FORMS THE VERY FOUNDATION AND STRUCTURE OF OUR UNIVERSE? WHAT IS THE GLUE THAT HOLDS IT ALL TOGETHER?
DARK ENERGY...
EXACTLY.
...AND YEARS BEFORE, BEFORE ANY OF THIS, WHILE HE WAS STILL FOLLOWING THE SCIENTIFIC PATH OF LEAST RESISTANCE...
THAT WAS THE THEORY YOUR FATHER CAME UP WITH AND WAS KEEPING TO HIMSELF WHEN HE DIED.
I DON'T UNDERSTAND.
DARK ENERGY MAKES UP 70% OF THE UNIVERSE AND NO MATTER HOW MUCH THE UNIVERSE EXPANDS, DARK ENERGY, LIKE EVERYTHING IN THE UNIVERSE, IS A FINITE RESOURCE.
SO WE'RE RUNNING OUT OF DARK ENERGY?
NOT RUNNING, I'M AFRAID. RAN...

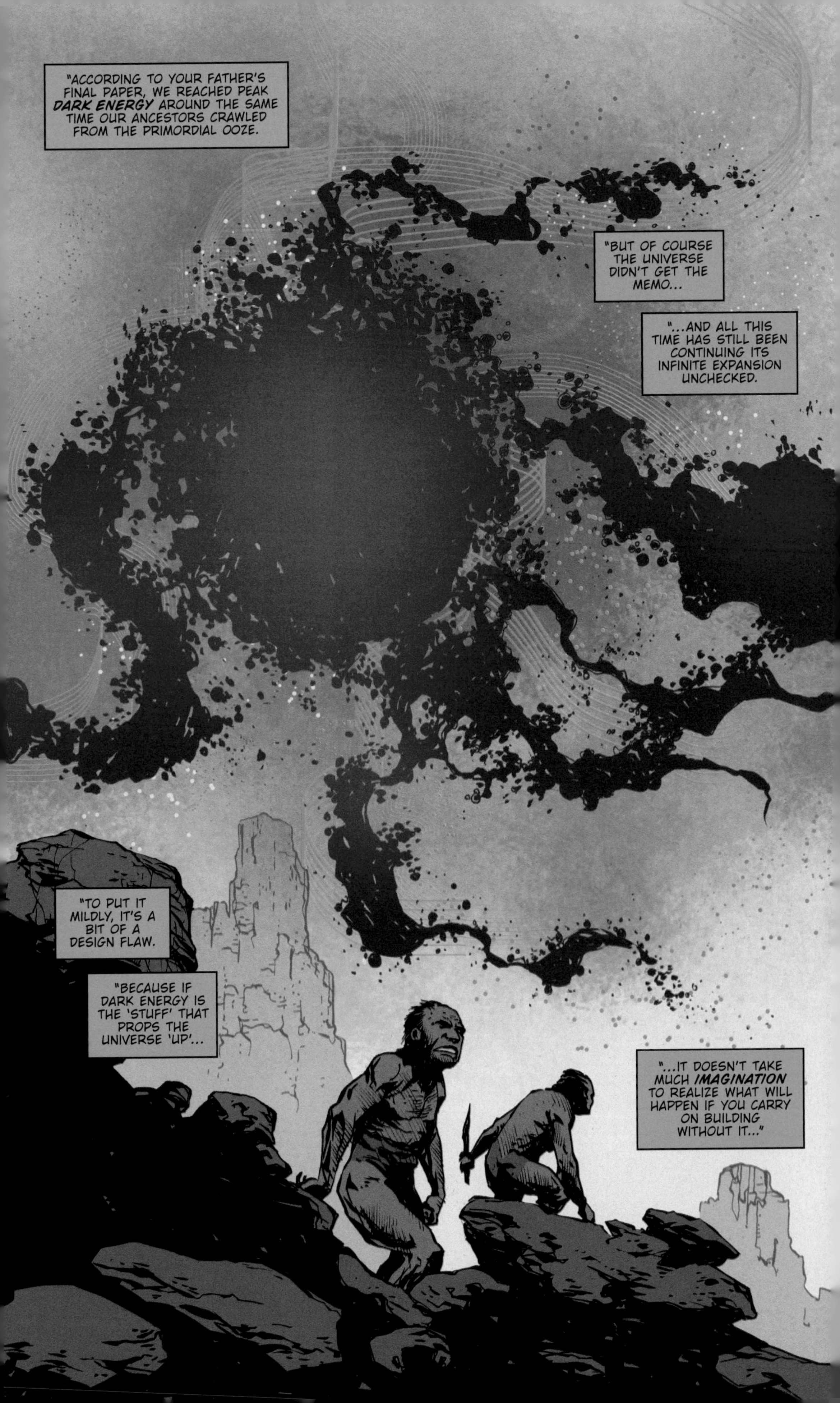
"ACCORDING TO YOUR FATHER'S FINAL PAPER, WE REACHED PEAK **DARK ENERGY** AROUND THE SAME TIME OUR ANCESTORS CRAWLED FROM THE PRIMORDIAL OOZE.
"BUT OF COURSE THE UNIVERSE DIDN'T GET THE MEMO...
"...AND ALL THIS TIME HAS STILL BEEN CONTINUING ITS INFINITE EXPANSION UNCHECKED.
"TO PUT IT MILDLY, IT'S A BIT OF A DESIGN FLAW.
"BECAUSE IF DARK ENERGY IS THE 'STUFF' THAT PROPS THE UNIVERSE 'UP'...
"...IT DOESN'T TAKE MUCH **IMAGINATION** TO REALIZE WHAT WILL HAPPEN IF YOU CARRY ON BUILDING WITHOUT IT..."

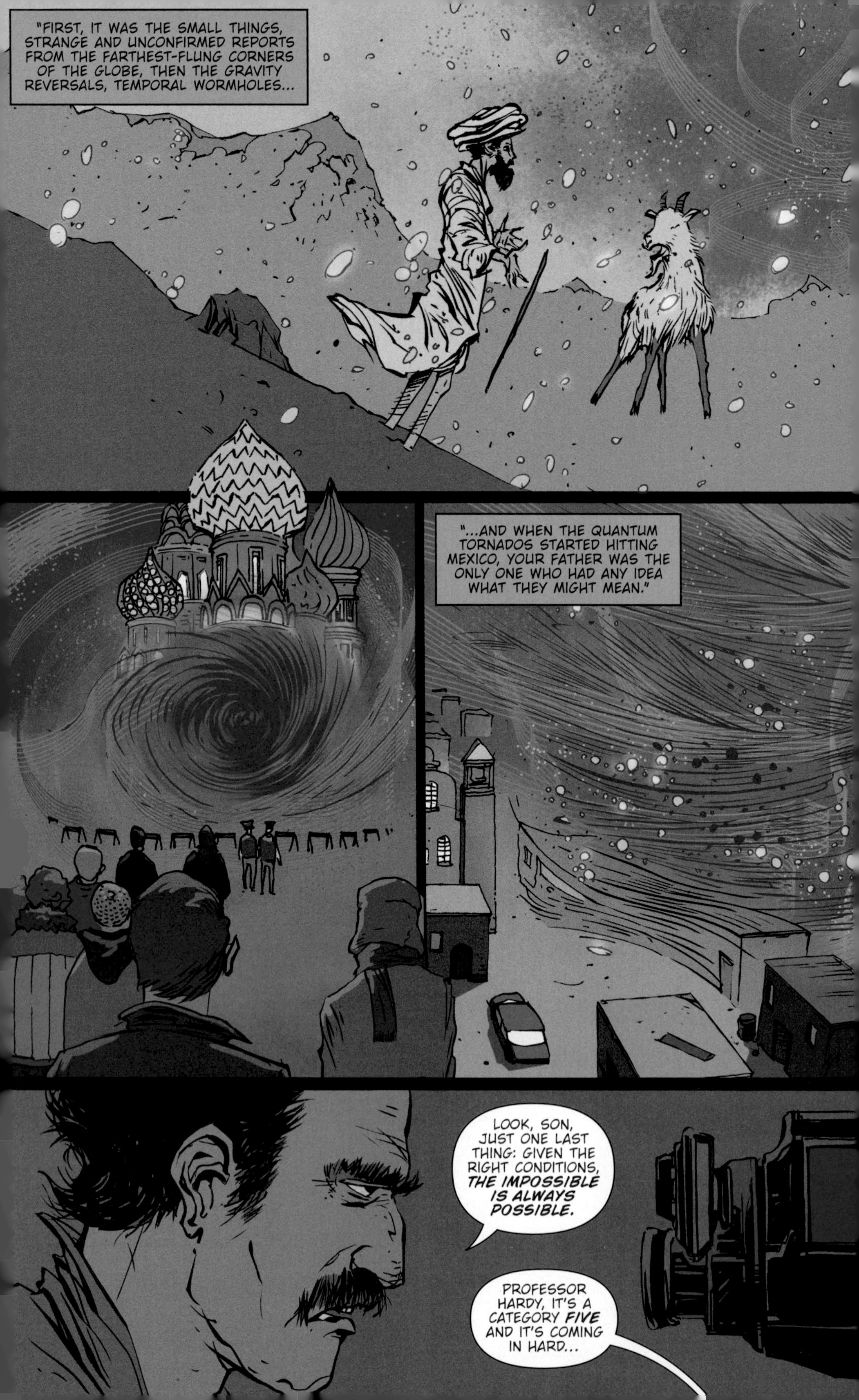
"FIRST, IT WAS THE SMALL THINGS, STRANGE AND UNCONFIRMED REPORTS FROM THE FARTHEST-FLUNG CORNERS OF THE GLOBE, THEN THE GRAVITY REVERSALS, TEMPORAL WORMHOLES...
"...AND WHEN THE QUANTUM TORNADOS STARTED HITTING MEXICO, YOUR FATHER WAS THE ONLY ONE WHO HAD ANY IDEA WHAT THEY MIGHT MEAN."
LOOK, SON, JUST ONE LAST THING: GIVEN THE RIGHT CONDITIONS, *THE IMPOSSIBLE IS ALWAYS POSSIBLE.*
PROFESSOR HARDY, IT'S A CATEGORY *FIVE* AND IT'S COMING IN HARD...

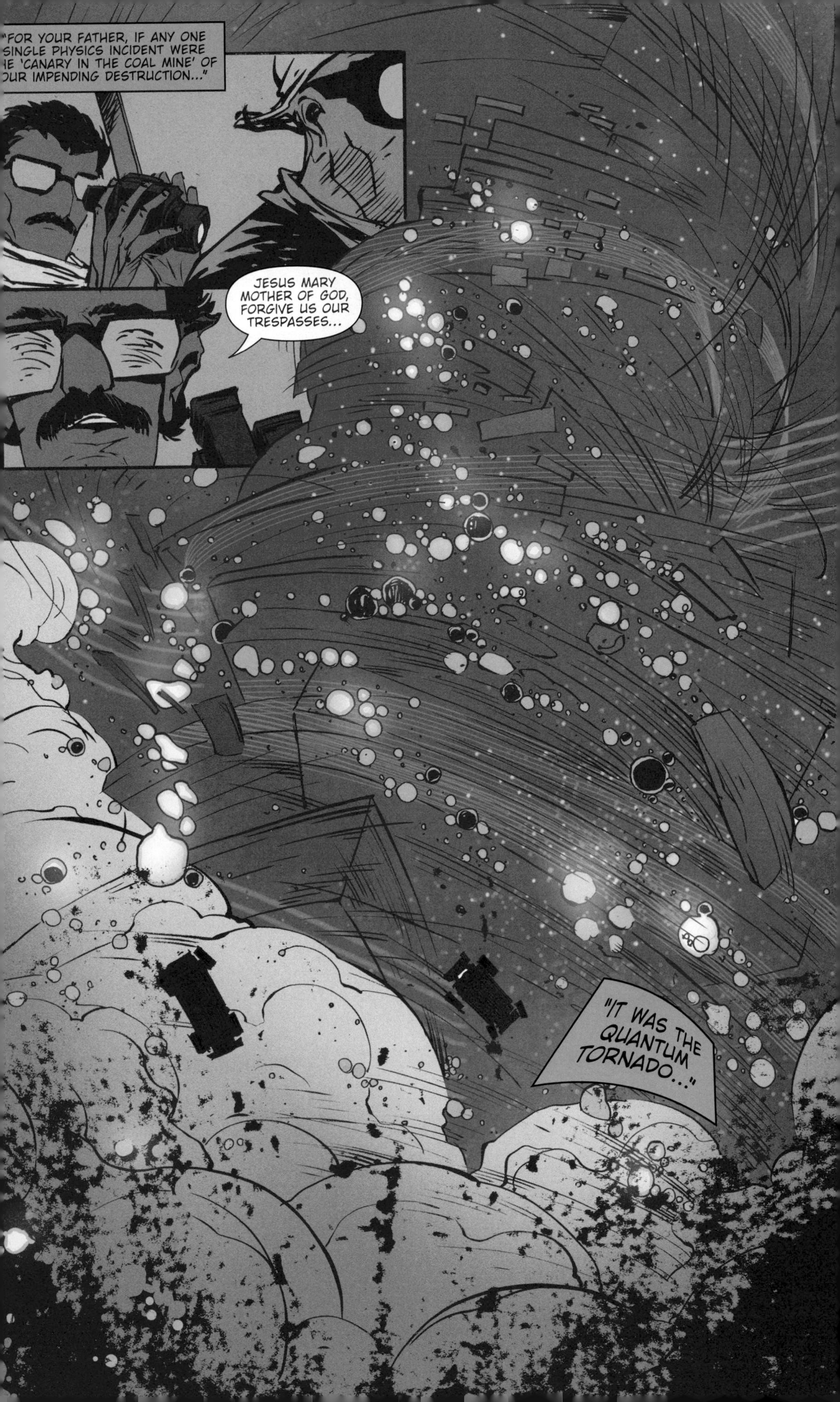
"FOR YOUR FATHER, IF ANY ONE SINGLE PHYSICS INCIDENT WERE THE 'CANARY IN THE COAL MINE' OF OUR IMPENDING DESTRUCTION..."
JESUS MARY MOTHER OF GOD, FORGIVE US OUR TRESPASSES...
"IT WAS THE QUANTUM TORNADO..."

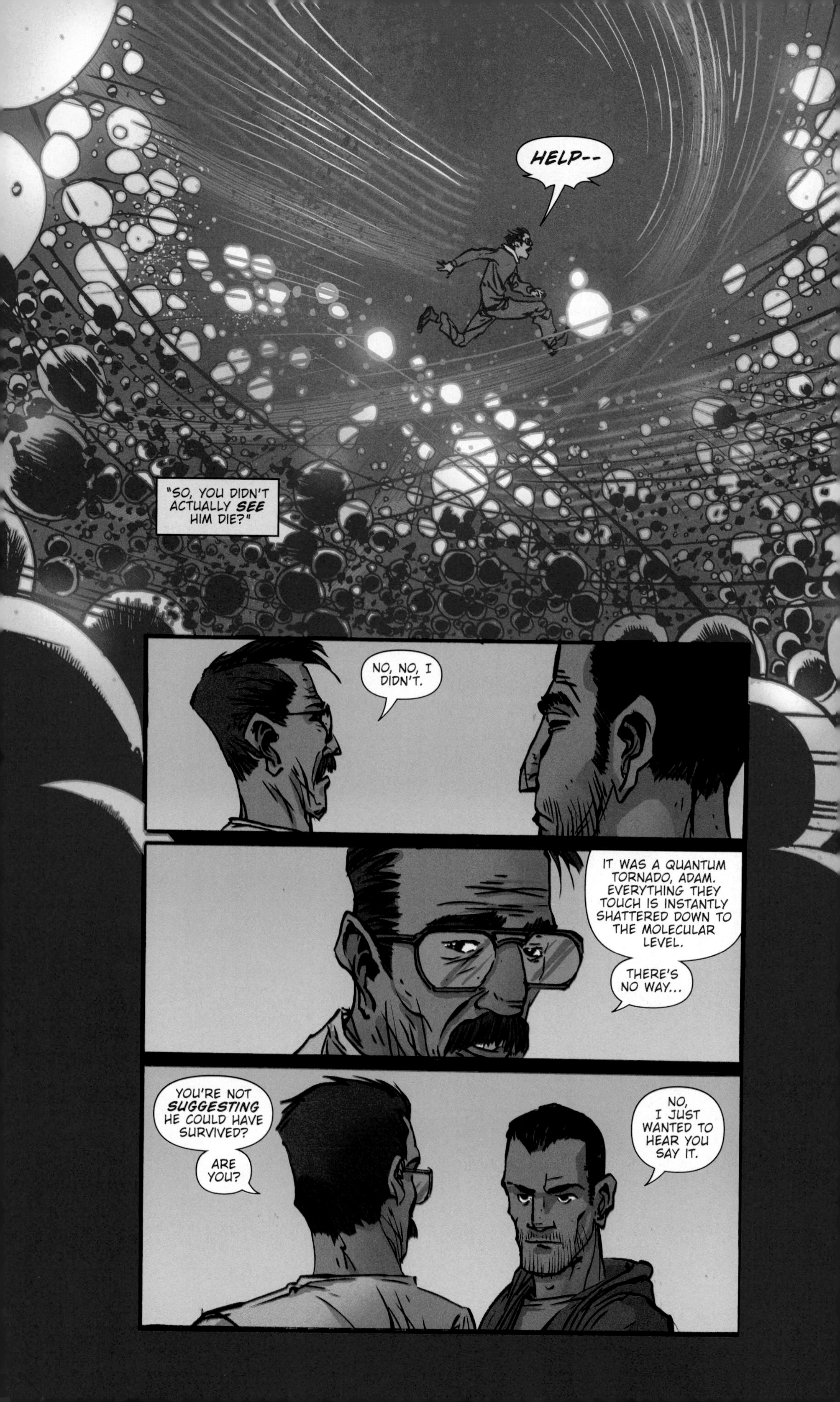
HELP--
"SO, YOU DIDN'T ACTUALLY SEE HIM DIE?"
NO, NO, I DIDN'T.
IT WAS A QUANTUM TORNADO, ADAM. EVERYTHING THEY TOUCH IS INSTANTLY SHATTERED DOWN TO THE MOLECULAR LEVEL.
THERE'S NO WAY...
YOU'RE NOT SUGGESTING HE COULD HAVE SURVIVED?
ARE YOU?
NO, I JUST WANTED TO HEAR YOU SAY IT.

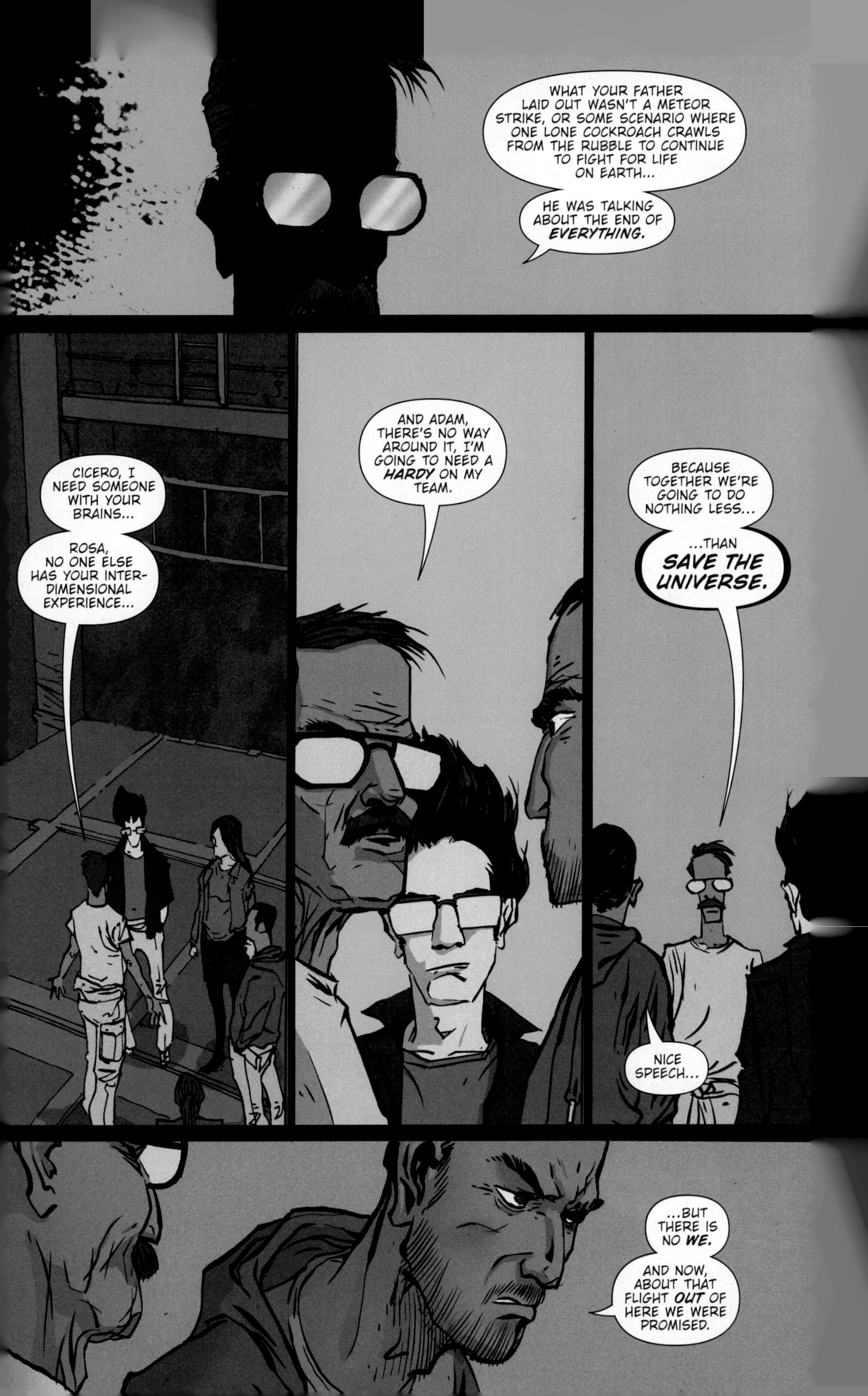
WHAT YOUR FATHER LAID OUT WASN'T A METEOR STRIKE, OR SOME SCENARIO WHERE ONE LONE COCKROACH CRAWLS FROM THE RUBBLE TO CONTINUE TO FIGHT FOR LIFE ON EARTH...
HE WAS TALKING ABOUT THE END OF *EVERYTHING.*
CICERO, I NEED SOMEONE WITH YOUR BRAINS...
ROSA, NO ONE ELSE HAS YOUR INTER-DIMENSIONAL EXPERIENCE...
AND ADAM, THERE'S NO WAY AROUND IT, I'M GOING TO NEED A *HARDY* ON MY TEAM.
BECAUSE TOGETHER WE'RE GOING TO DO NOTHING LESS...
...THAN **SAVE THE UNIVERSE.**
NICE SPEECH...
...BUT THERE IS NO *WE.*
AND NOW, ABOUT THAT FLIGHT *OUT* OF HERE WE WERE PROMISED.

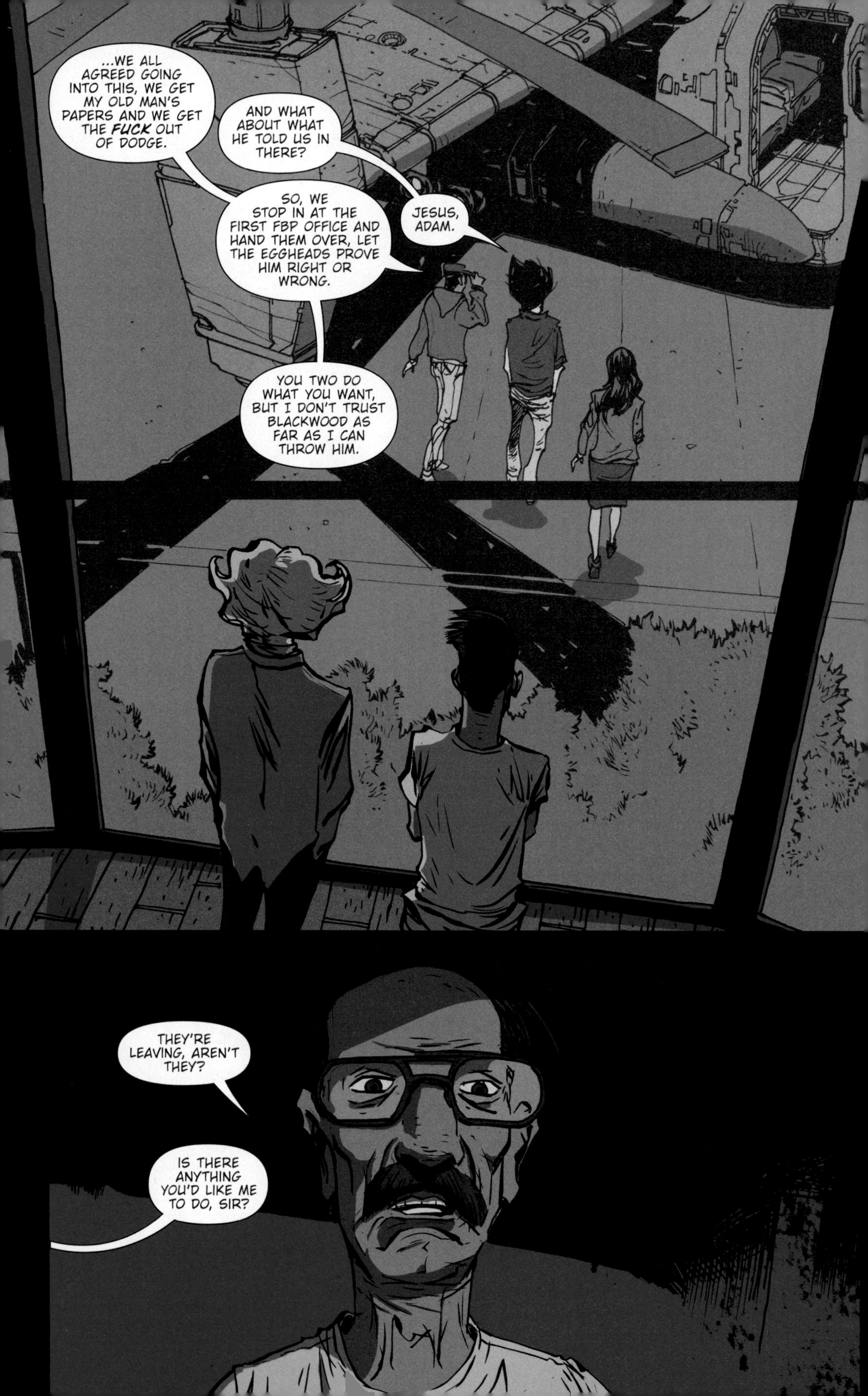

...WE ALL AGREED GOING INTO THIS, WE GET MY OLD MAN'S PAPERS AND WE GET THE ***FUCK*** OUT OF DODGE.
AND WHAT ABOUT WHAT HE TOLD US IN THERE?
SO, WE STOP IN AT THE FIRST FBP OFFICE AND HAND THEM OVER, LET THE EGGHEADS PROVE HIM RIGHT OR WRONG.
JESUS, ADAM.
YOU TWO DO WHAT YOU WANT, BUT I DON'T TRUST BLACKWOOD AS FAR AS I CAN THROW HIM.
THEY'RE LEAVING, AREN'T THEY?
IS THERE ANYTHING YOU'D LIKE ME TO DO, SIR?

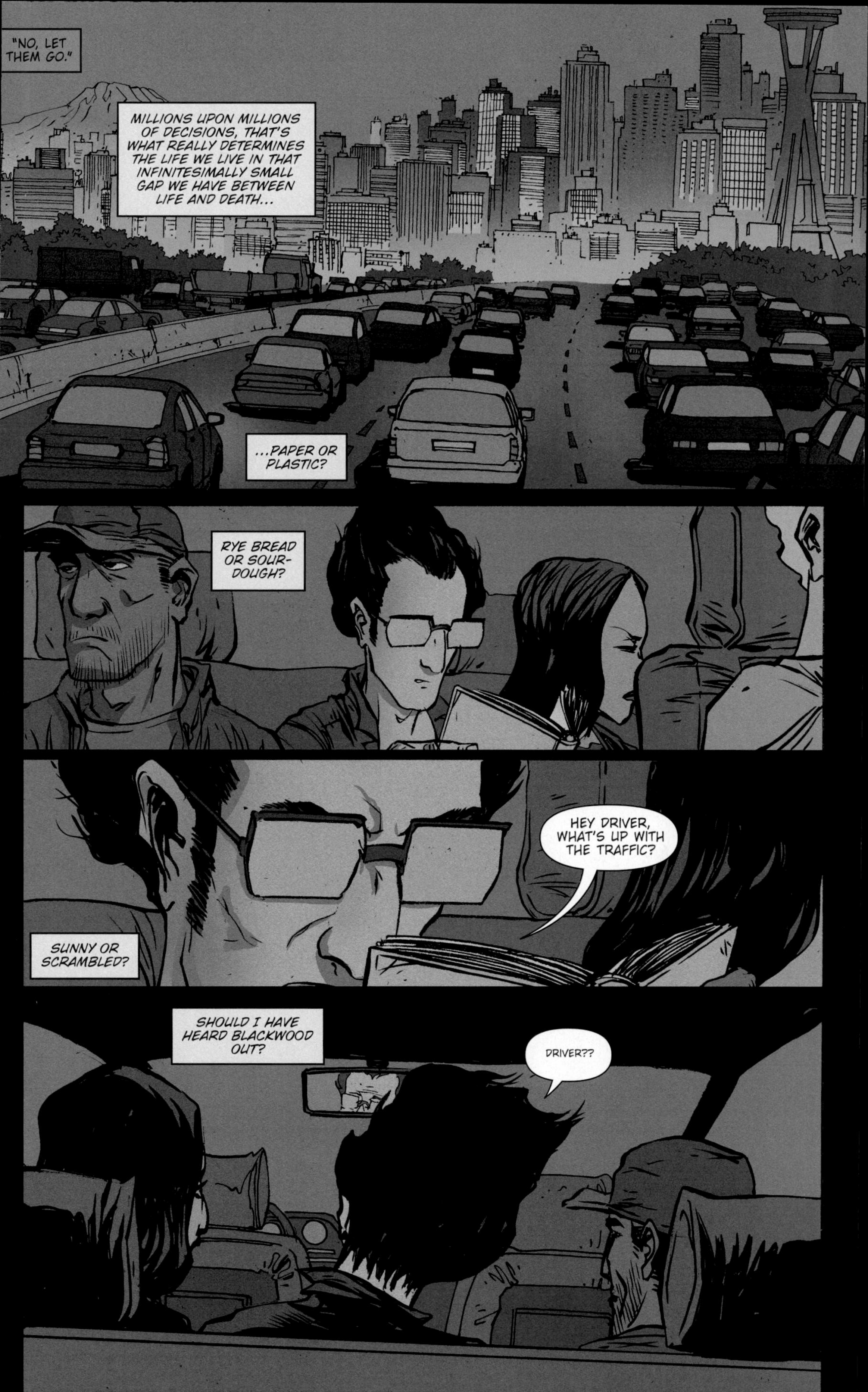
"NO, LET THEM GO."
MILLIONS UPON MILLIONS OF DECISIONS, THAT'S WHAT REALLY DETERMINES THE LIFE WE LIVE IN THAT INFINITESIMALLY SMALL GAP WE HAVE BETWEEN LIFE AND DEATH...
...PAPER OR PLASTIC?
RYE BREAD OR SOUR-DOUGH?
HEY DRIVER, WHAT'S UP WITH THE TRAFFIC?
SUNNY OR SCRAMBLED?
SHOULD I HAVE HEARD BLACKWOOD OUT?
DRIVER??

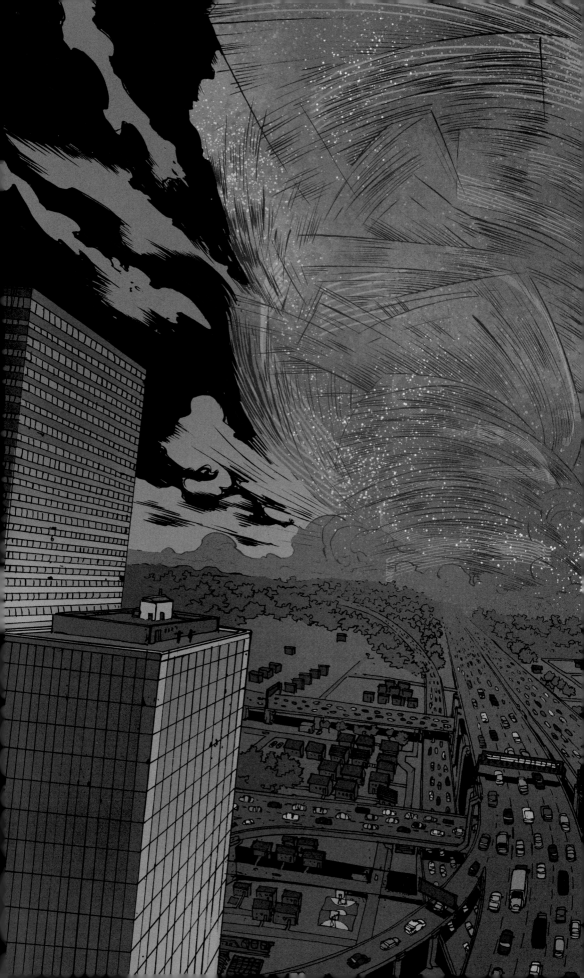

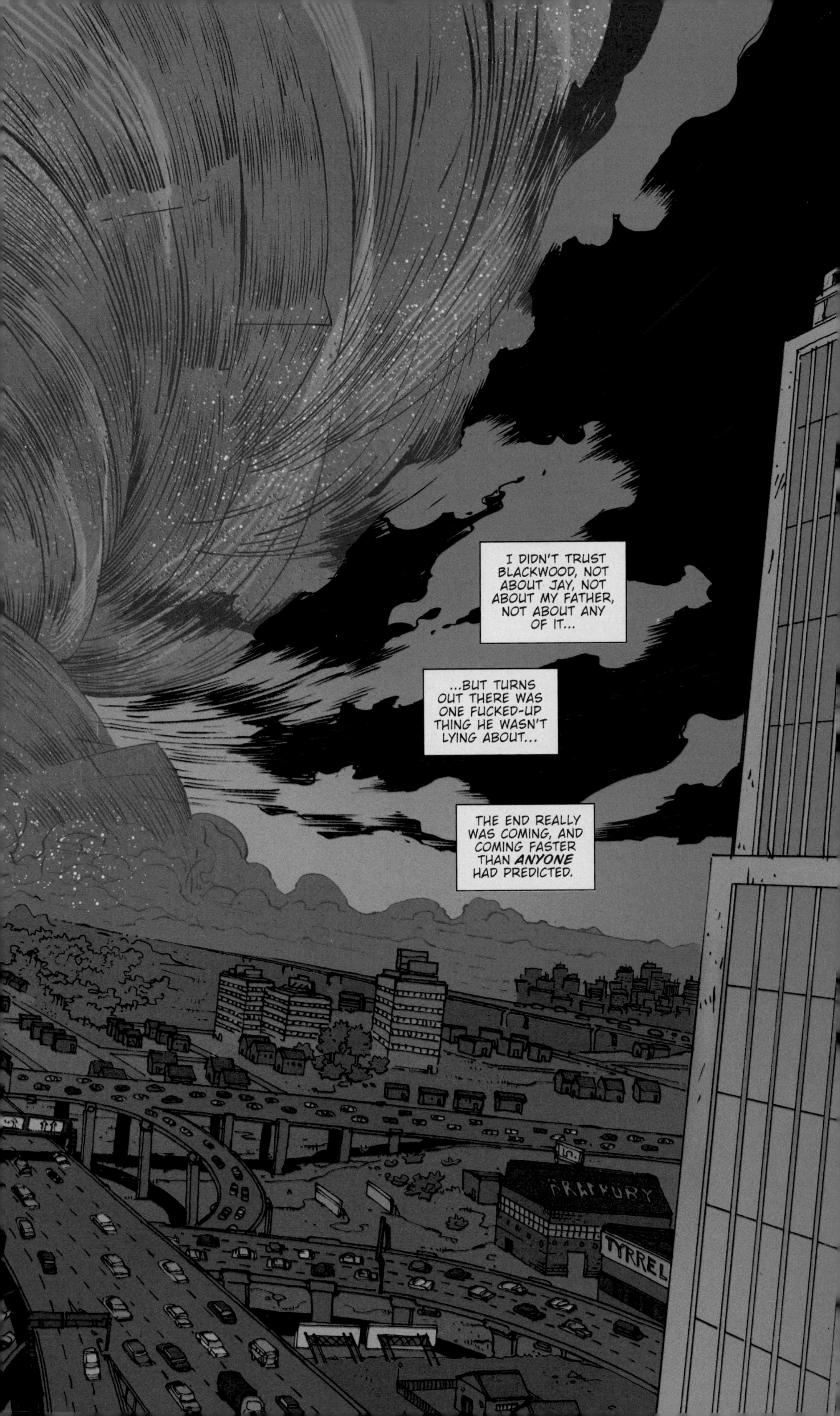
I DIDN'T TRUST BLACKWOOD, NOT ABOUT JAY, NOT ABOUT MY FATHER, NOT ABOUT ANY OF IT...
...BUT TURNS OUT THERE WAS ONE FUCKED-UP THING HE WASN'T LYING ABOUT...
THE END REALLY WAS COMING, AND COMING FASTER THAN ***ANYONE*** HAD PREDICTED.
TYRREL

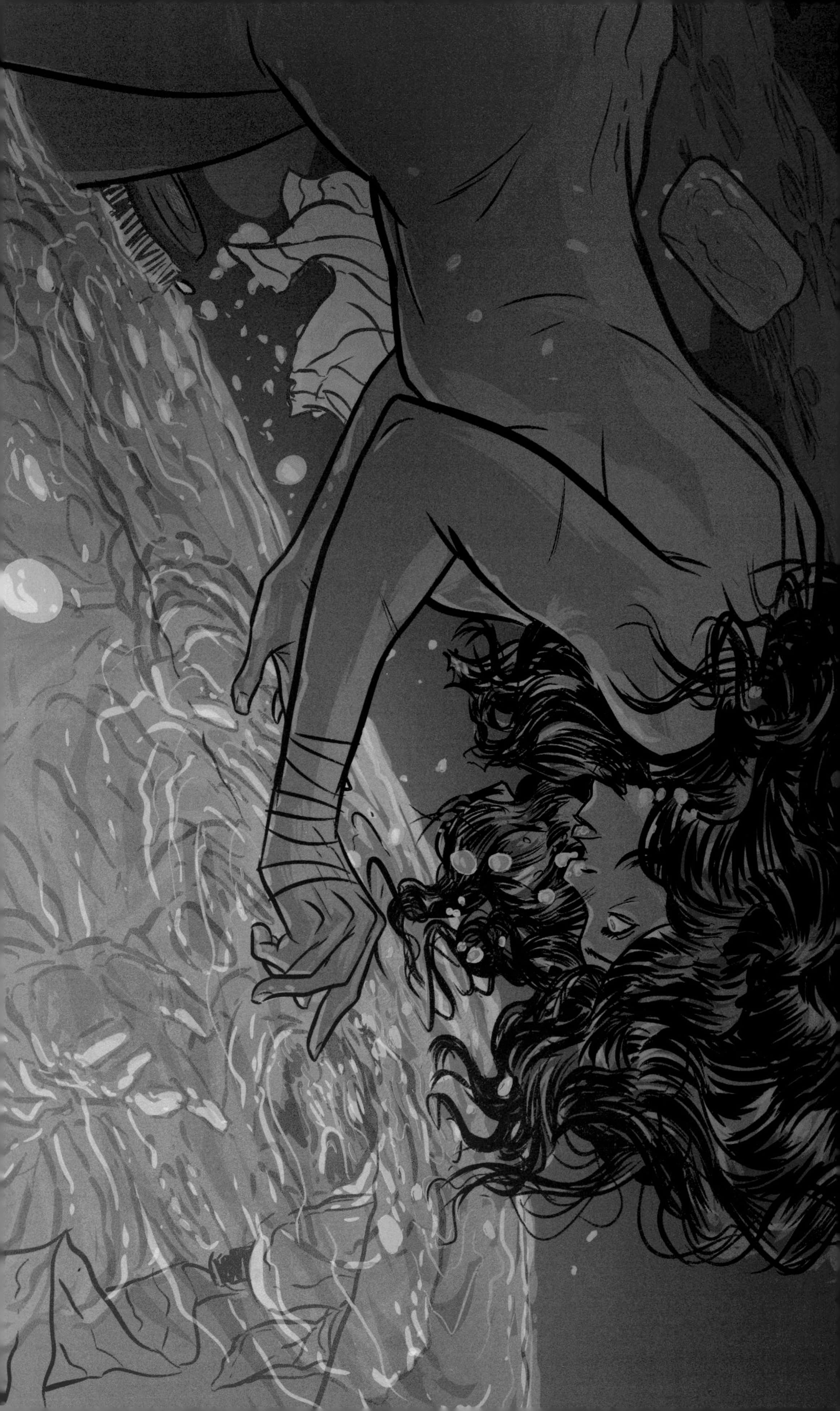

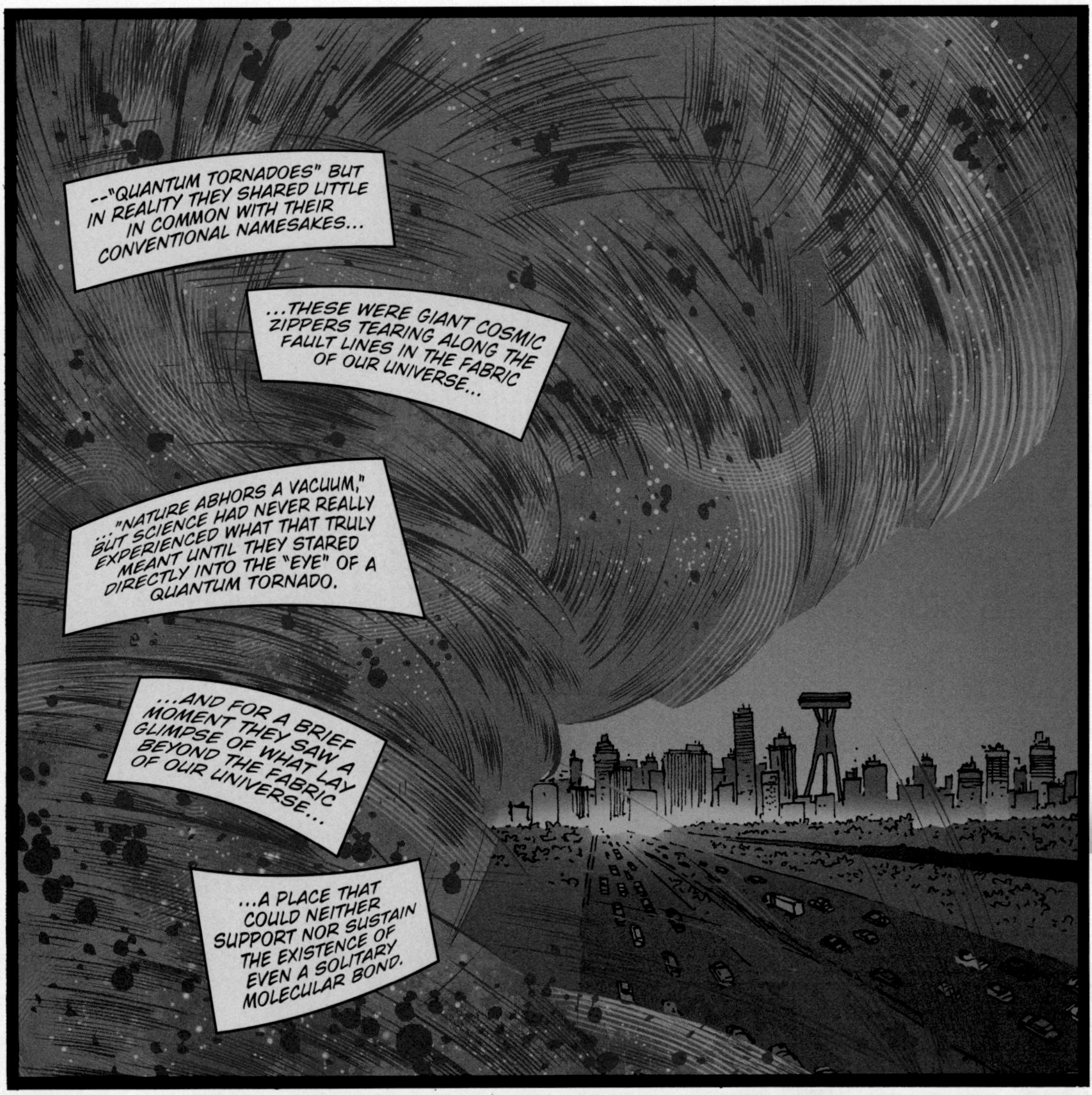
--"QUANTUM TORNADOES" BUT IN REALITY THEY SHARED LITTLE IN COMMON WITH THEIR CONVENTIONAL NAMESAKES...
...THESE WERE GIANT COSMIC ZIPPERS TEARING ALONG THE FAULT LINES IN THE FABRIC OF OUR UNIVERSE...
..."NATURE ABHORS A VACUUM," BUT SCIENCE HAD NEVER REALLY EXPERIENCED WHAT THAT TRULY MEANT UNTIL THEY STARED DIRECTLY INTO THE "EYE" OF A QUANTUM TORNADO.
...AND FOR A BRIEF MOMENT THEY SAW A GLIMPSE OF WHAT LAY BEYOND THE FABRIC OF OUR UNIVERSE...
...A PLACE THAT COULD NEITHER SUPPORT NOR SUSTAIN THE EXISTENCE OF EVEN A SOLITARY MOLECULAR BOND.

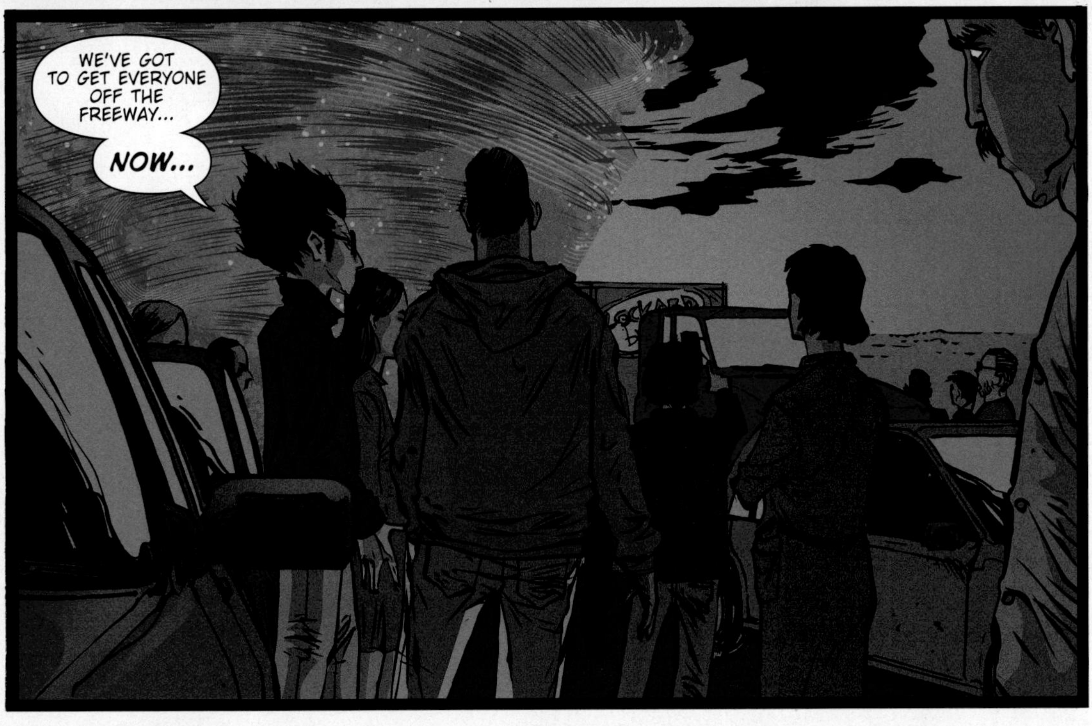
WE'VE GOT TO GET EVERYONE OFF THE FREEWAY... NOW...

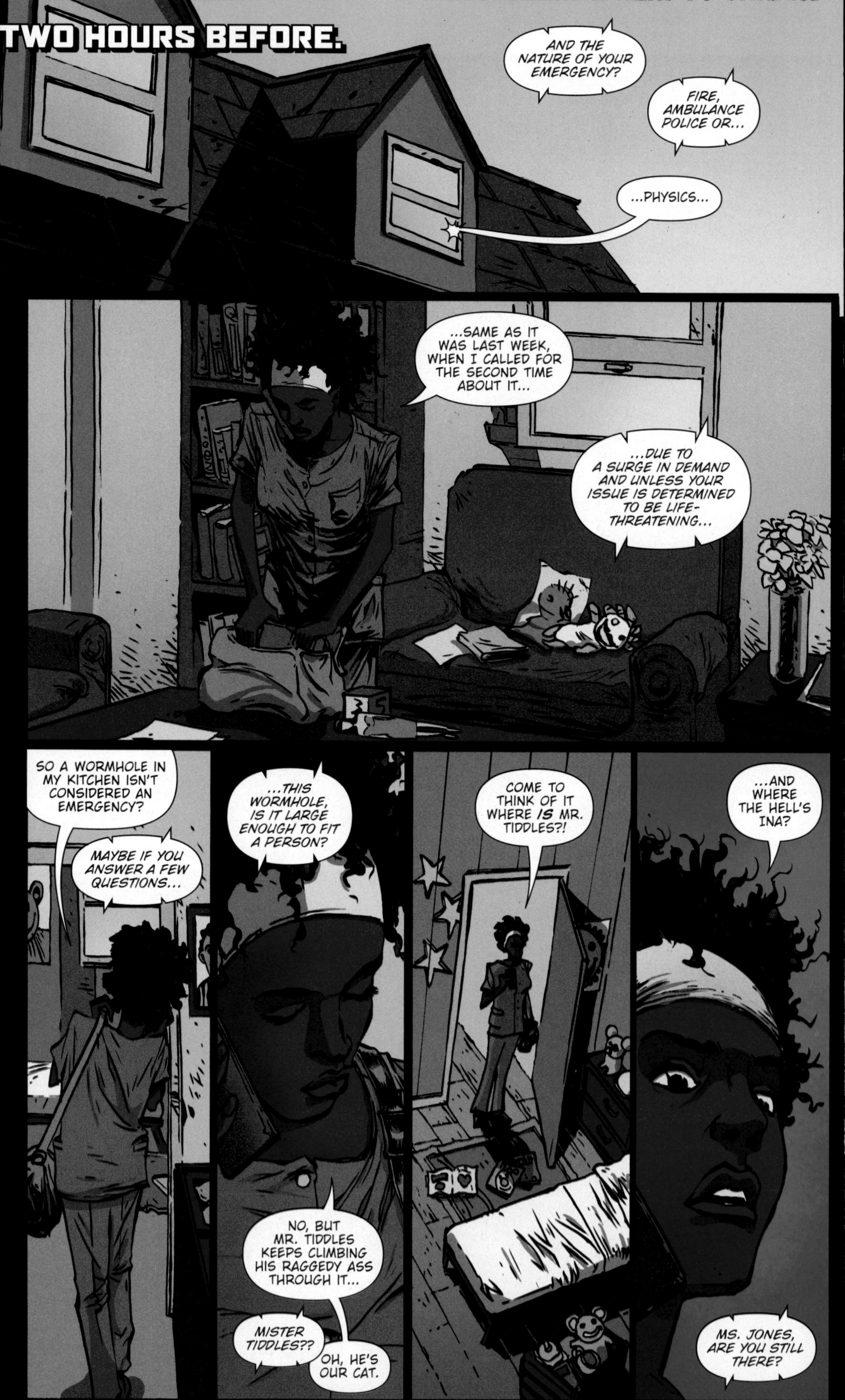
TWO HOURS BEFORE.
AND THE NATURE OF YOUR EMERGENCY?
FIRE, AMBULANCE POLICE OR...
...PHYSICS...
...SAME AS IT WAS LAST WEEK, WHEN I CALLED FOR THE SECOND TIME ABOUT IT...
...DUE TO A SURGE IN DEMAND AND UNLESS YOUR ISSUE IS DETERMINED TO BE LIFE-THREATENING...
SO A WORMHOLE IN MY KITCHEN ISN'T CONSIDERED AN EMERGENCY?
MAYBE IF YOU ANSWER A FEW QUESTIONS...
...THIS WORMHOLE, IS IT LARGE ENOUGH TO FIT A PERSON?
NO, BUT MR. TIDDLES KEEPS CLIMBING HIS RAGGEDY ASS THROUGH IT...
MISTER TIDDLES??
OH, HE'S OUR CAT.
COME TO THINK OF IT WHERE IS MR. TIDDLES?!
...AND WHERE THE HELL'S INA?
MS. JONES, ARE YOU STILL THERE?

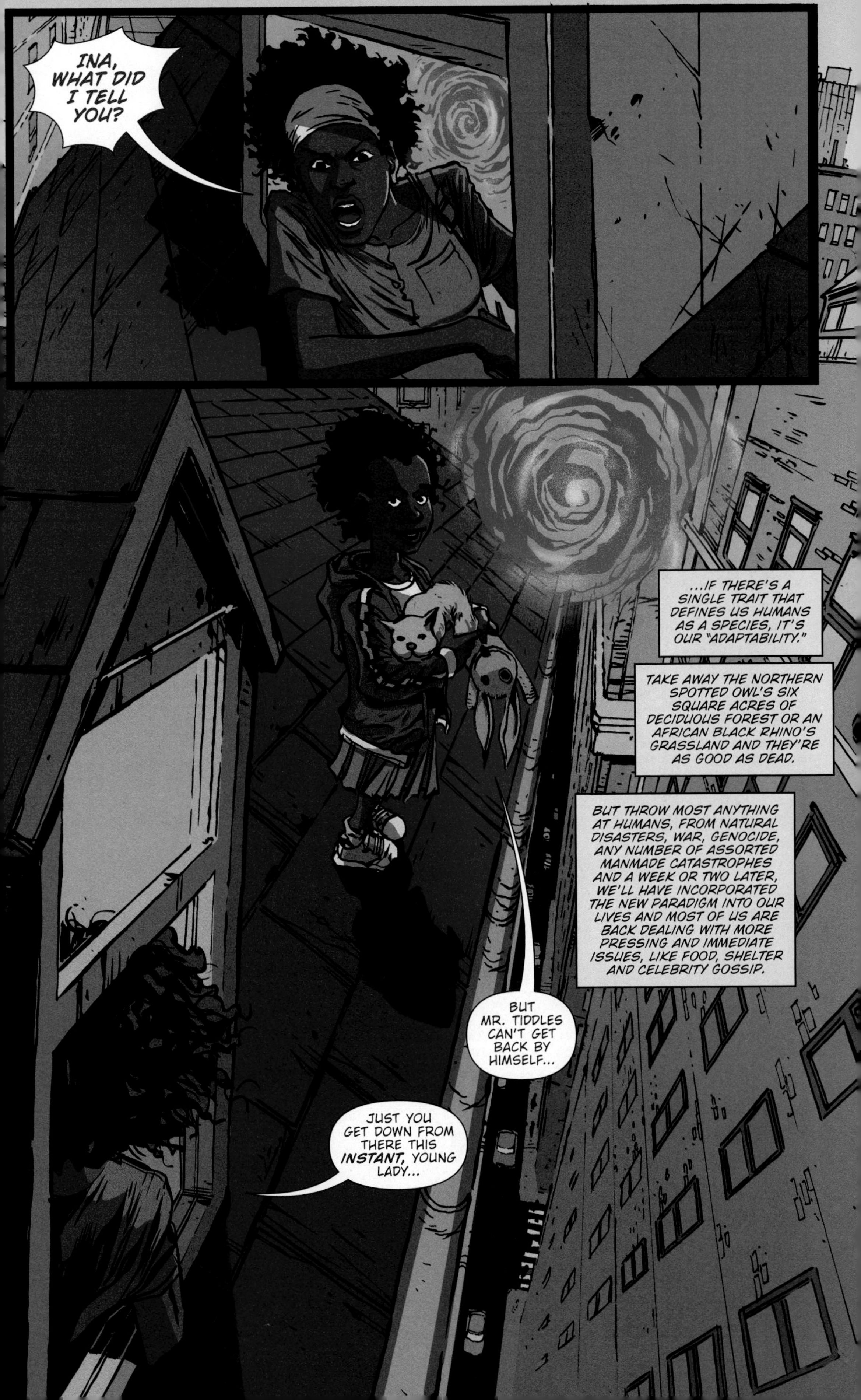
INA, WHAT DID I TELL YOU?
...IF THERE'S A SINGLE TRAIT THAT DEFINES US HUMANS AS A SPECIES, IT'S OUR "ADAPTABILITY."
TAKE AWAY THE NORTHERN SPOTTED OWL'S SIX SQUARE ACRES OF DECIDUOUS FOREST OR AN AFRICAN BLACK RHINO'S GRASSLAND AND THEY'RE AS GOOD AS DEAD.
BUT THROW MOST ANYTHING AT HUMANS, FROM NATURAL DISASTERS, WAR, GENOCIDE, ANY NUMBER OF ASSORTED MANMADE CATASTROPHES AND A WEEK OR TWO LATER, WE'LL HAVE INCORPORATED THE NEW PARADIGM INTO OUR LIVES AND MOST OF US ARE BACK DEALING WITH MORE PRESSING AND IMMEDIATE ISSUES, LIKE FOOD, SHELTER AND CELEBRITY GOSSIP.
BUT MR. TIDDLES CAN'T GET BACK BY HIMSELF...
JUST YOU GET DOWN FROM THERE THIS INSTANT, YOUNG LADY...

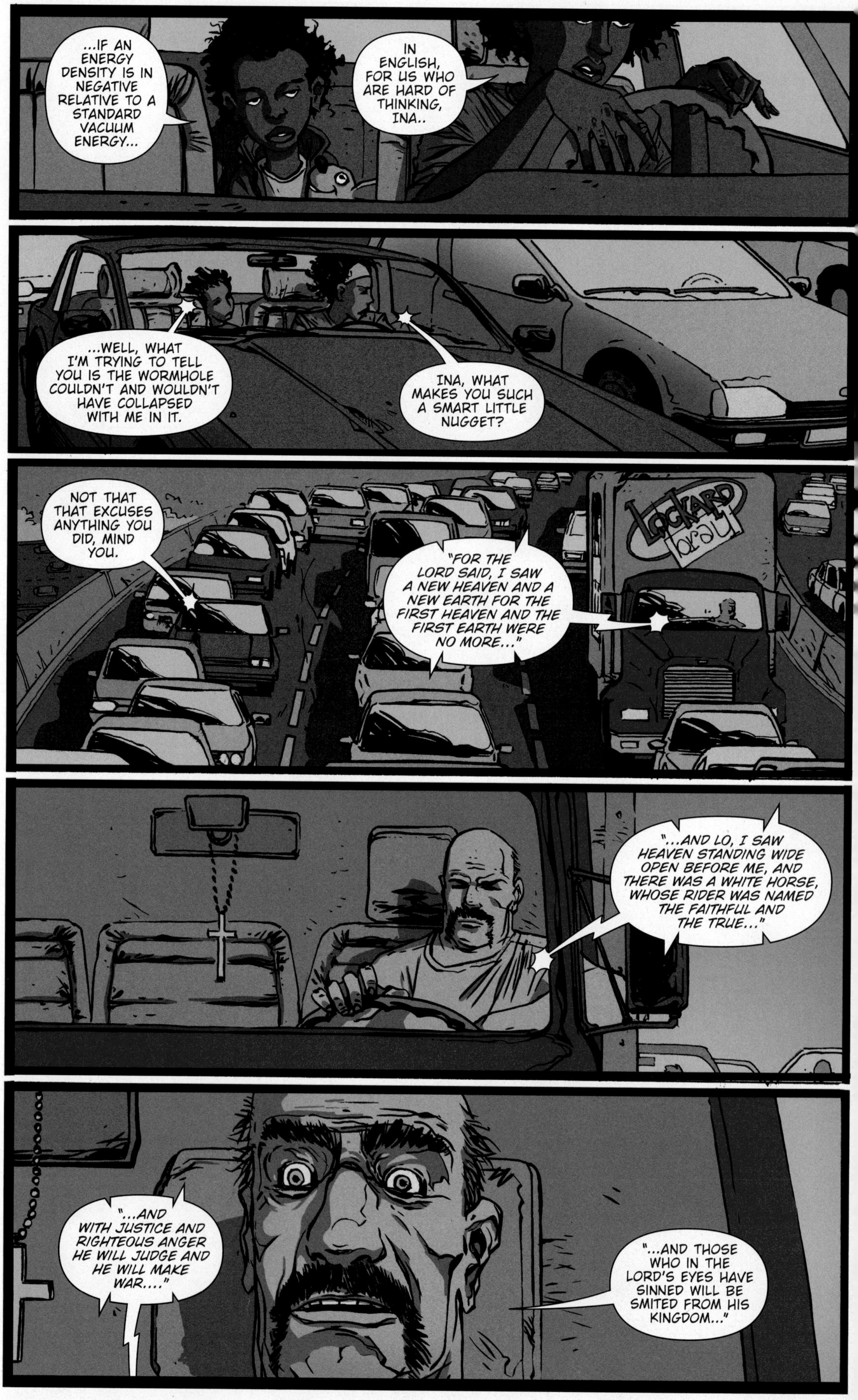

...IF AN ENERGY DENSITY IS IN NEGATIVE RELATIVE TO A STANDARD VACUUM ENERGY...
IN ENGLISH, FOR US WHO ARE HARD OF THINKING, INA..
...WELL, WHAT I'M TRYING TO TELL YOU IS THE WORMHOLE COULDN'T AND WOULDN'T HAVE COLLAPSED WITH ME IN IT.
INA, WHAT MAKES YOU SUCH A SMART LITTLE NUGGET?
NOT THAT THAT EXCUSES ANYTHING YOU DID, MIND YOU.
LOCKARD
"FOR THE LORD SAID, I SAW A NEW HEAVEN AND A NEW EARTH FOR THE FIRST HEAVEN AND THE FIRST EARTH WERE NO MORE..."
"...AND LO, I SAW HEAVEN STANDING WIDE OPEN BEFORE ME, AND THERE WAS A WHITE HORSE, WHOSE RIDER WAS NAMED THE FAITHFUL AND THE TRUE..."
"...AND WITH JUSTICE AND RIGHTEOUS ANGER HE WILL JUDGE AND HE WILL MAKE WAR...."
"...AND THOSE WHO IN THE LORD'S EYES HAVE SINNED WILL BE SMITED FROM HIS KINGDOM..."

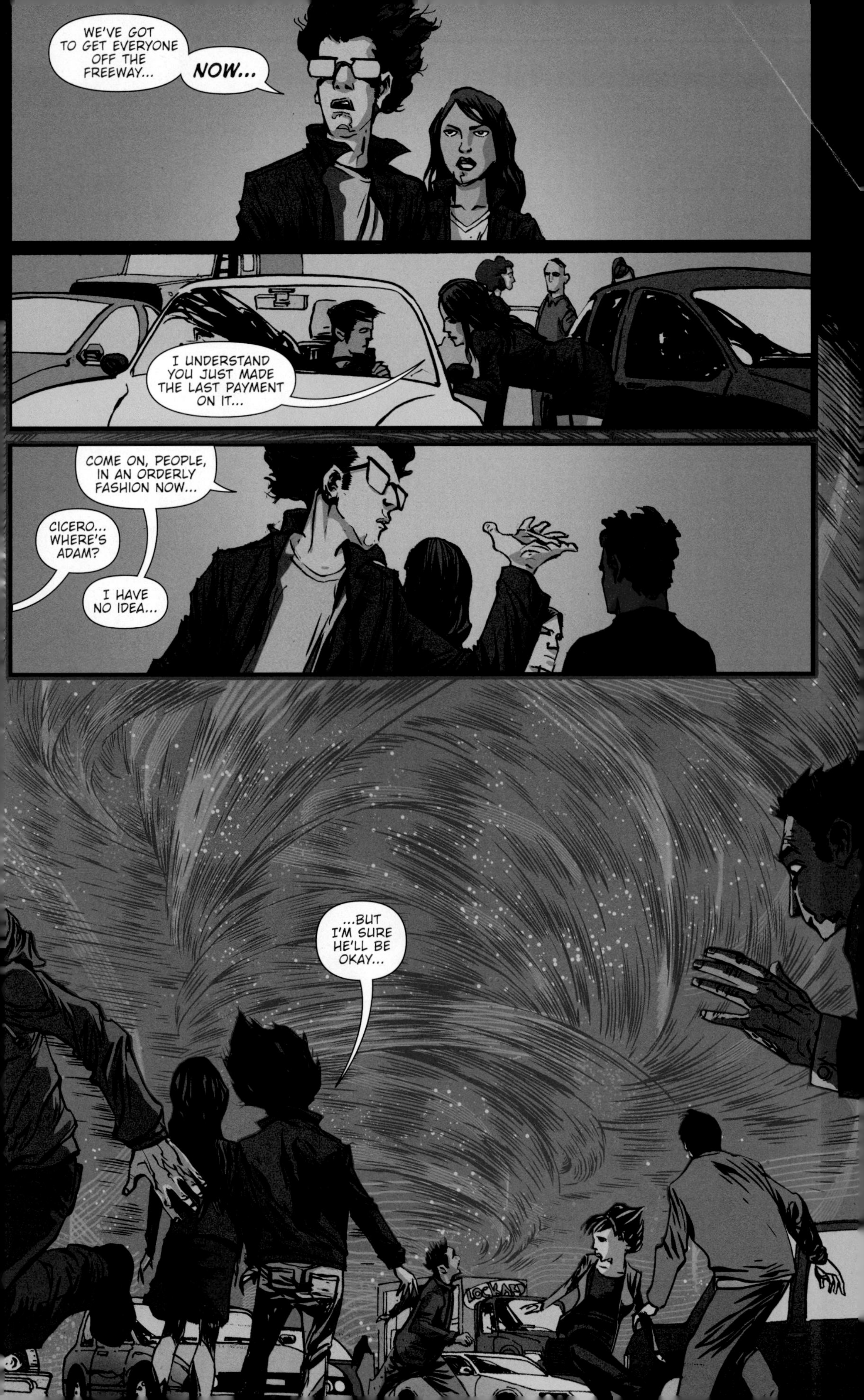
WE'VE GOT TO GET EVERYONE OFF THE FREEWAY...
NOW...
I UNDERSTAND YOU JUST MADE THE LAST PAYMENT ON IT...
COME ON, PEOPLE, IN AN ORDERLY FASHION NOW...
CICERO... WHERE'S ADAM?
I HAVE NO IDEA...
...BUT I'M SURE HE'LL BE OKAY...

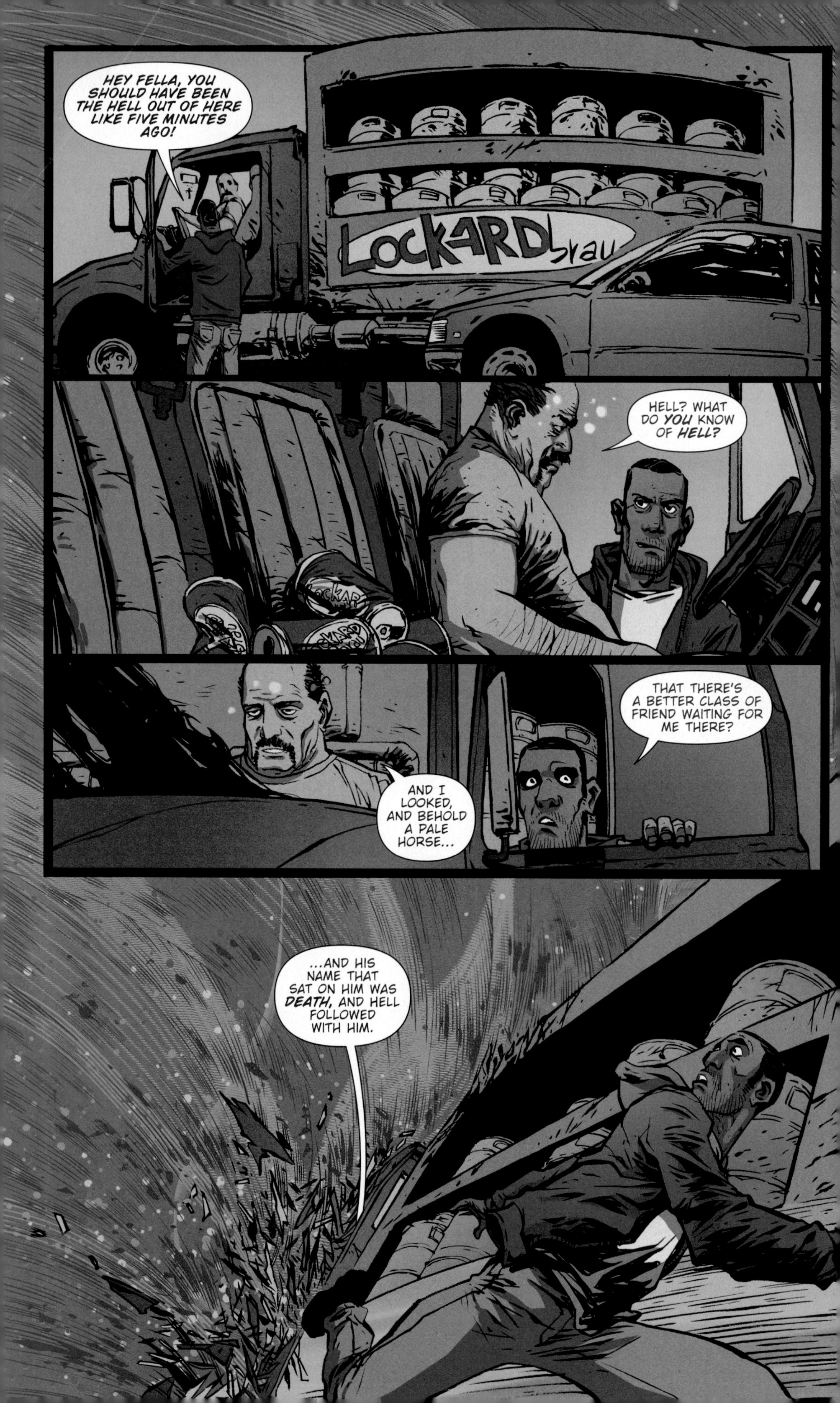
HEY FELLA, YOU SHOULD HAVE BEEN THE HELL OUT OF HERE LIKE FIVE MINUTES AGO!
LOCKARD brau
HELL? WHAT DO *YOU* KNOW OF *HELL?*
THAT THERE'S A BETTER CLASS OF FRIEND WAITING FOR ME THERE?
AND I LOOKED, AND BEHOLD A PALE HORSE...
...AND HIS NAME THAT SAT ON HIM WAS *DEATH,* AND HELL FOLLOWED WITH HIM.

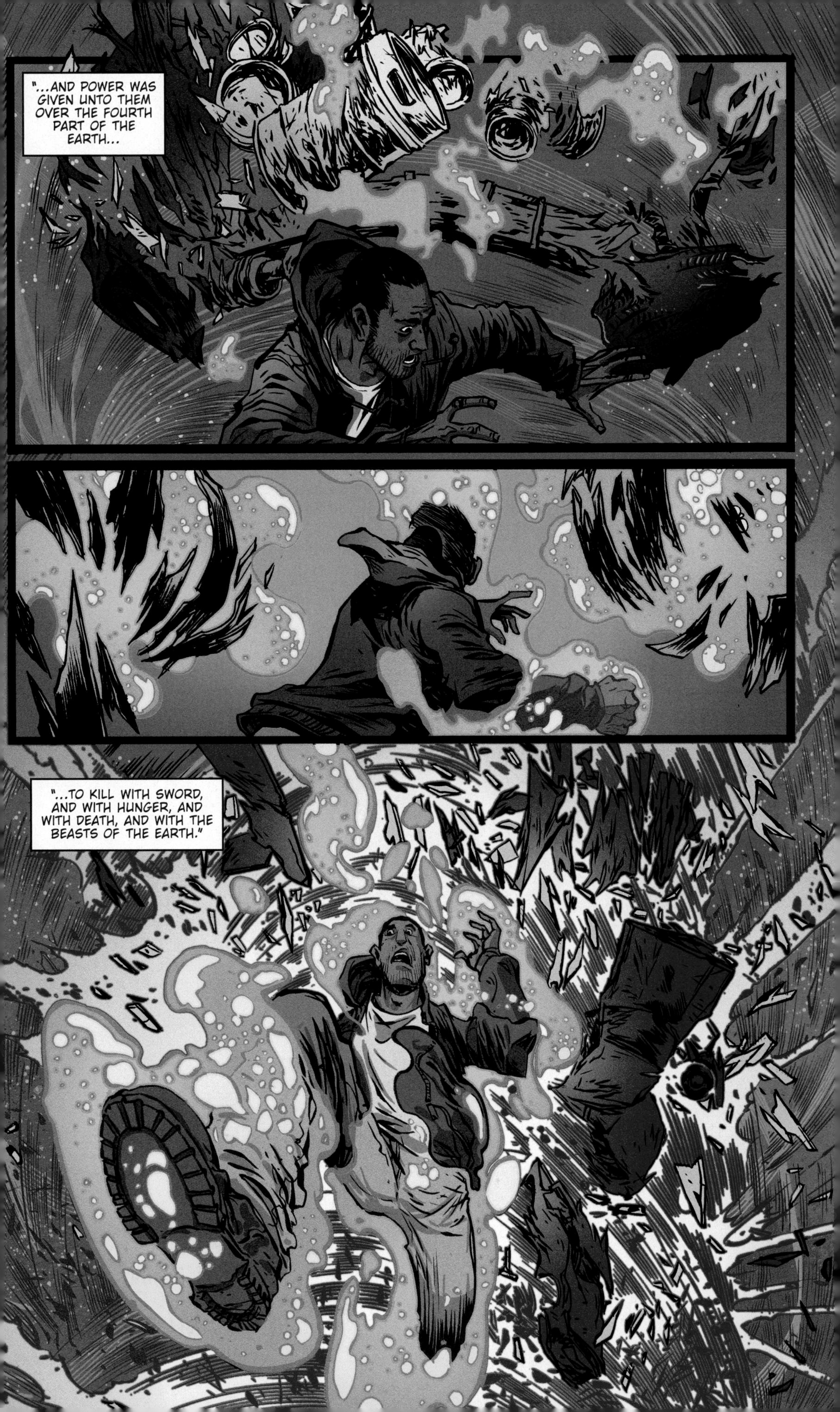
"...AND POWER WAS GIVEN UNTO THEM OVER THE FOURTH PART OF THE EARTH...
"...TO KILL WITH SWORD, AND WITH HUNGER, AND WITH DEATH, AND WITH THE BEASTS OF THE EARTH."

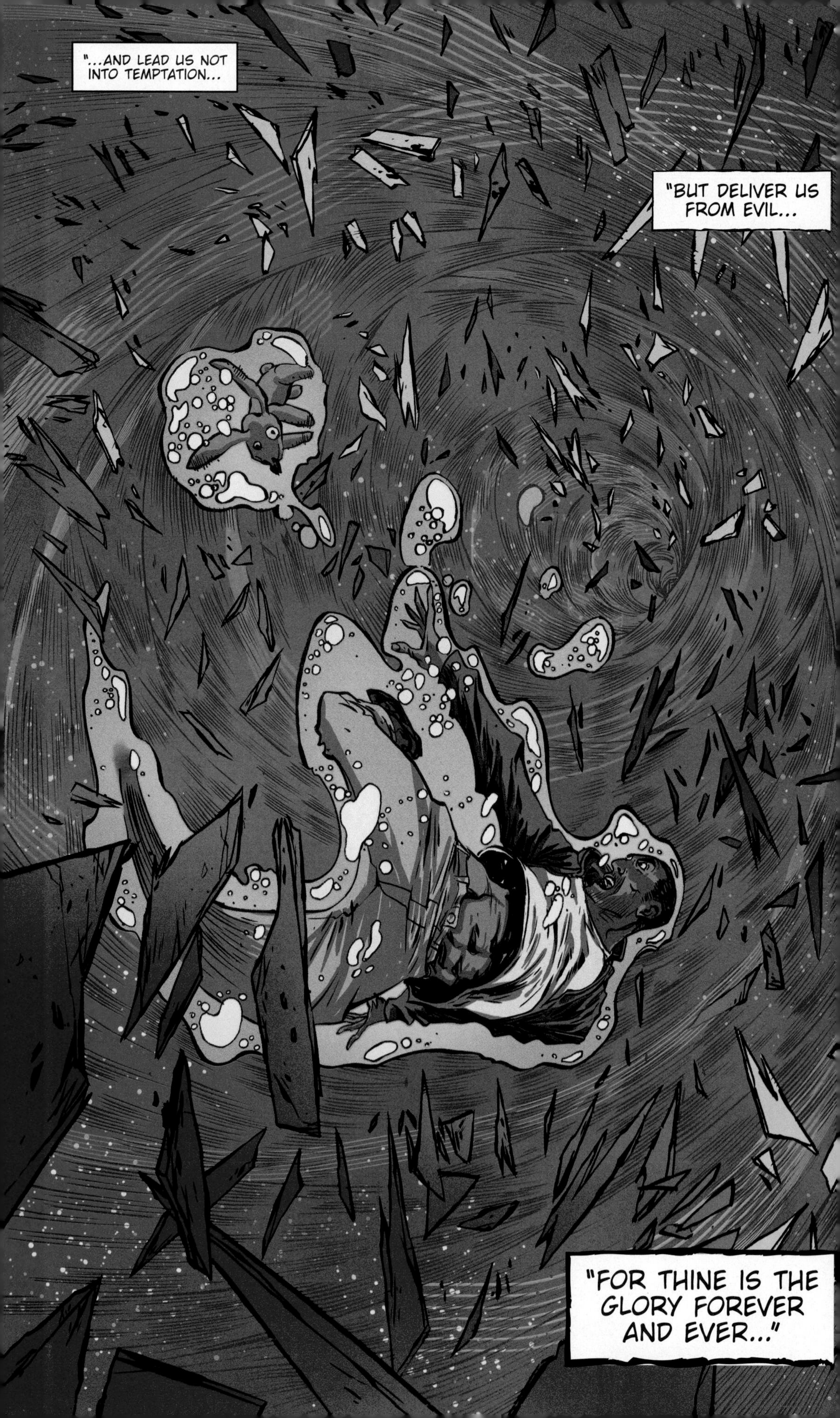
"...AND LEAD US NOT INTO TEMPTATION...
"BUT DELIVER US FROM EVIL...
"FOR THINE IS THE GLORY FOREVER AND EVER..."

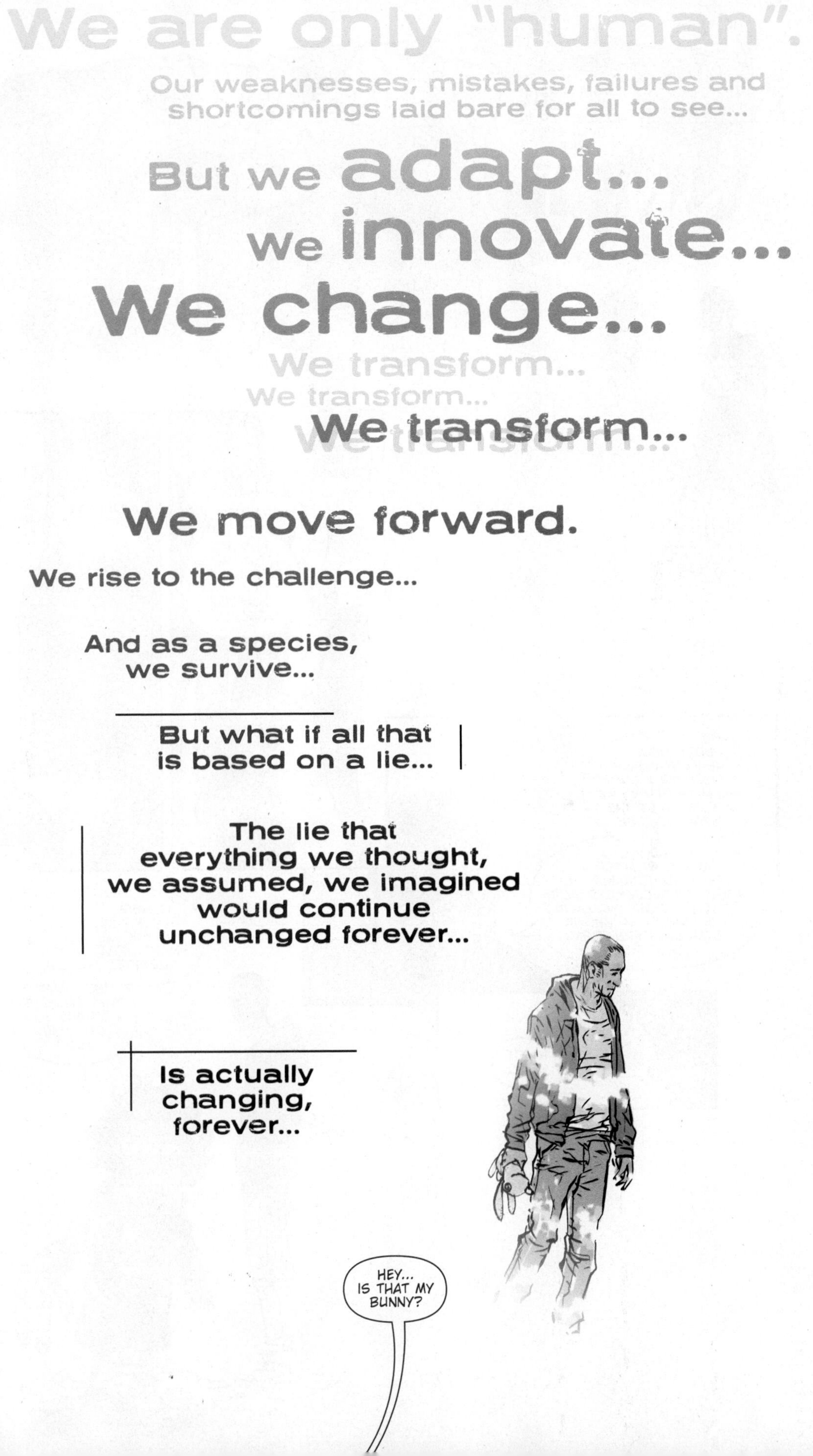
We are only "human".
Our weaknesses, mistakes, failures and shortcomings laid bare for all to see...
But we adapt...
We innovate...
We change...
We transform...
We transform...
We transform...
We move forward.
We rise to the challenge...
And as a species, we survive...
But what if all that is based on a lie...
The lie that everything we thought, we assumed, we imagined would continue unchanged forever...
Is actually changing, forever...
HEY... IS THAT MY BUNNY?

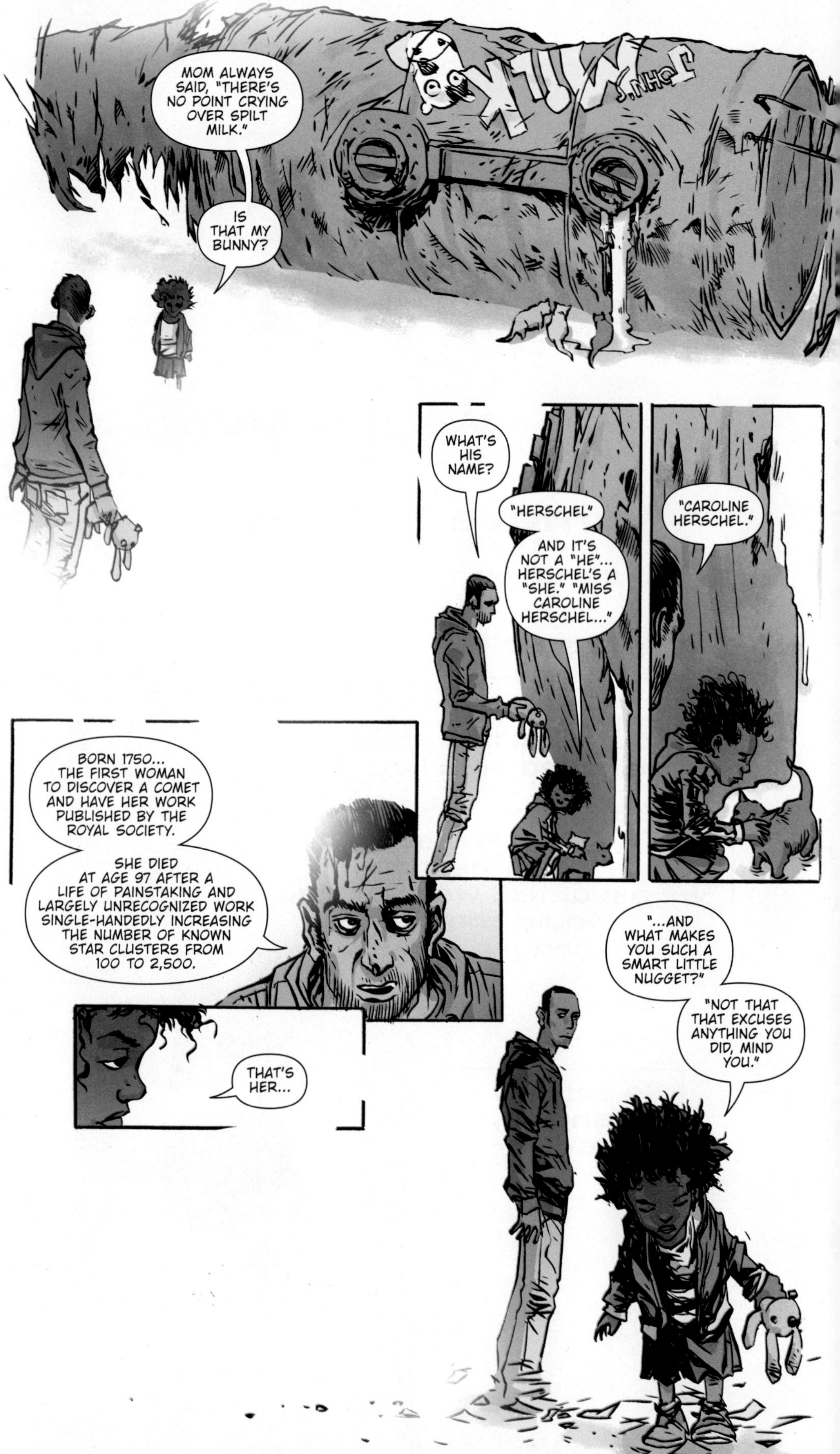
MOM ALWAYS SAID, "THERE'S NO POINT CRYING OVER SPILT MILK."
IS THAT MY BUNNY?
WHAT'S HIS NAME?
"HERSCHEL"
AND IT'S NOT A "HE"... HERSCHEL'S A "SHE." "MISS CAROLINE HERSCHEL..."
"CAROLINE HERSCHEL."
BORN 1750... THE FIRST WOMAN TO DISCOVER A COMET AND HAVE HER WORK PUBLISHED BY THE ROYAL SOCIETY.
SHE DIED AT AGE 97 AFTER A LIFE OF PAINSTAKING AND LARGELY UNRECOGNIZED WORK SINGLE-HANDEDLY INCREASING THE NUMBER OF KNOWN STAR CLUSTERS FROM 100 TO 2,500.
THAT'S HER...
"...AND WHAT MAKES YOU SUCH A SMART LITTLE NUGGET?"
"NOT THAT THAT EXCUSES ANYTHING YOU DID, MIND YOU."

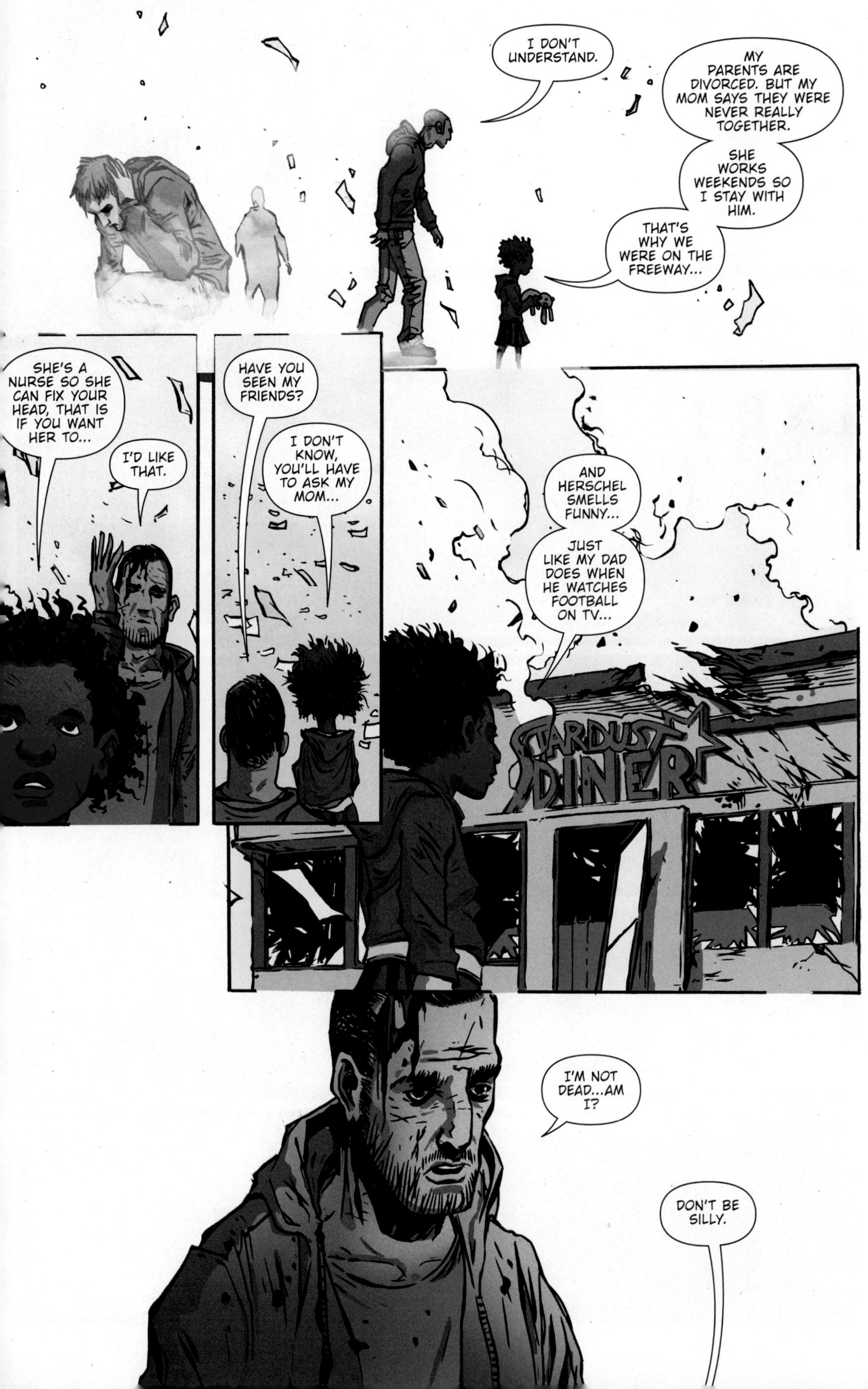
I DON'T UNDERSTAND.
MY PARENTS ARE DIVORCED. BUT MY MOM SAYS THEY WERE NEVER REALLY TOGETHER.
SHE WORKS WEEKENDS SO I STAY WITH HIM.
THAT'S WHY WE WERE ON THE FREEWAY...
SHE'S A NURSE SO SHE CAN FIX YOUR HEAD, THAT IS IF YOU WANT HER TO...
I'D LIKE THAT.
HAVE YOU SEEN MY FRIENDS?
I DON'T KNOW, YOU'LL HAVE TO ASK MY MOM...
AND HERSCHEL SMELLS FUNNY...
JUST LIKE MY DAD DOES WHEN HE WATCHES FOOTBALL ON TV...
STARDUST DINER
I'M NOT DEAD...AM I?
DON'T BE SILLY.

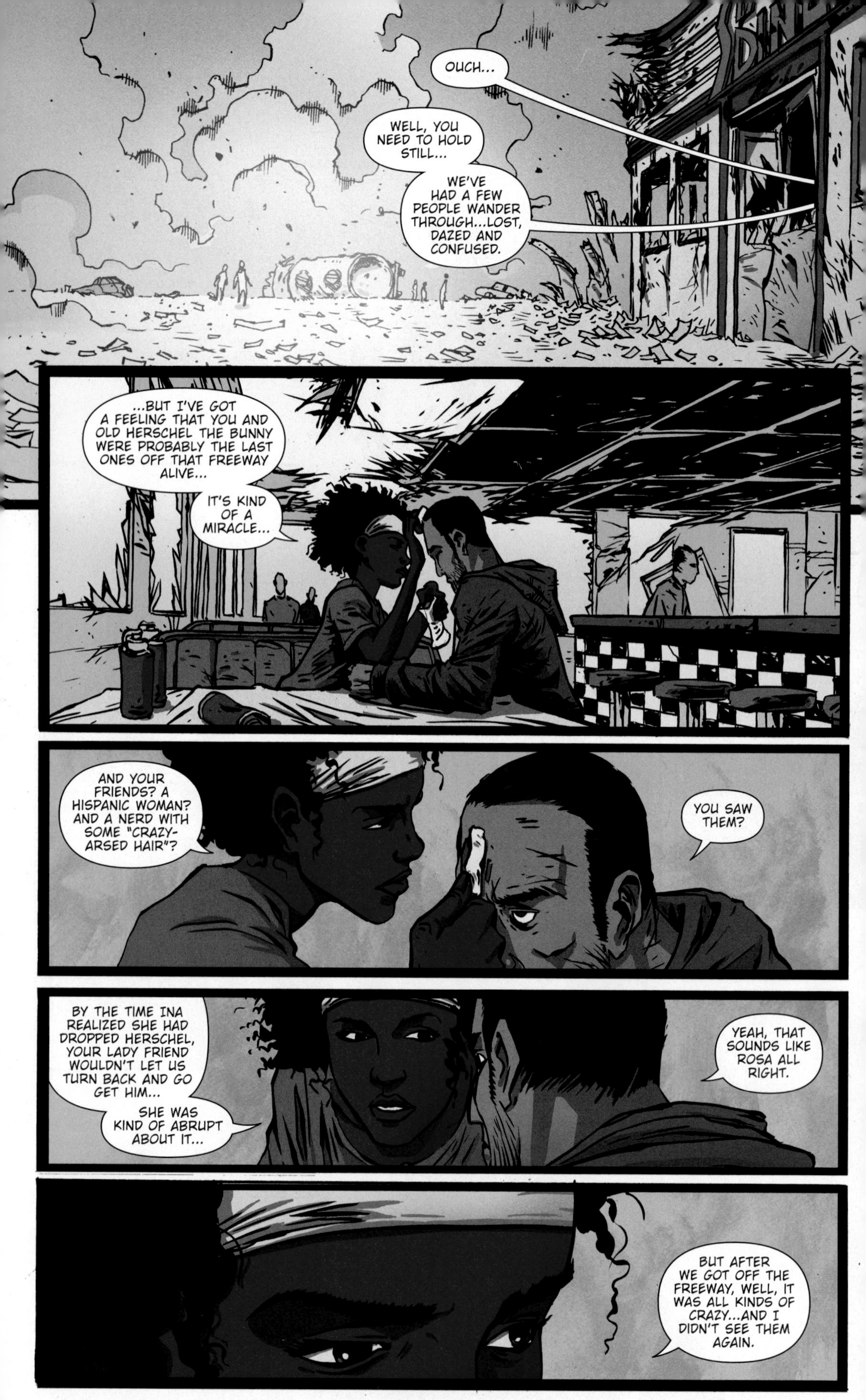
OUCH...
WELL, YOU NEED TO HOLD STILL...
WE'VE HAD A FEW PEOPLE WANDER THROUGH...LOST, DAZED AND CONFUSED.
...BUT I'VE GOT A FEELING THAT YOU AND OLD HERSCHEL THE BUNNY WERE PROBABLY THE LAST ONES OFF THAT FREEWAY ALIVE...
IT'S KIND OF A MIRACLE...
AND YOUR FRIENDS? A HISPANIC WOMAN? AND A NERD WITH SOME "CRAZY-ARSED HAIR"?
YOU SAW THEM?
BY THE TIME INA REALIZED SHE HAD DROPPED HERSCHEL, YOUR LADY FRIEND WOULDN'T LET US TURN BACK AND GO GET HIM...
SHE WAS KIND OF ABRUPT ABOUT IT...
YEAH, THAT SOUNDS LIKE ROSA ALL RIGHT.
BUT AFTER WE GOT OFF THE FREEWAY, WELL, IT WAS ALL KINDS OF CRAZY...AND I DIDN'T SEE THEM AGAIN.

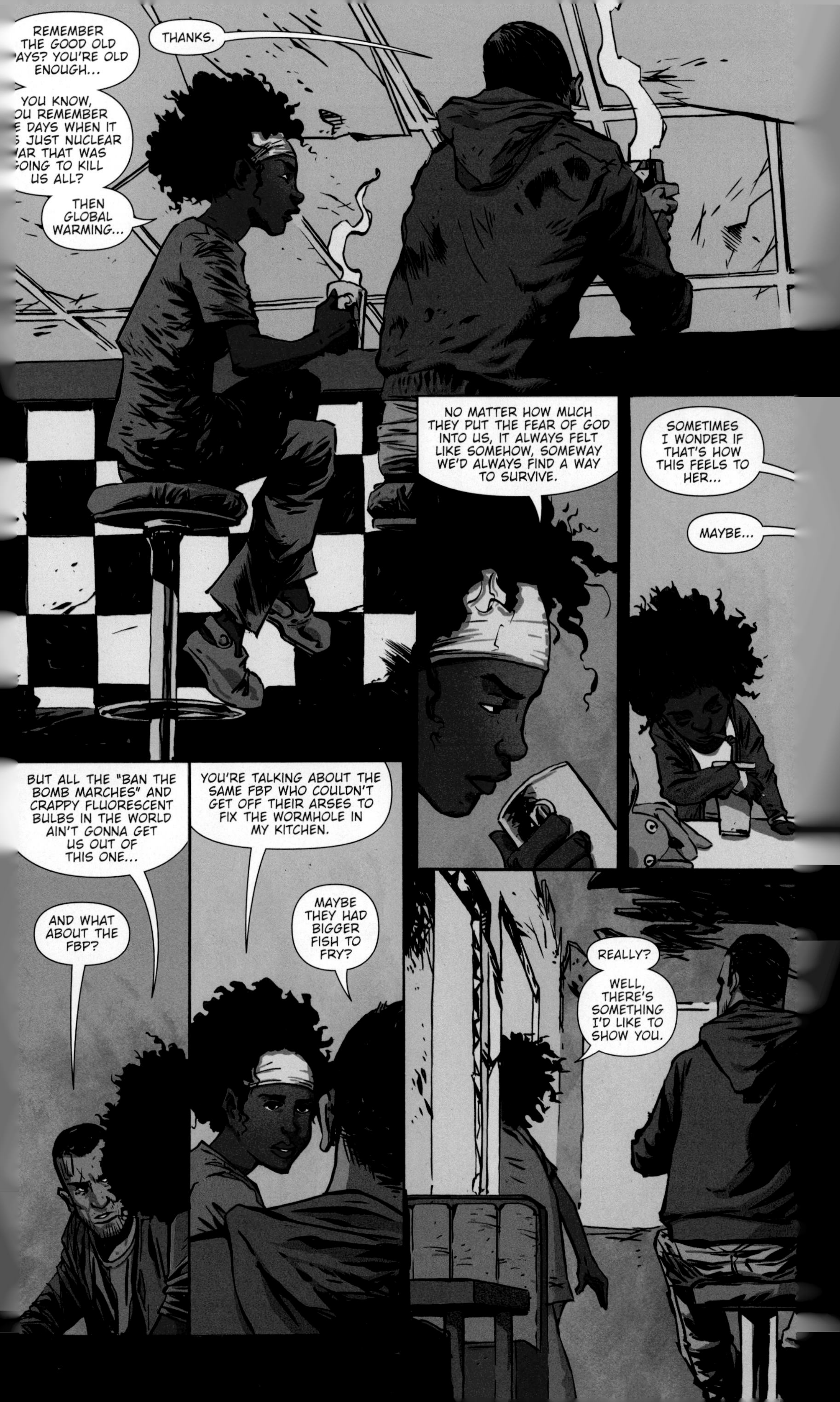

REMEMBER THE GOOD OLD AYS? YOU'RE OLD ENOUGH...
THANKS.
YOU KNOW, OU REMEMBER E DAYS WHEN IT S JUST NUCLEAR AR THAT WAS OING TO KILL US ALL?
THEN GLOBAL WARMING...
NO MATTER HOW MUCH THEY PUT THE FEAR OF GOD INTO US, IT ALWAYS FELT LIKE SOMEHOW, SOMEWAY WE'D ALWAYS FIND A WAY TO SURVIVE.
SOMETIMES I WONDER IF THAT'S HOW THIS FEELS TO HER...
MAYBE...
BUT ALL THE "BAN THE BOMB MARCHES" AND CRAPPY FLUORESCENT BULBS IN THE WORLD AIN'T GONNA GET US OUT OF THIS ONE...
AND WHAT ABOUT THE FBP?
YOU'RE TALKING ABOUT THE SAME FBP WHO COULDN'T GET OFF THEIR ARSES TO FIX THE WORMHOLE IN MY KITCHEN.
MAYBE THEY HAD BIGGER FISH TO FRY?
REALLY?
WELL, THERE'S SOMETHING I'D LIKE TO SHOW YOU.

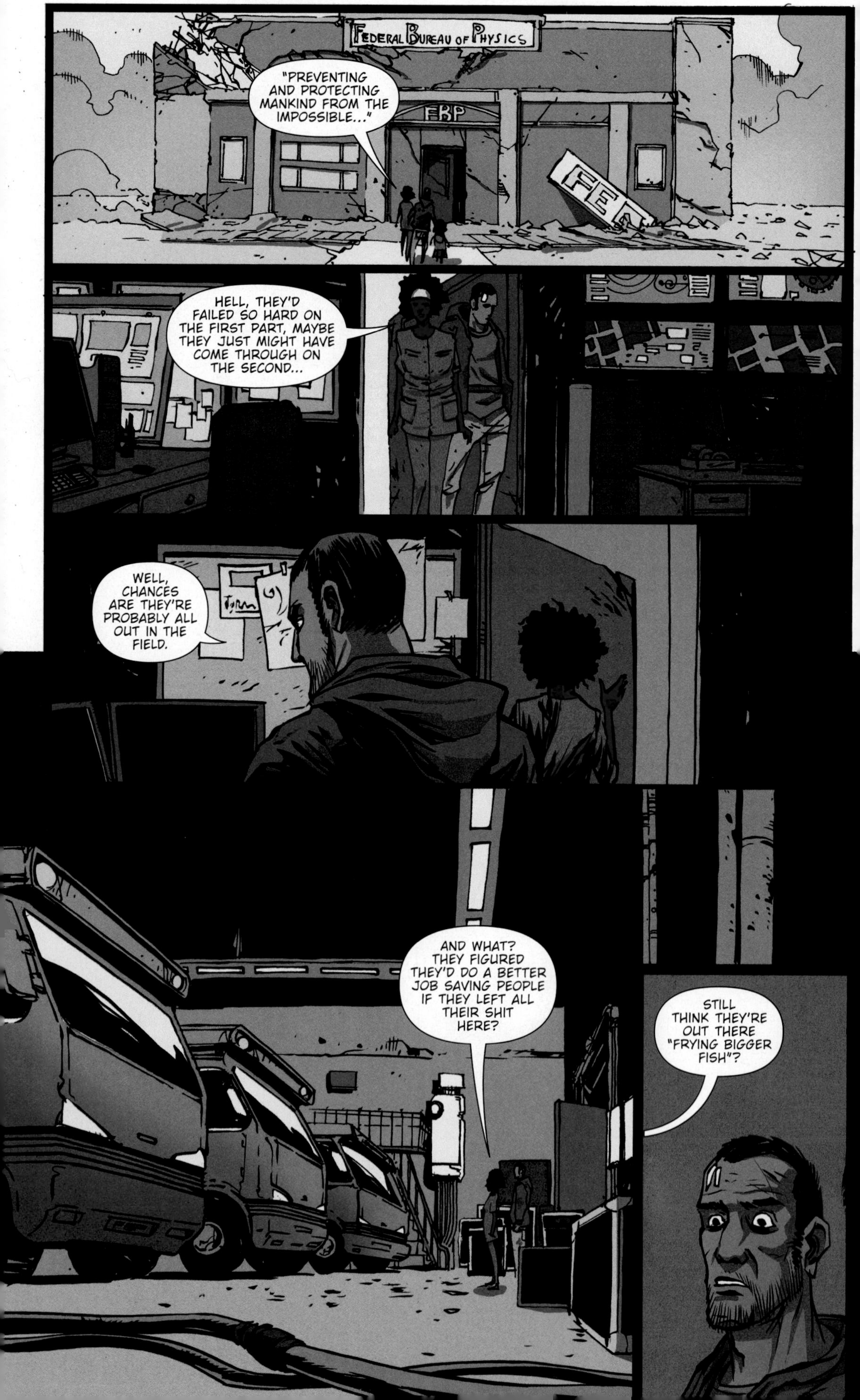

FEDERAL BUREAU OF PHYSICS
FBP
"PREVENTING AND PROTECTING MANKIND FROM THE IMPOSSIBLE..."
HELL, THEY'D FAILED SO HARD ON THE FIRST PART, MAYBE THEY JUST MIGHT HAVE COME THROUGH ON THE SECOND...
WELL, CHANCES ARE THEY'RE PROBABLY ALL OUT IN THE FIELD.
AND WHAT? THEY FIGURED THEY'D DO A BETTER JOB SAVING PEOPLE IF THEY LEFT ALL THEIR SHIT HERE?
STILL THINK THEY'RE OUT THERE "FRYING BIGGER FISH"?

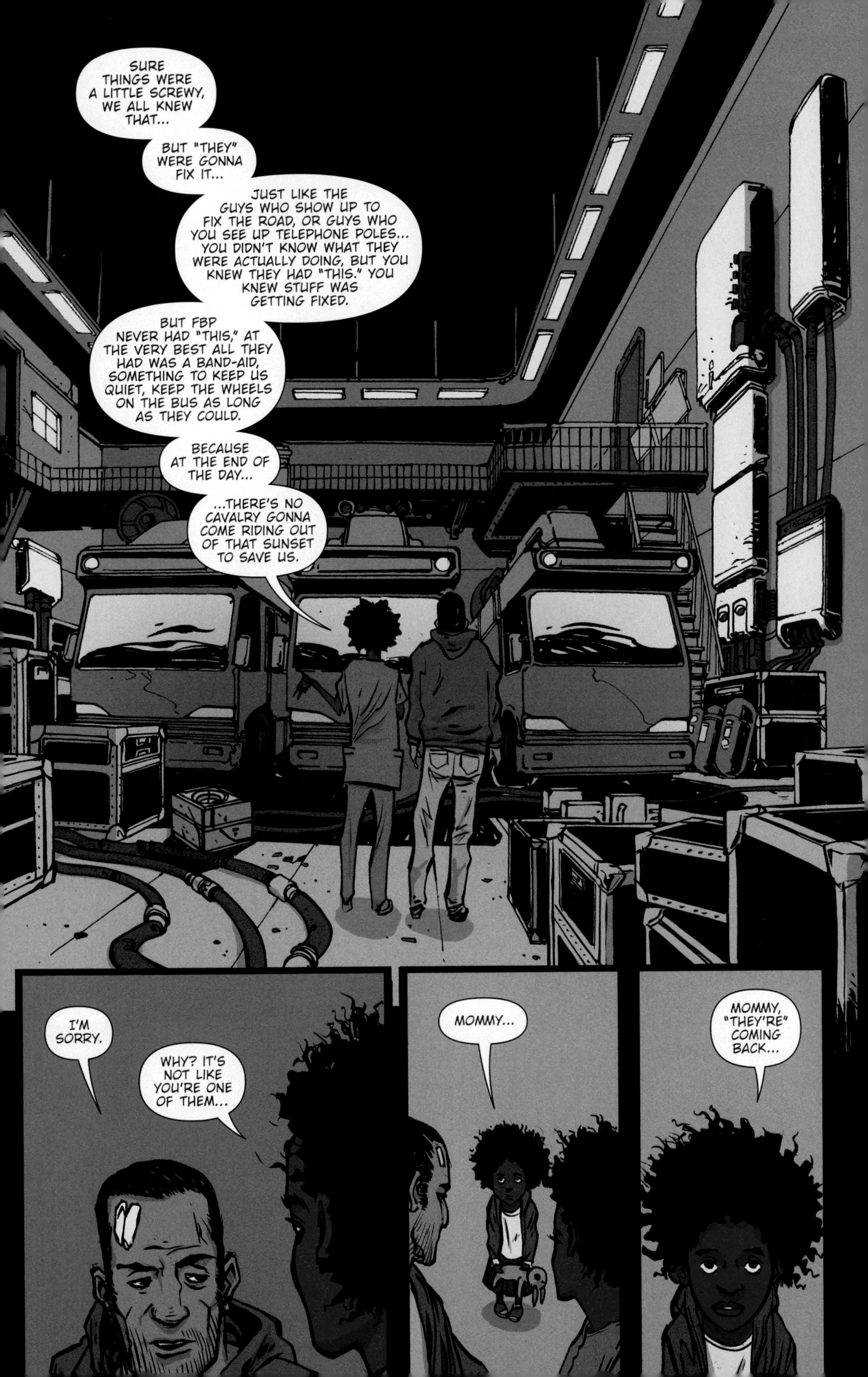
SURE THINGS WERE A LITTLE SCREWY, WE ALL KNEW THAT...
BUT "THEY" WERE GONNA FIX IT...
JUST LIKE THE GUYS WHO SHOW UP TO FIX THE ROAD, OR GUYS WHO YOU SEE UP TELEPHONE POLES... YOU DIDN'T KNOW WHAT THEY WERE ACTUALLY DOING, BUT YOU KNEW THEY HAD "THIS." YOU KNEW STUFF WAS GETTING FIXED.
BUT FBP NEVER HAD "THIS," AT THE VERY BEST ALL THEY HAD WAS A BAND-AID, SOMETHING TO KEEP US QUIET, KEEP THE WHEELS ON THE BUS AS LONG AS THEY COULD.
BECAUSE AT THE END OF THE DAY...
...THERE'S NO CAVALRY GONNA COME RIDING OUT OF THAT SUNSET TO SAVE US.
I'M SORRY.
WHY? IT'S NOT LIKE YOU'RE ONE OF THEM...
MOMMY...
MOMMY, "THEY'RE" COMING BACK...

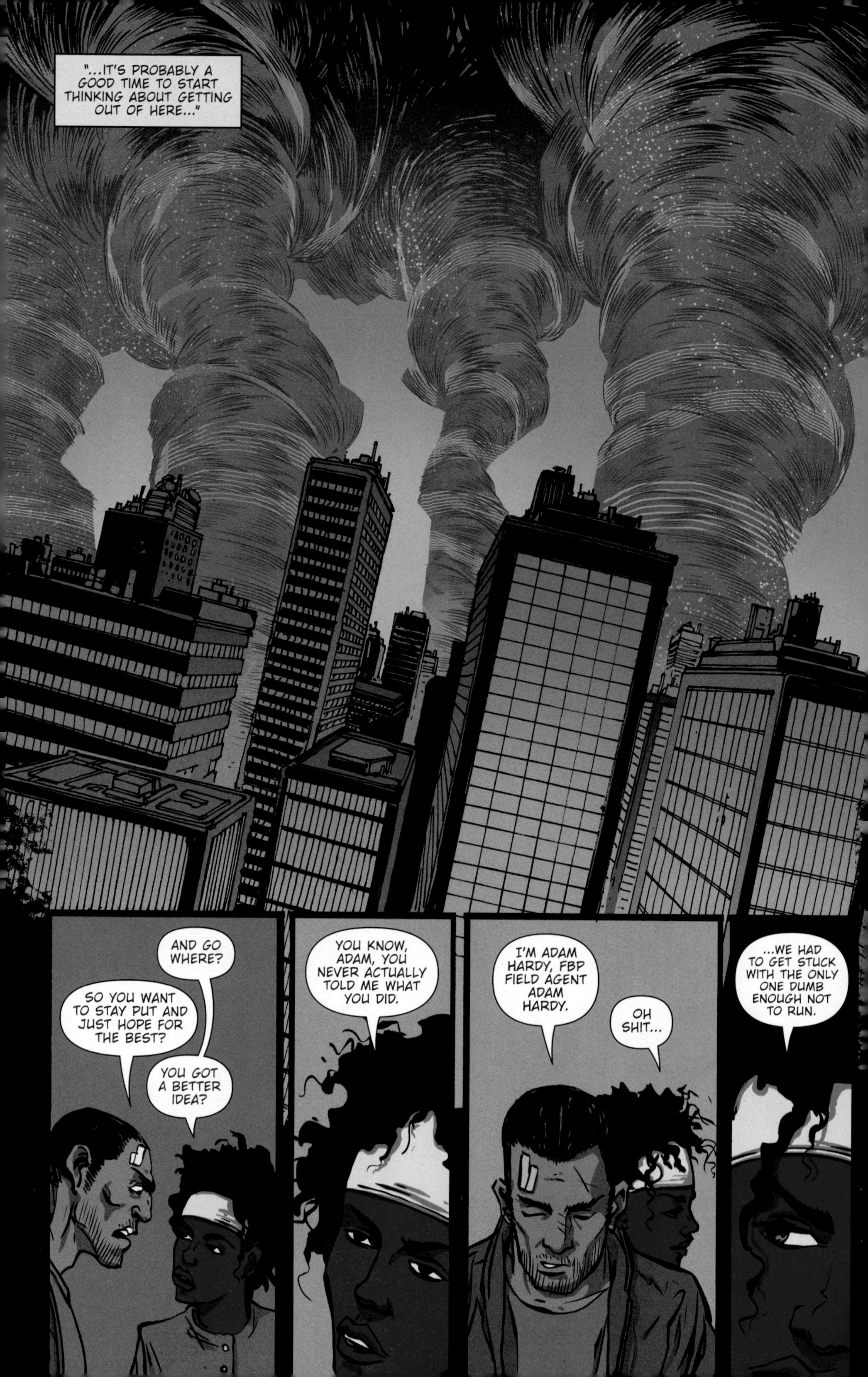
"...IT'S PROBABLY A GOOD TIME TO START THINKING ABOUT GETTING OUT OF HERE..."
AND GO WHERE?
SO YOU WANT TO STAY PUT AND JUST HOPE FOR THE BEST?
YOU GOT A BETTER IDEA?
YOU KNOW, ADAM, YOU NEVER ACTUALLY TOLD ME WHAT YOU DID.
I'M ADAM HARDY, FBP FIELD AGENT ADAM HARDY.
OH SHIT...
...WE HAD TO GET STUCK WITH THE ONLY ONE DUMB ENOUGH NOT TO RUN.

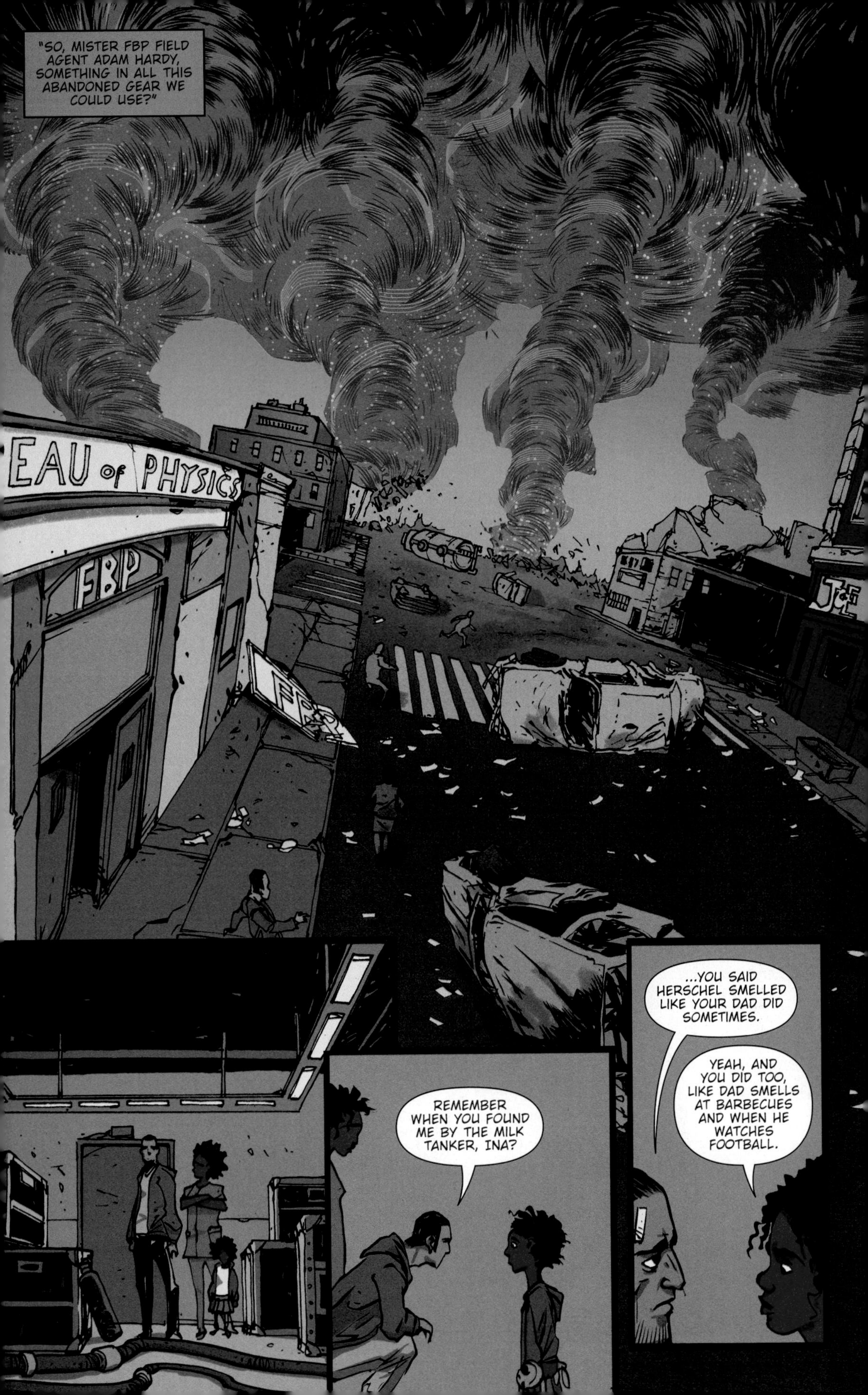
"SO, MISTER FBP FIELD AGENT ADAM HARDY, SOMETHING IN ALL THIS ABANDONED GEAR WE COULD USE?"
EAU of PHYSICS
FBP
...YOU SAID HERSCHEL SMELLED LIKE YOUR DAD DID SOMETIMES.
REMEMBER WHEN YOU FOUND ME BY THE MILK TANKER, INA?
YEAH, AND YOU DID TOO, LIKE DAD SMELLS AT BARBECUES AND WHEN HE WATCHES FOOTBALL.

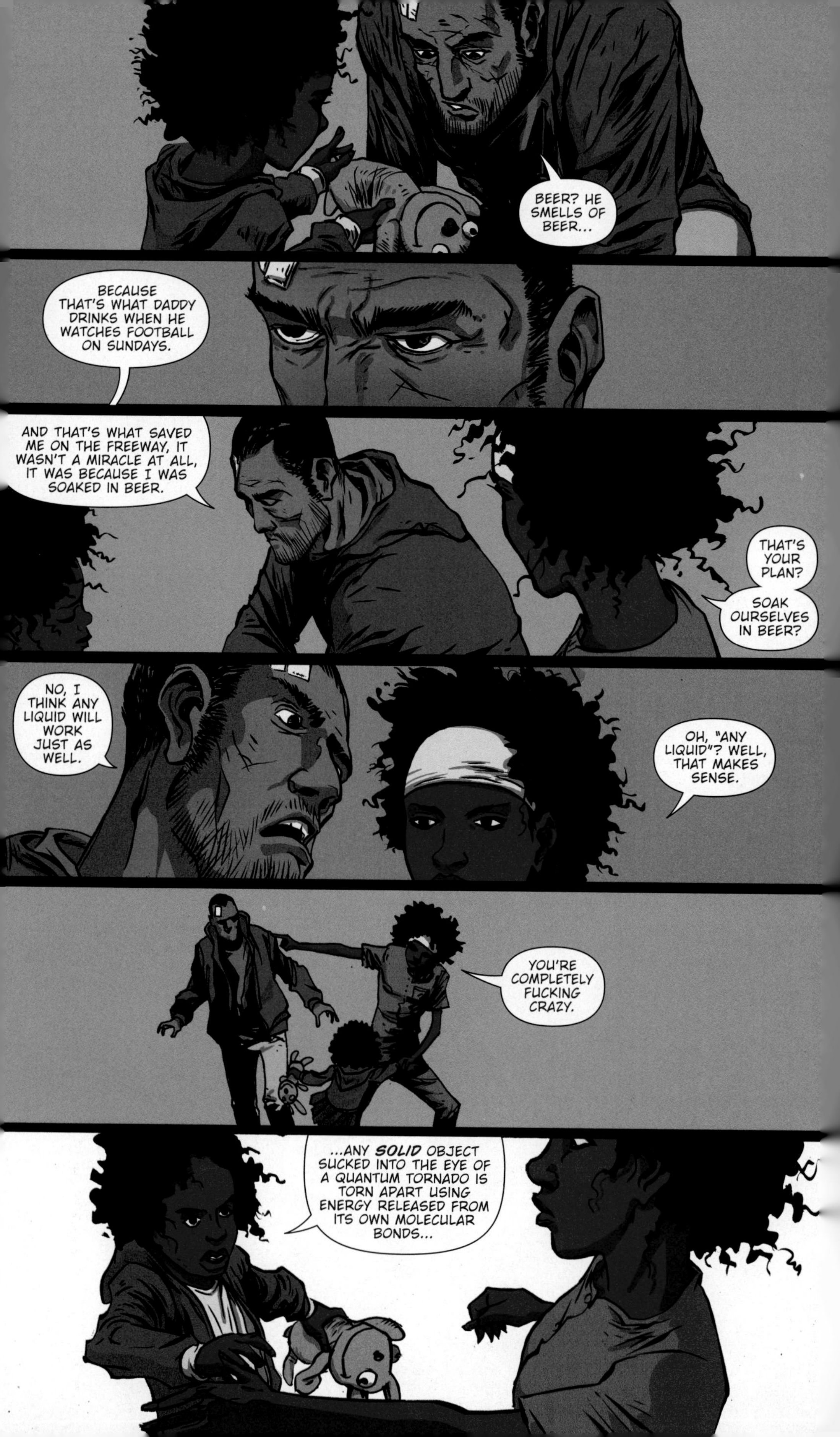
BEER? HE SMELLS OF BEER...
BECAUSE THAT'S WHAT DADDY DRINKS WHEN HE WATCHES FOOTBALL ON SUNDAYS.
AND THAT'S WHAT SAVED ME ON THE FREEWAY, IT WASN'T A MIRACLE AT ALL, IT WAS BECAUSE I WAS SOAKED IN BEER.
THAT'S YOUR PLAN?
SOAK OURSELVES IN BEER?
NO, I THINK ANY LIQUID WILL WORK JUST AS WELL.
OH, "ANY LIQUID"? WELL, THAT MAKES SENSE.
YOU'RE COMPLETELY FUCKING CRAZY.
...ANY SOLID OBJECT SUCKED INTO THE EYE OF A QUANTUM TORNADO IS TORN APART USING ENERGY RELEASED FROM ITS OWN MOLECULAR BONDS...

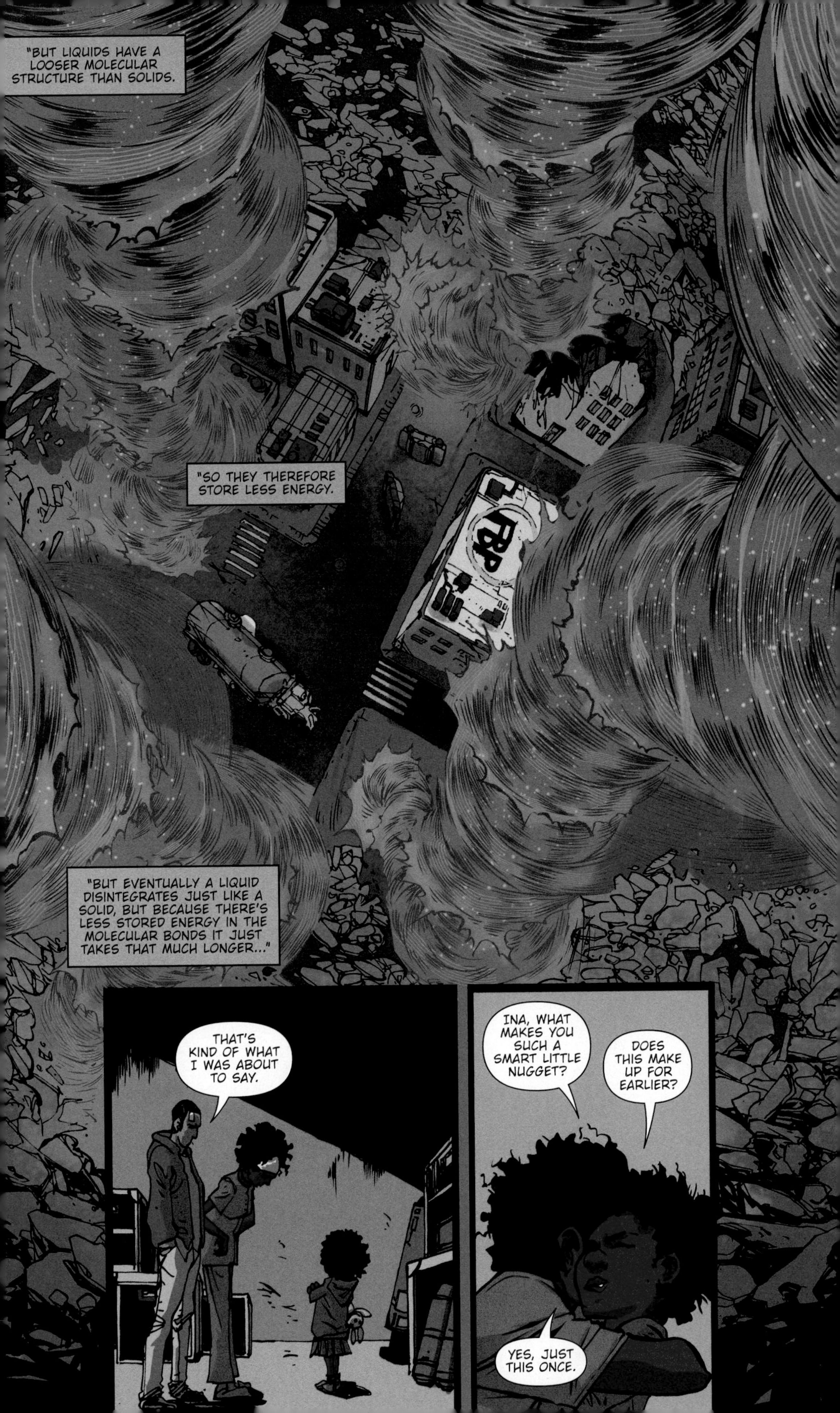
"BUT LIQUIDS HAVE A LOOSER MOLECULAR STRUCTURE THAN SOLIDS.
"SO THEY THEREFORE STORE LESS ENERGY.
FBP
"BUT EVENTUALLY A LIQUID DISINTEGRATES JUST LIKE A SOLID, BUT BECAUSE THERE'S LESS STORED ENERGY IN THE MOLECULAR BONDS IT JUST TAKES THAT MUCH LONGER..."
THAT'S KIND OF WHAT I WAS ABOUT TO SAY.
INA, WHAT MAKES YOU SUCH A SMART LITTLE NUGGET?
DOES THIS MAKE UP FOR EARLIER?
YES, JUST THIS ONCE.

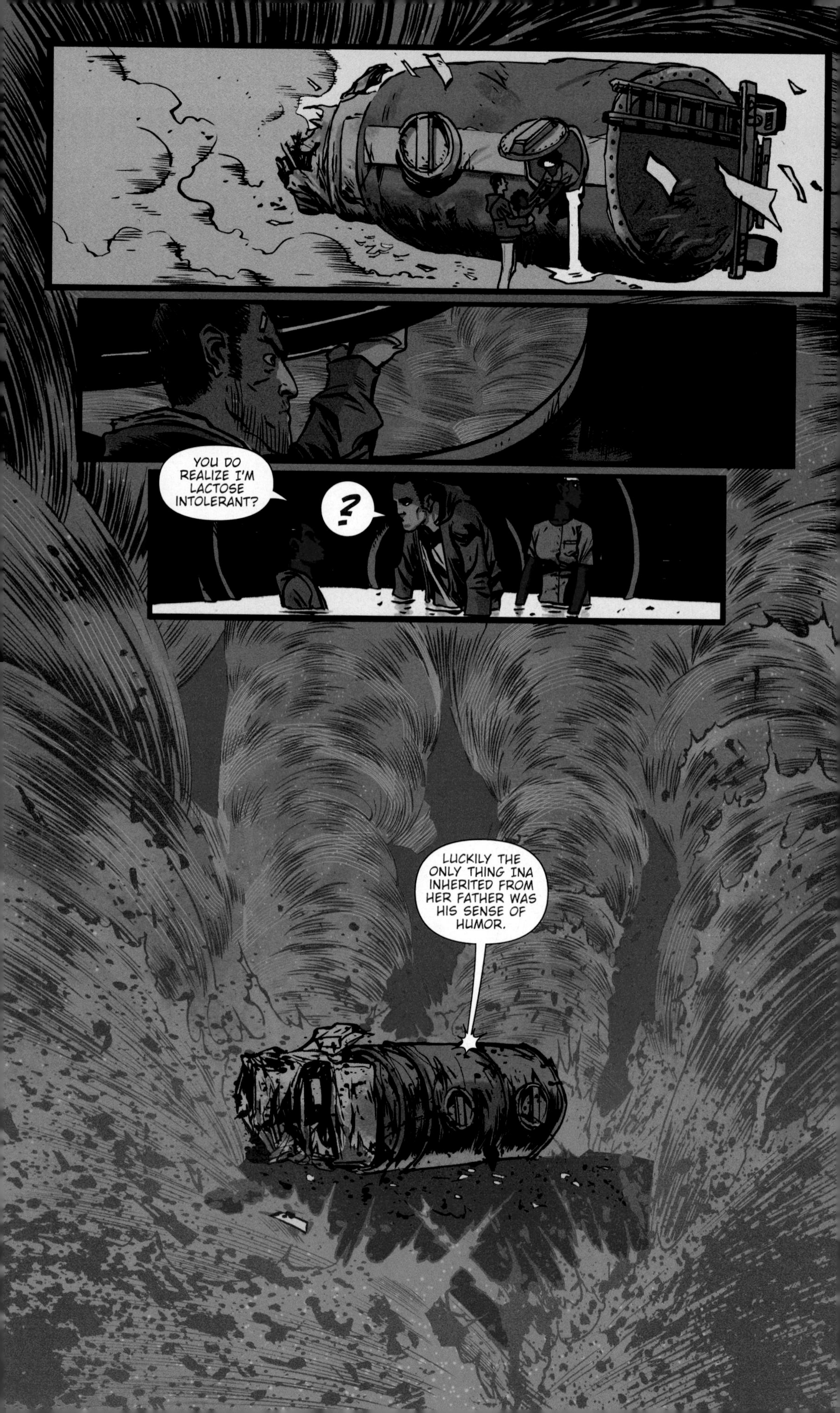
YOU DO REALIZE I'M LACTOSE INTOLERANT?
?
LUCKILY THE ONLY THING INA INHERITED FROM HER FATHER WAS HIS SENSE OF HUMOR.

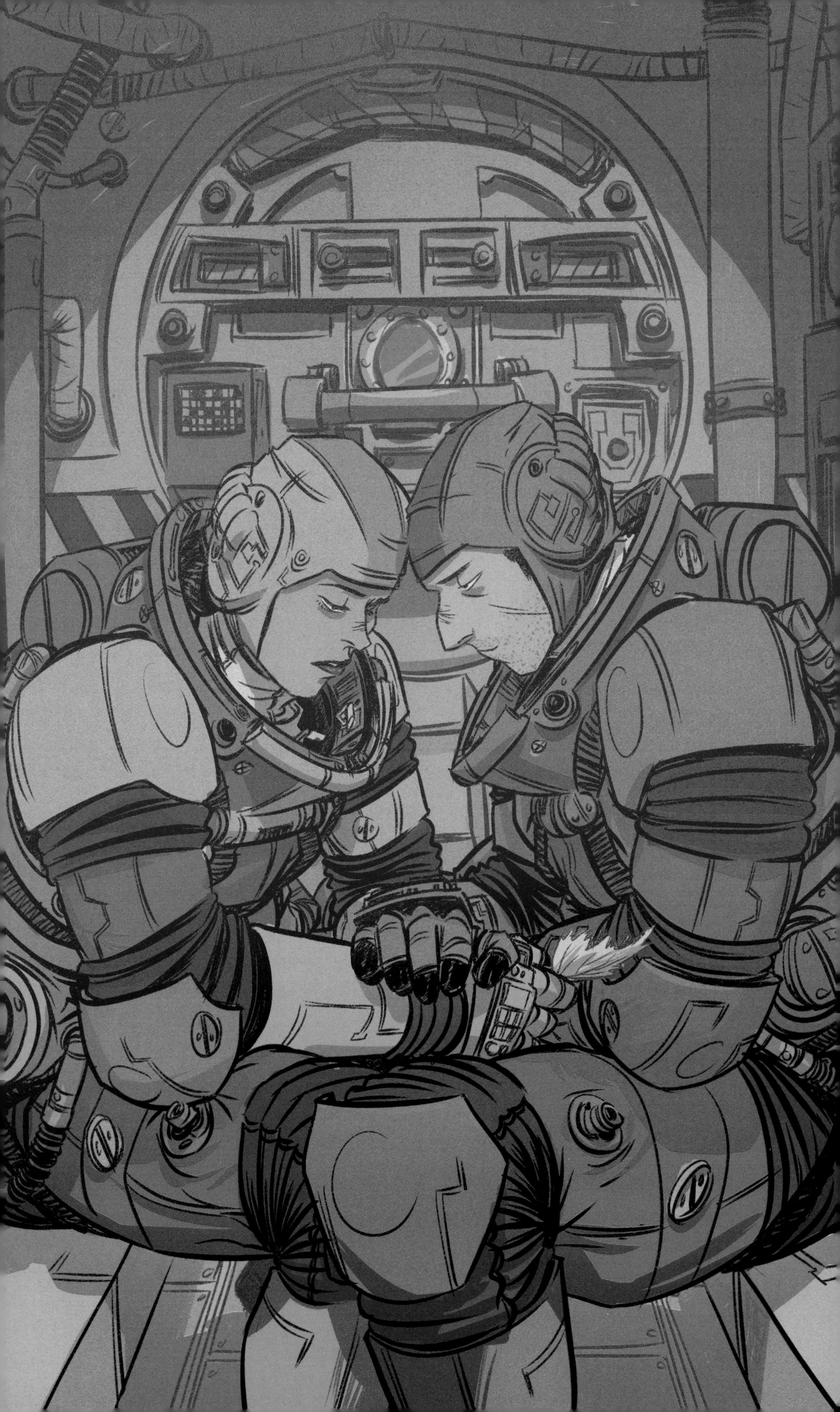

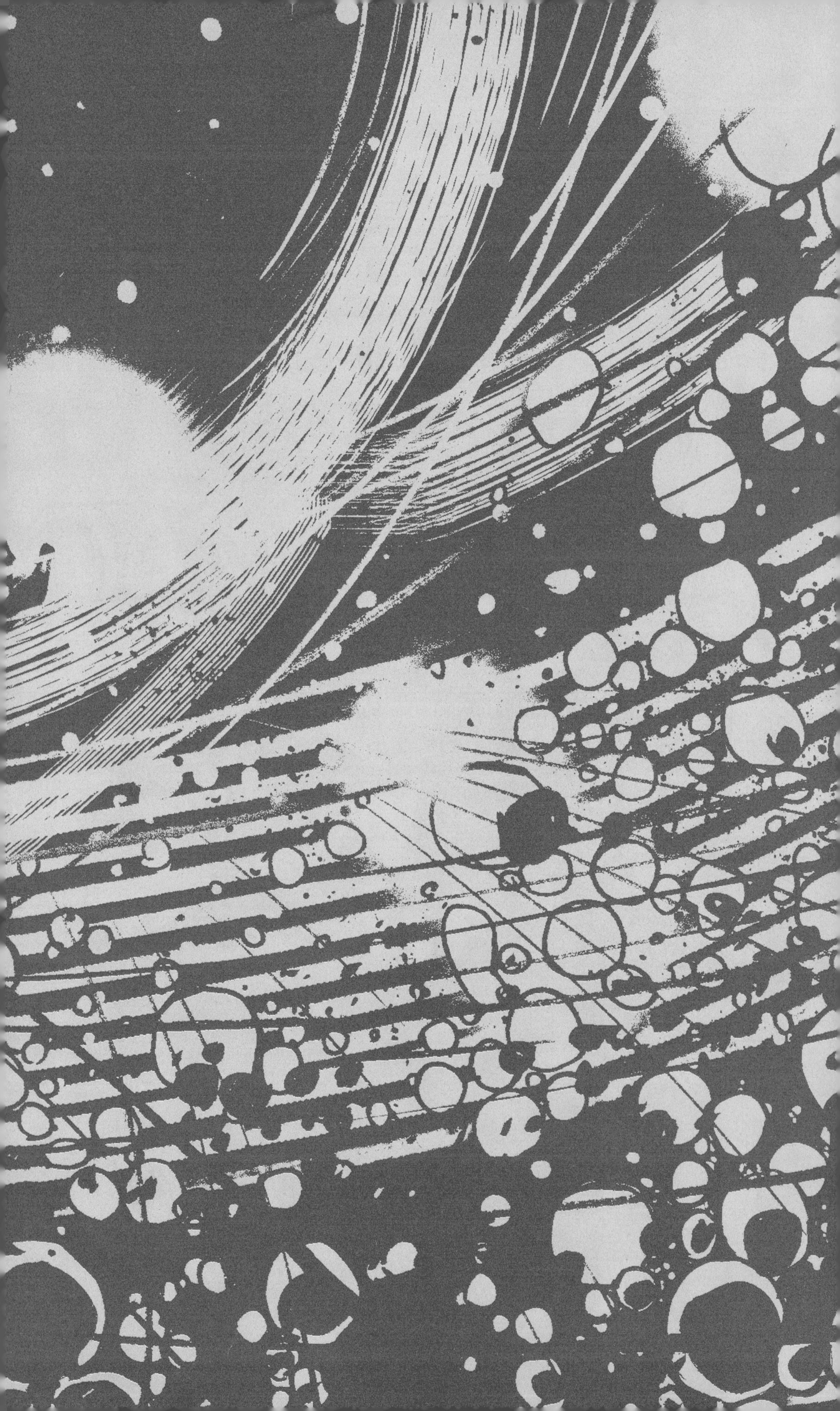

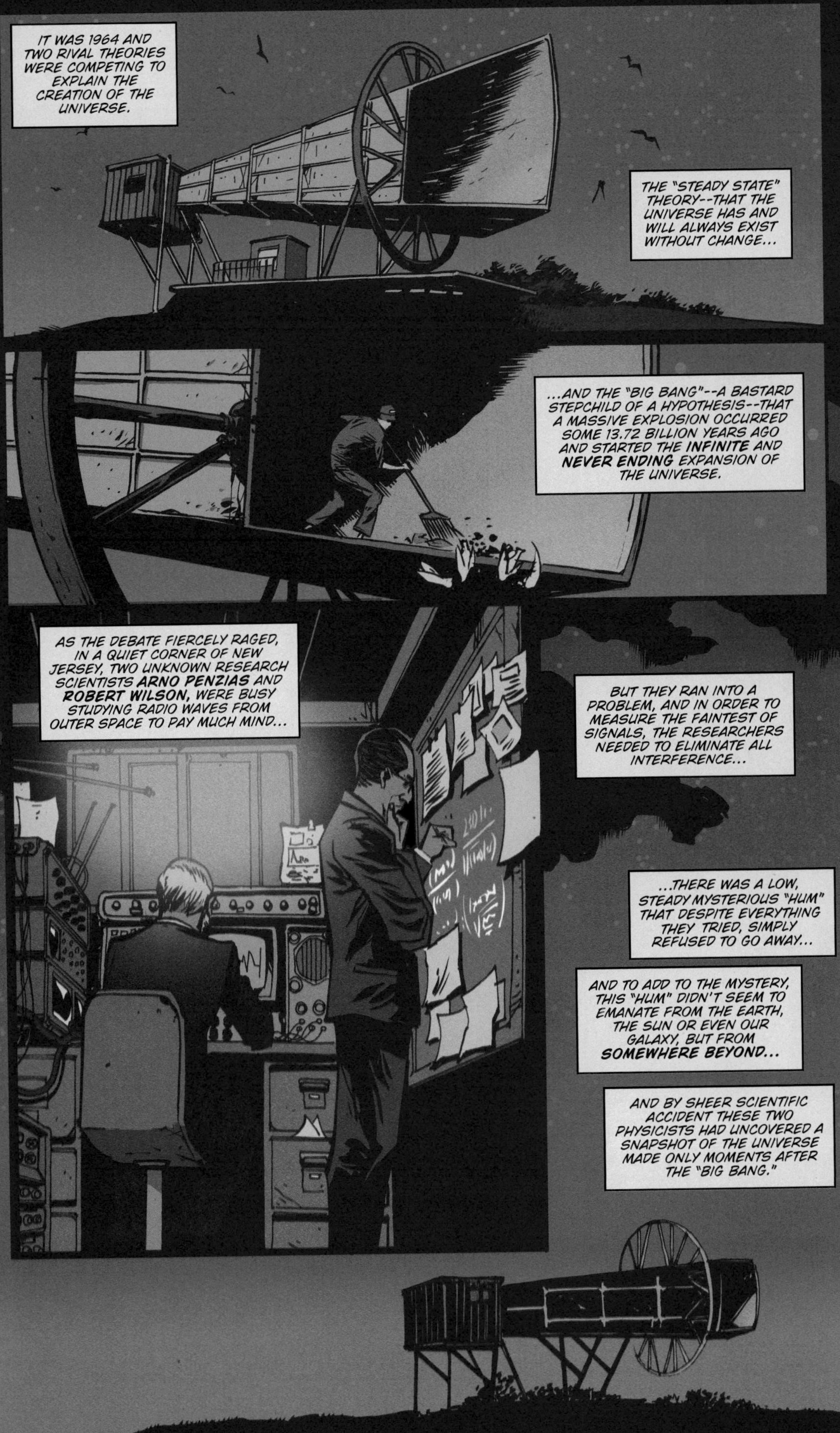
IT WAS 1964 AND TWO RIVAL THEORIES WERE COMPETING TO EXPLAIN THE CREATION OF THE UNIVERSE.
THE "STEADY STATE" THEORY--THAT THE UNIVERSE HAS AND WILL ALWAYS EXIST WITHOUT CHANGE...
...AND THE "BIG BANG"--A BASTARD STEPCHILD OF A HYPOTHESIS--THAT A MASSIVE EXPLOSION OCCURRED SOME 13.72 BILLION YEARS AGO AND STARTED THE **INFINITE** AND **NEVER ENDING** EXPANSION OF THE UNIVERSE.
AS THE DEBATE FIERCELY RAGED, IN A QUIET CORNER OF NEW JERSEY, TWO UNKNOWN RESEARCH SCIENTISTS **ARNO PENZIAS** AND **ROBERT WILSON,** WERE BUSY STUDYING RADIO WAVES FROM OUTER SPACE TO PAY MUCH MIND...
BUT THEY RAN INTO A PROBLEM, AND IN ORDER TO MEASURE THE FAINTEST OF SIGNALS, THE RESEARCHERS NEEDED TO ELIMINATE ALL INTERFERENCE...
...THERE WAS A LOW, STEADY MYSTERIOUS "HUM" THAT DESPITE EVERYTHING THEY TRIED, SIMPLY REFUSED TO GO AWAY...
AND TO ADD TO THE MYSTERY, THIS "HUM" DIDN'T SEEM TO EMANATE FROM THE EARTH, THE SUN OR EVEN OUR GALAXY, BUT FROM **SOMEWHERE BEYOND...**
AND BY SHEER SCIENTIFIC ACCIDENT THESE TWO PHYSICISTS HAD UNCOVERED A SNAPSHOT OF THE UNIVERSE MADE ONLY MOMENTS AFTER THE "BIG BANG."

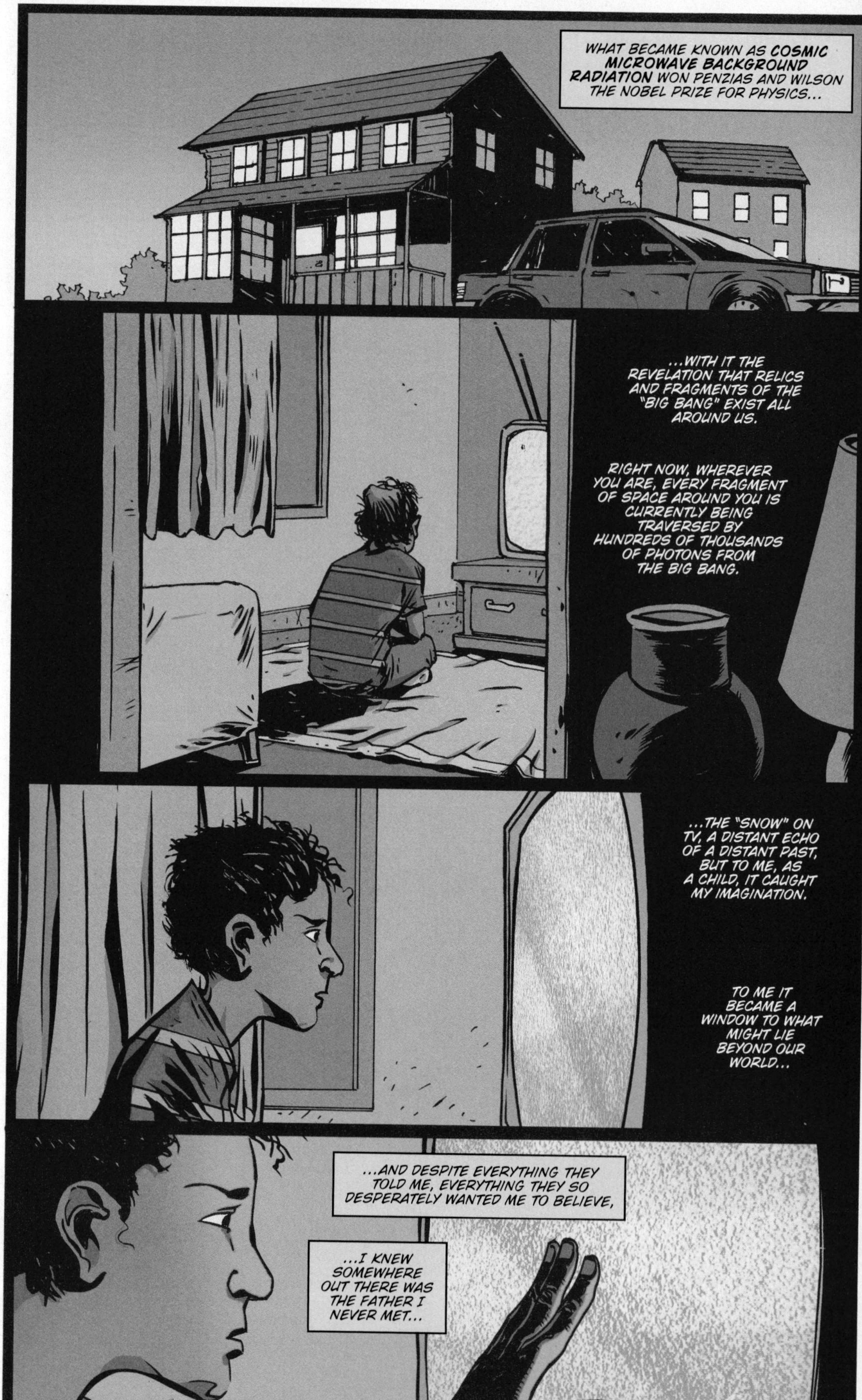
WHAT BECAME KNOWN AS **COSMIC MICROWAVE BACKGROUND RADIATION** WON PENZIAS AND WILSON THE NOBEL PRIZE FOR PHYSICS...
...WITH IT THE REVELATION THAT RELICS AND FRAGMENTS OF THE "BIG BANG" EXIST ALL AROUND US.
RIGHT NOW, WHEREVER YOU ARE, EVERY FRAGMENT OF SPACE AROUND YOU IS CURRENTLY BEING TRAVERSED BY HUNDREDS OF THOUSANDS OF PHOTONS FROM THE BIG BANG.
...THE "SNOW" ON TV, A DISTANT ECHO OF A DISTANT PAST, BUT TO ME, AS A CHILD, IT CAUGHT MY IMAGINATION.
TO ME IT BECAME A WINDOW TO WHAT MIGHT LIE BEYOND OUR WORLD...
...AND DESPITE EVERYTHING THEY TOLD ME, EVERYTHING THEY SO DESPERATELY WANTED ME TO BELIEVE,
...I KNEW SOMEWHERE OUT THERE WAS THE FATHER I NEVER MET...

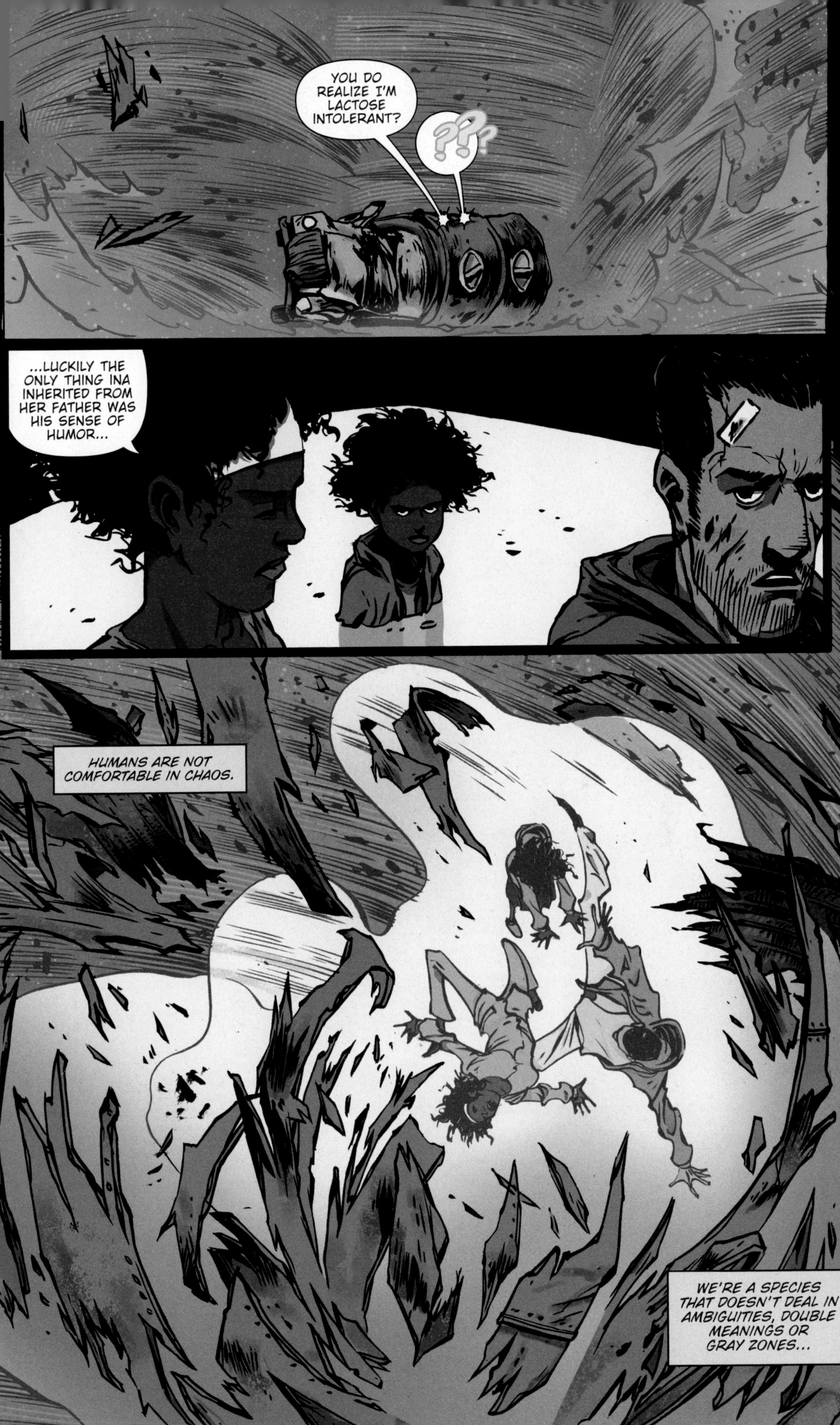
YOU DO REALIZE I'M LACTOSE INTOLERANT?
??
...LUCKILY THE ONLY THING INA INHERITED FROM HER FATHER WAS HIS SENSE OF HUMOR...
HUMANS ARE NOT COMFORTABLE IN CHAOS.
WE'RE A SPECIES THAT DOESN'T DEAL IN AMBIGUITIES, DOUBLE MEANINGS OR GRAY ZONES...

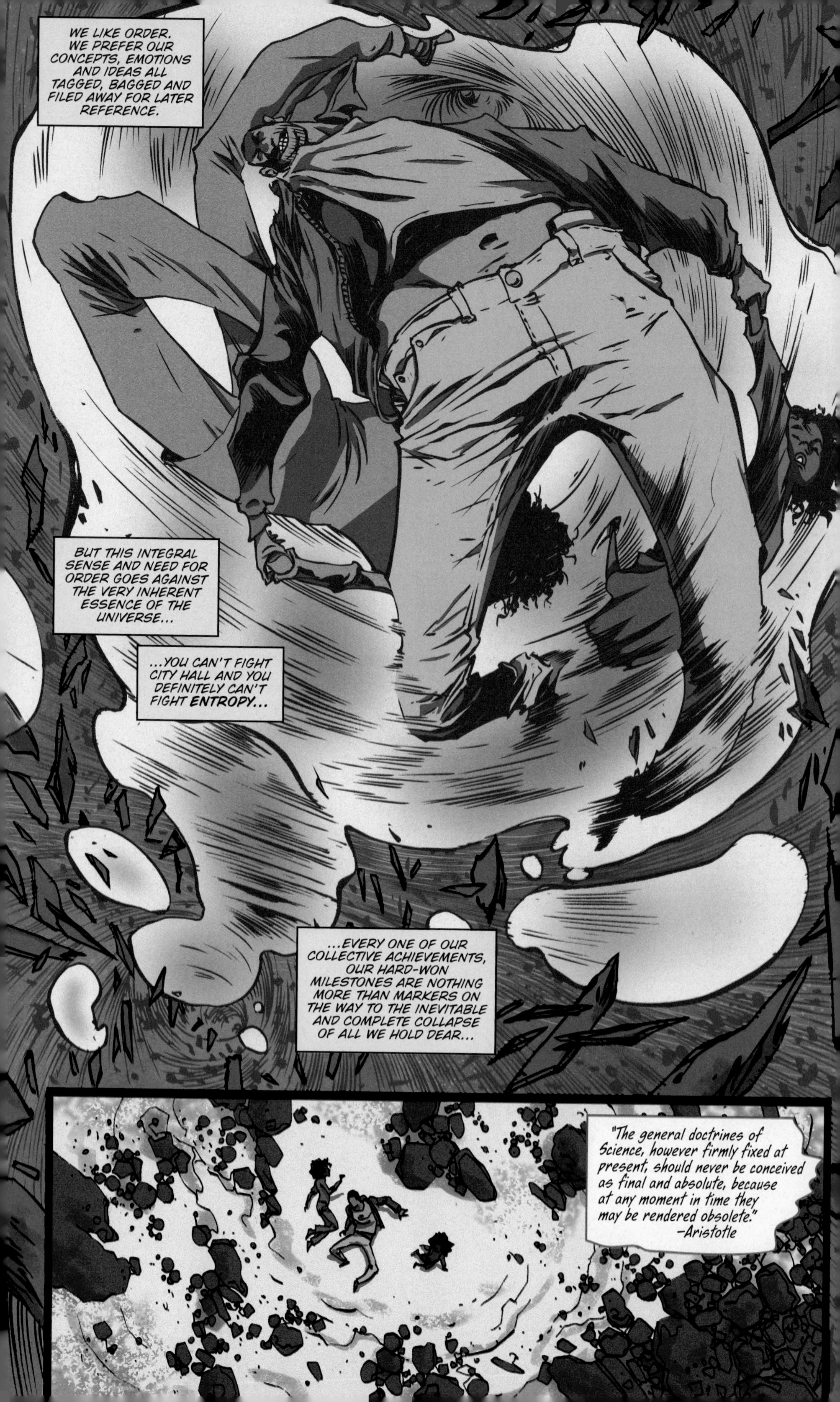
WE LIKE ORDER. WE PREFER OUR CONCEPTS, EMOTIONS AND IDEAS ALL TAGGED, BAGGED AND FILED AWAY FOR LATER REFERENCE.
BUT THIS INTEGRAL SENSE AND NEED FOR ORDER GOES AGAINST THE VERY INHERENT ESSENCE OF THE UNIVERSE...
...YOU CAN'T FIGHT CITY HALL AND YOU DEFINITELY CAN'T FIGHT **ENTROPY...**
...EVERY ONE OF OUR COLLECTIVE ACHIEVEMENTS, OUR HARD-WON MILESTONES ARE NOTHING MORE THAN MARKERS ON THE WAY TO THE INEVITABLE AND COMPLETE COLLAPSE OF ALL WE HOLD DEAR...
"The general doctrines of Science, however firmly fixed at present, should never be conceived as final and absolute, because at any moment in time they may be rendered obsolete." –Aristotle

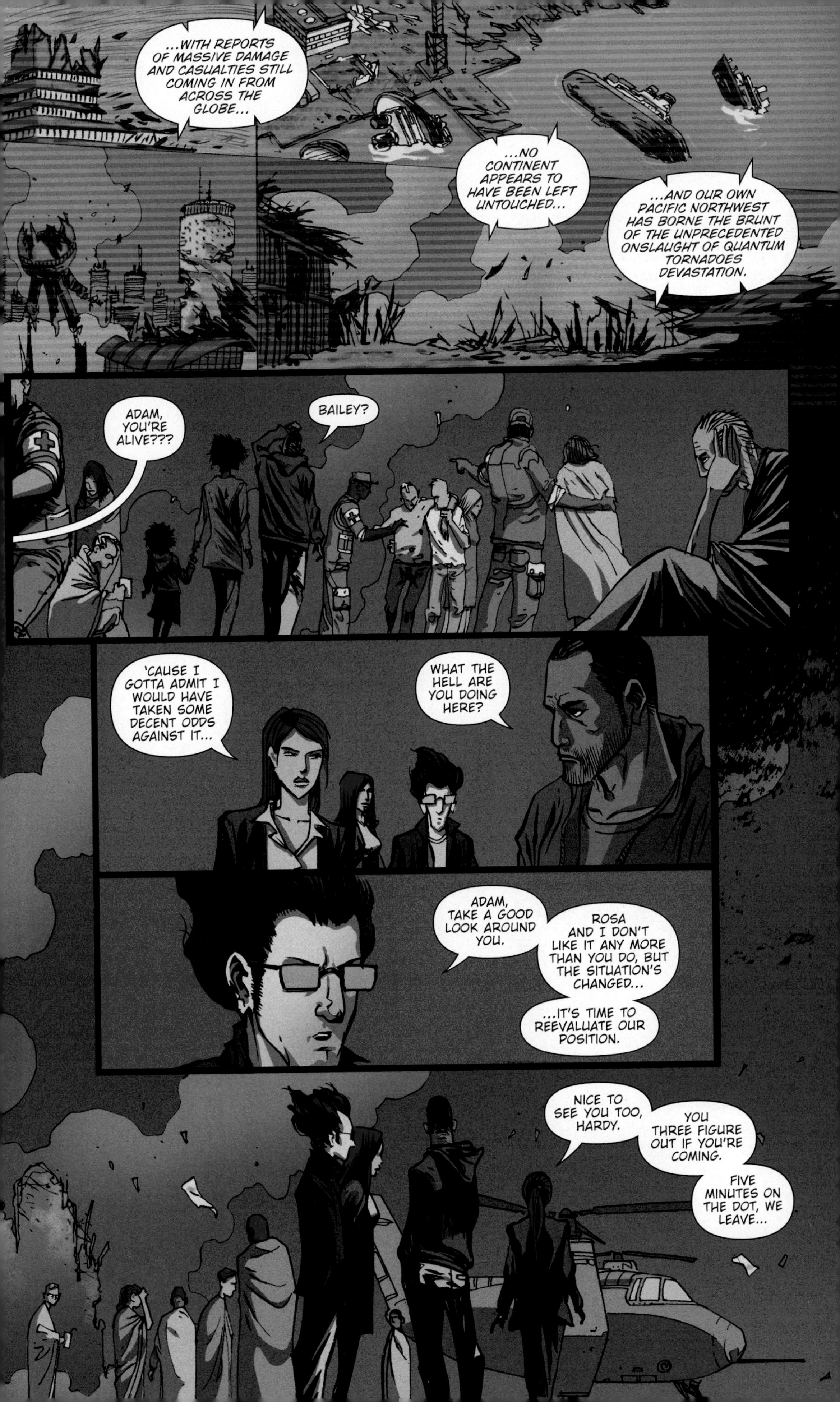
...WITH REPORTS OF MASSIVE DAMAGE AND CASUALTIES STILL COMING IN FROM ACROSS THE GLOBE...
...NO CONTINENT APPEARS TO HAVE BEEN LEFT UNTOUCHED...
...AND OUR OWN PACIFIC NORTHWEST HAS BORNE THE BRUNT OF THE UNPRECEDENTED ONSLAUGHT OF QUANTUM TORNADOES DEVASTATION.
ADAM, YOU'RE ALIVE???
BAILEY?
'CAUSE I GOTTA ADMIT I WOULD HAVE TAKEN SOME DECENT ODDS AGAINST IT...
WHAT THE HELL ARE YOU DOING HERE?
ADAM, TAKE A GOOD LOOK AROUND YOU.
ROSA AND I DON'T LIKE IT ANY MORE THAN YOU DO, BUT THE SITUATION'S CHANGED...
...IT'S TIME TO REEVALUATE OUR POSITION.
NICE TO SEE YOU TOO, HARDY.
YOU THREE FIGURE OUT IF YOU'RE COMING.
FIVE MINUTES ON THE DOT, WE LEAVE...

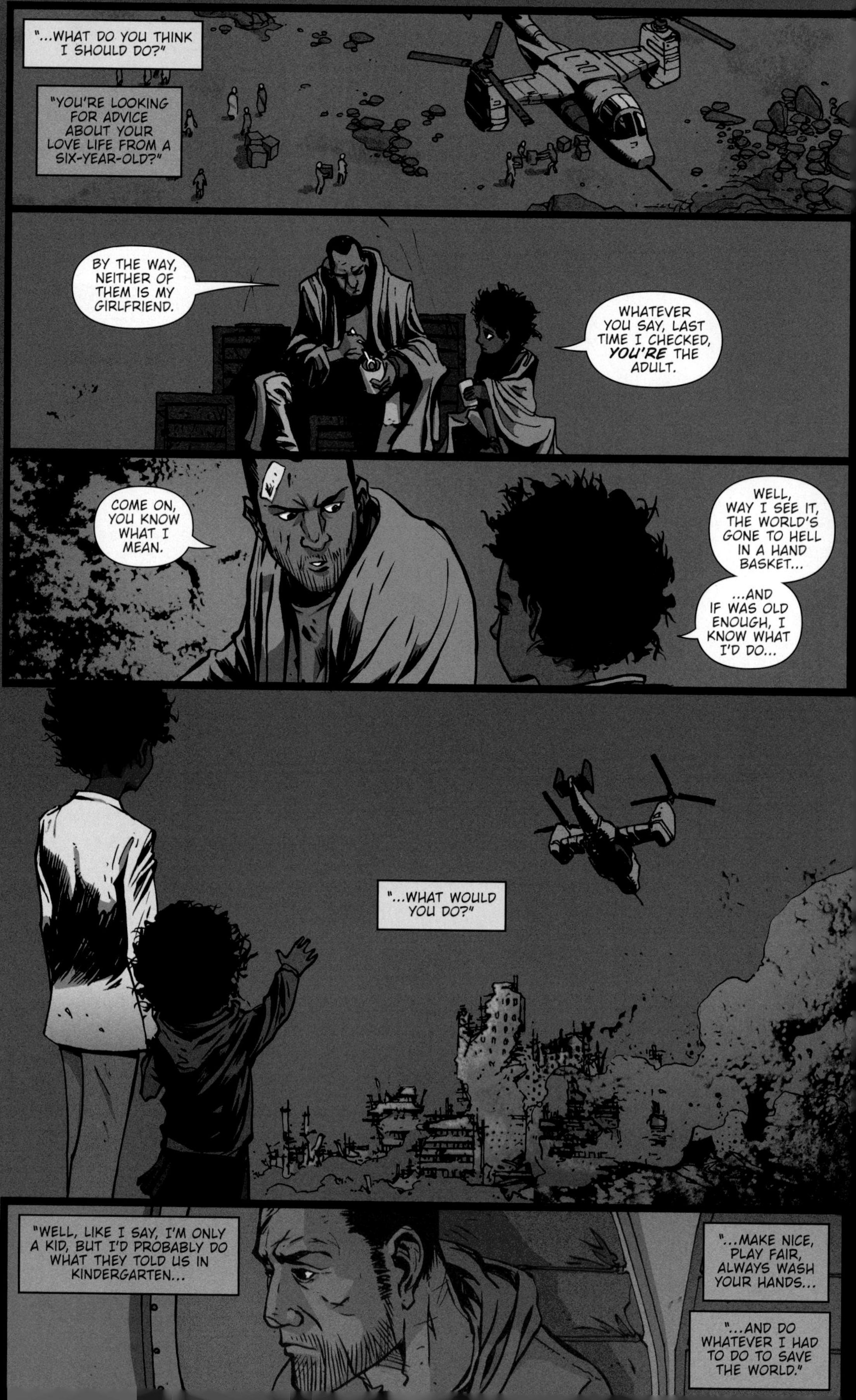
"...WHAT DO YOU THINK I SHOULD DO?"
"YOU'RE LOOKING FOR ADVICE ABOUT YOUR LOVE LIFE FROM A SIX-YEAR-OLD?"
BY THE WAY, NEITHER OF THEM IS MY GIRLFRIEND.
WHATEVER YOU SAY, LAST TIME I CHECKED, *YOU'RE* THE ADULT.
COME ON, YOU KNOW WHAT I MEAN.
WELL, WAY I SEE IT, THE WORLD'S GONE TO HELL IN A HAND BASKET...
...AND IF WAS OLD ENOUGH, I KNOW WHAT I'D DO...
"...WHAT WOULD YOU DO?"
"WELL, LIKE I SAY, I'M ONLY A KID, BUT I'D PROBABLY DO WHAT THEY TOLD US IN KINDERGARTEN...
"...MAKE NICE, PLAY FAIR, ALWAYS WASH YOUR HANDS...
"...AND DO WHATEVER I HAD TO DO TO SAVE THE WORLD."

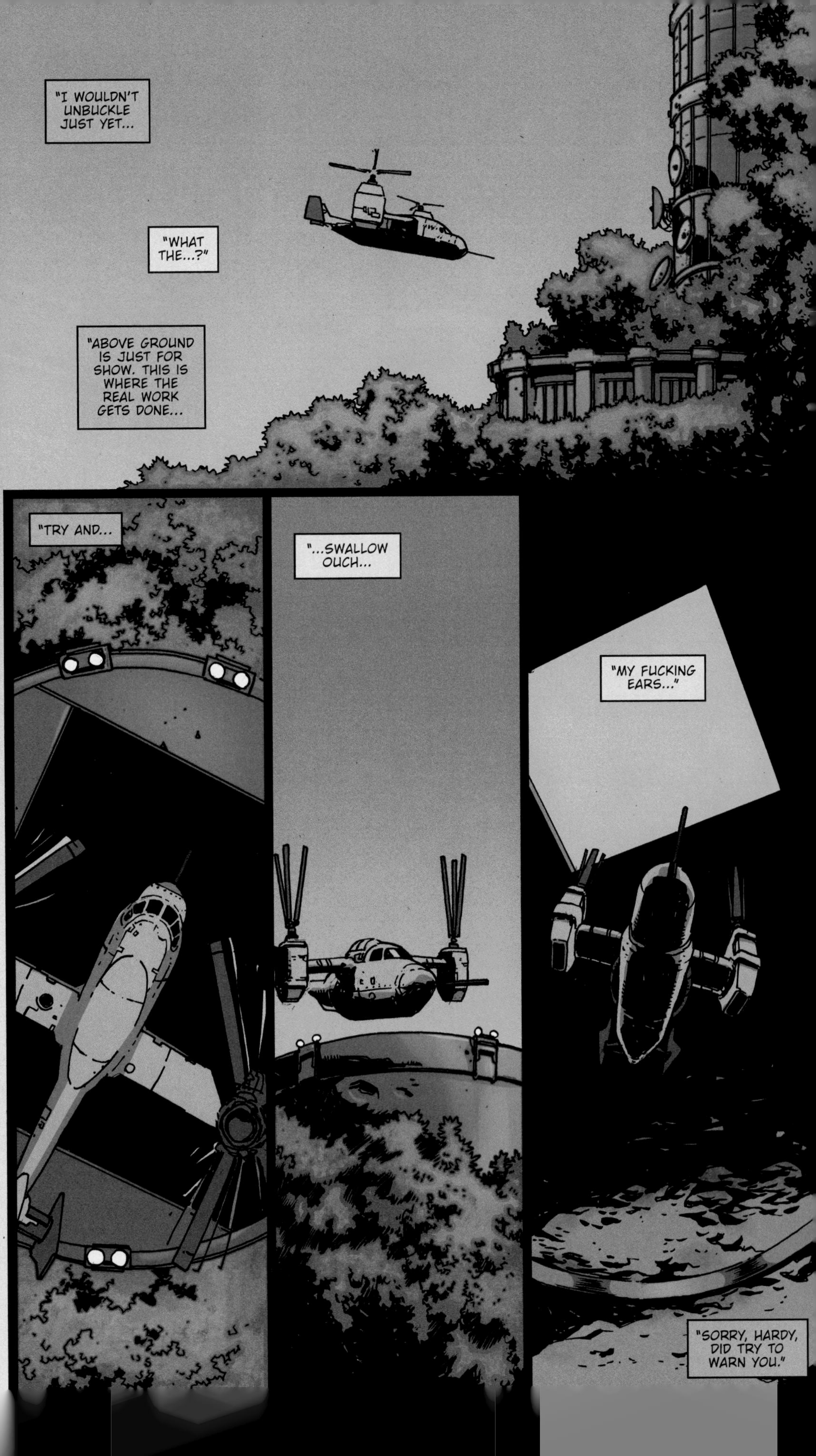
"I WOULDN'T UNBUCKLE JUST YET...
"WHAT THE...?"
"ABOVE GROUND IS JUST FOR SHOW. THIS IS WHERE THE REAL WORK GETS DONE...
"TRY AND...
"...SWALLOW OUCH...
"MY FUCKING EARS..."
"SORRY, HARDY, DID TRY TO WARN YOU."

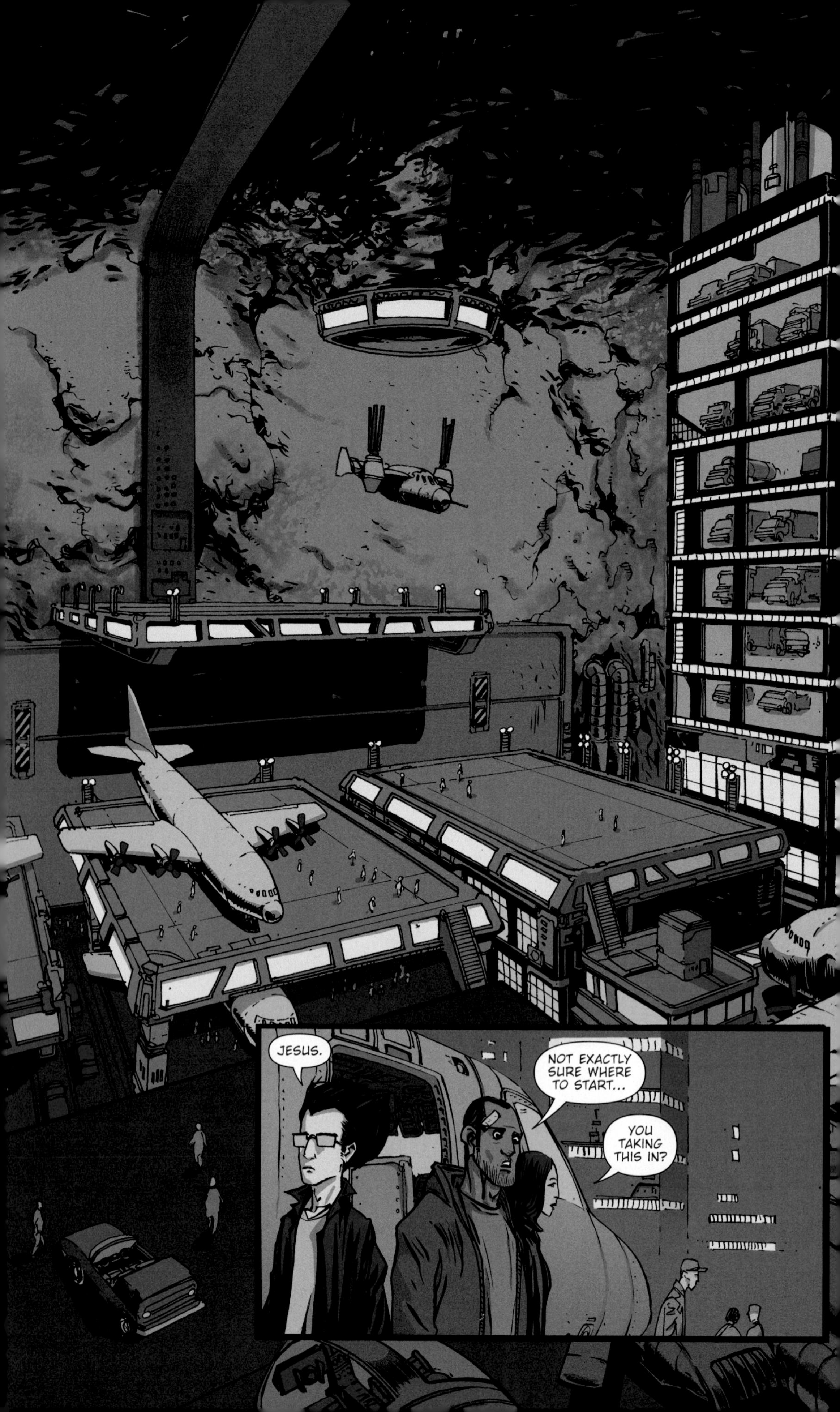
JESUS.
NOT EXACTLY SURE WHERE TO START...
YOU TAKING THIS IN?

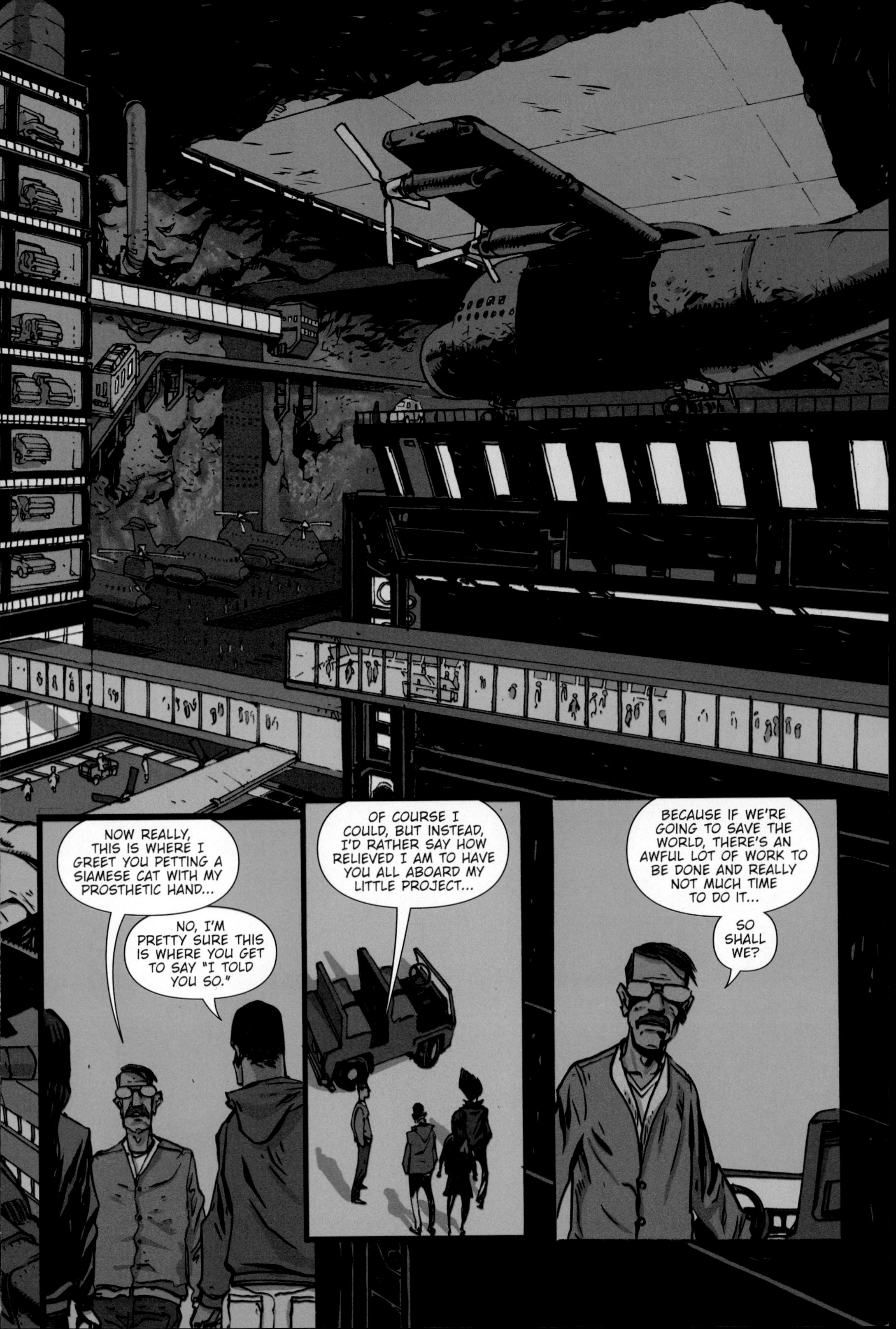
NOW REALLY, THIS IS WHERE I GREET YOU PETTING A SIAMESE CAT WITH MY PROSTHETIC HAND...
NO, I'M PRETTY SURE THIS IS WHERE YOU GET TO SAY "I TOLD YOU SO."
OF COURSE I COULD, BUT INSTEAD, I'D RATHER SAY HOW RELIEVED I AM TO HAVE YOU ALL ABOARD MY LITTLE PROJECT...
BECAUSE IF WE'RE GOING TO SAVE THE WORLD, THERE'S AN AWFUL LOT OF WORK TO BE DONE AND REALLY NOT MUCH TIME TO DO IT...
SO SHALL WE?

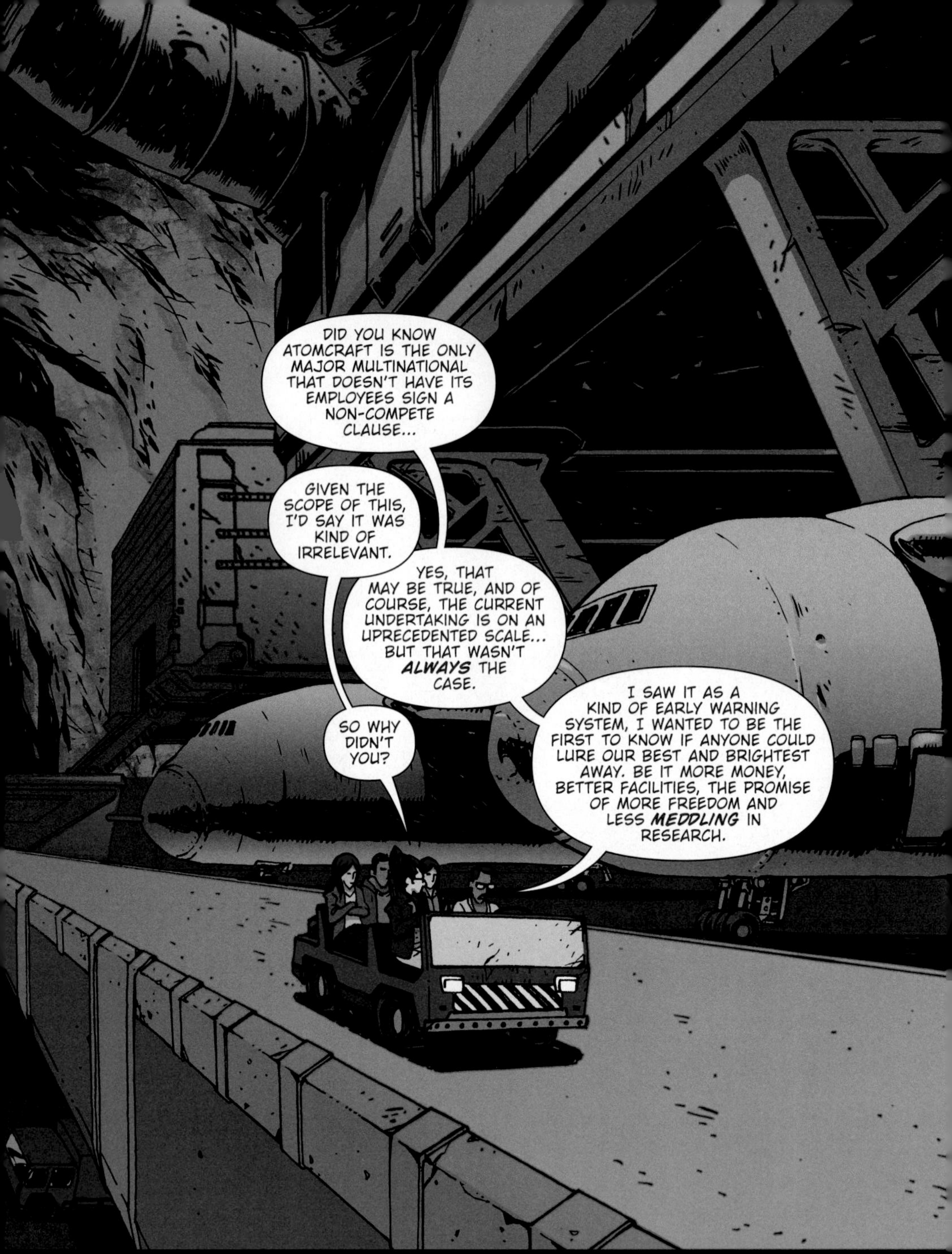
DID YOU KNOW ATOMCRAFT IS THE ONLY MAJOR MULTINATIONAL THAT DOESN'T HAVE ITS EMPLOYEES SIGN A NON-COMPETE CLAUSE...
GIVEN THE SCOPE OF THIS, I'D SAY IT WAS KIND OF IRRELEVANT.
YES, THAT MAY BE TRUE, AND OF COURSE, THE CURRENT UNDERTAKING IS ON AN UPRECEDENTED SCALE... BUT THAT WASN'T *ALWAYS* THE CASE.
SO WHY DIDN'T YOU?
I SAW IT AS A KIND OF EARLY WARNING SYSTEM, I WANTED TO BE THE FIRST TO KNOW IF ANYONE COULD LURE OUR BEST AND BRIGHTEST AWAY. BE IT MORE MONEY, BETTER FACILITIES, THE PROMISE OF MORE FREEDOM AND LESS *MEDDLING* IN RESEARCH.

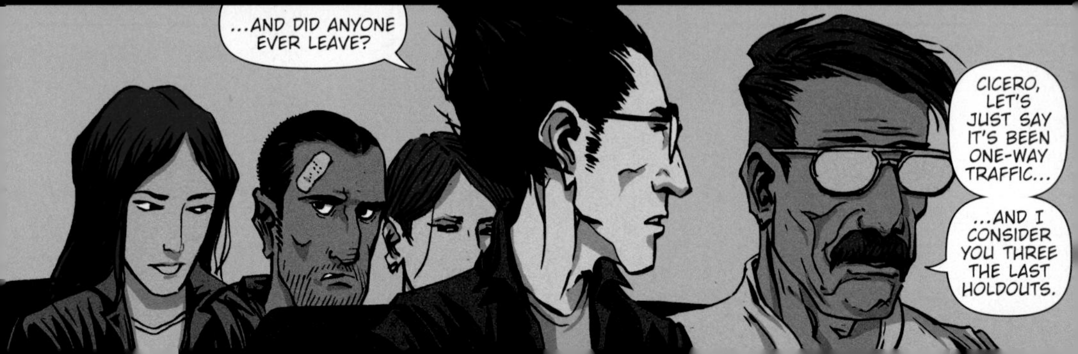
...AND DID ANYONE EVER LEAVE?
CICERO, LET'S JUST SAY IT'S BEEN ONE-WAY TRAFFIC...
...AND I CONSIDER YOU THREE THE LAST HOLDOUTS.

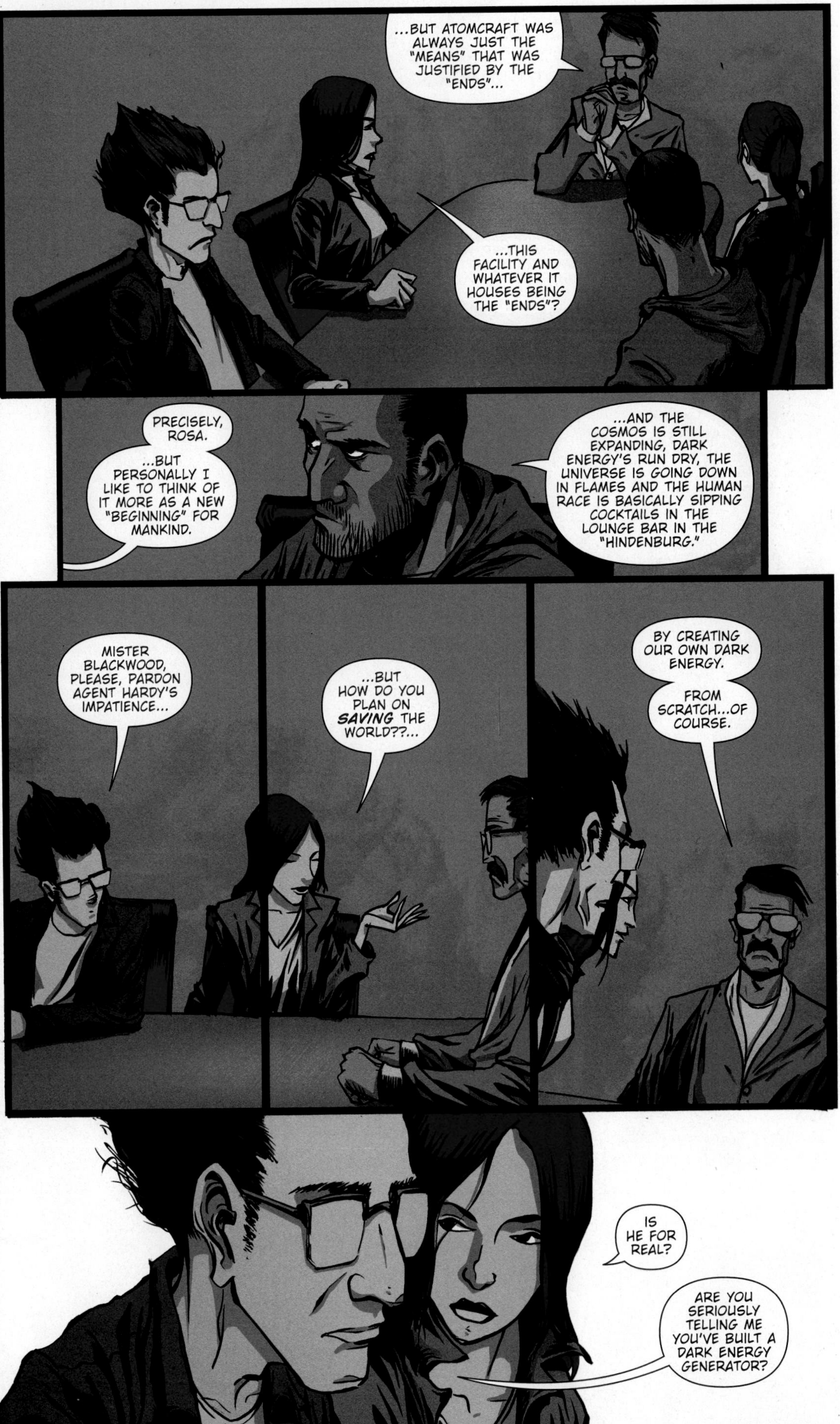
...BUT ATOMCRAFT WAS ALWAYS JUST THE "MEANS" THAT WAS JUSTIFIED BY THE "ENDS"...
...THIS FACILITY AND WHATEVER IT HOUSES BEING THE "ENDS"?
...AND THE COSMOS IS STILL EXPANDING, DARK ENERGY'S RUN DRY, THE UNIVERSE IS GOING DOWN IN FLAMES AND THE HUMAN RACE IS BASICALLY SIPPING COCKTAILS IN THE LOUNGE BAR IN THE "HINDENBURG."
PRECISELY, ROSA.
...BUT PERSONALLY I LIKE TO THINK OF IT MORE AS A NEW "BEGINNING" FOR MANKIND.
MISTER BLACKWOOD, PLEASE, PARDON AGENT HARDY'S IMPATIENCE...
...BUT HOW DO YOU PLAN ON *SAVING* THE WORLD??...
BY CREATING OUR OWN DARK ENERGY.
FROM SCRATCH...OF COURSE.
IS HE FOR REAL?
ARE YOU SERIOUSLY TELLING ME YOU'VE BUILT A DARK ENERGY GENERATOR?

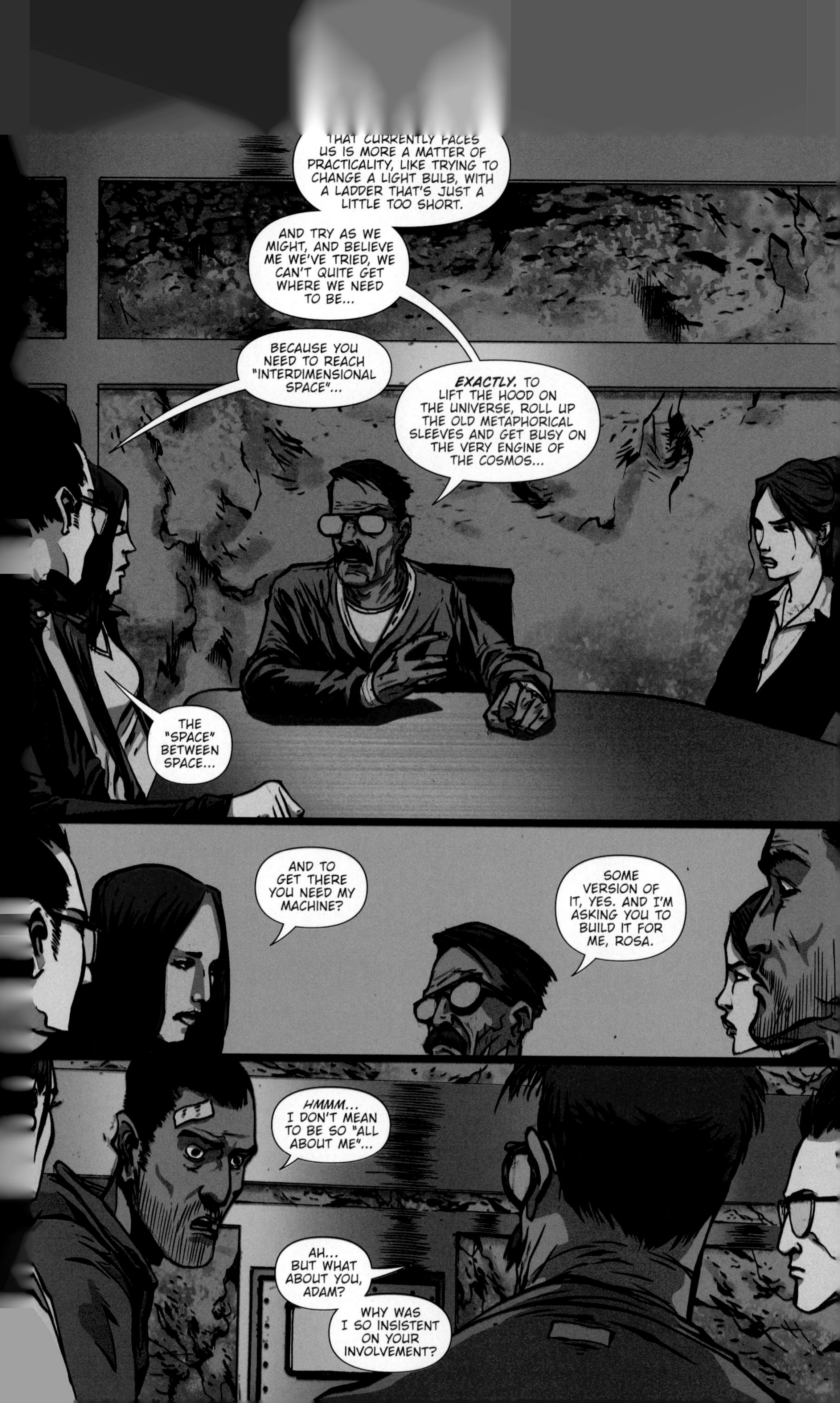

THAT CURRENTLY FACES US IS MORE A MATTER OF PRACTICALITY, LIKE TRYING TO CHANGE A LIGHT BULB, WITH A LADDER THAT'S JUST A LITTLE TOO SHORT.
AND TRY AS WE MIGHT, AND BELIEVE ME WE'VE TRIED, WE CAN'T QUITE GET WHERE WE NEED TO BE...
BECAUSE YOU NEED TO REACH "INTERDIMENSIONAL SPACE"...
EXACTLY. TO LIFT THE HOOD ON THE UNIVERSE, ROLL UP THE OLD METAPHORICAL SLEEVES AND GET BUSY ON THE VERY ENGINE OF THE COSMOS...
THE "SPACE" BETWEEN SPACE...
AND TO GET THERE YOU NEED MY MACHINE?
SOME VERSION OF IT, YES. AND I'M ASKING YOU TO BUILD IT FOR ME, ROSA.
HMMM... I DON'T MEAN TO BE SO "ALL ABOUT ME"...
AH... BUT WHAT ABOUT YOU, ADAM?
WHY WAS I SO INSISTENT ON YOUR INVOLVEMENT?

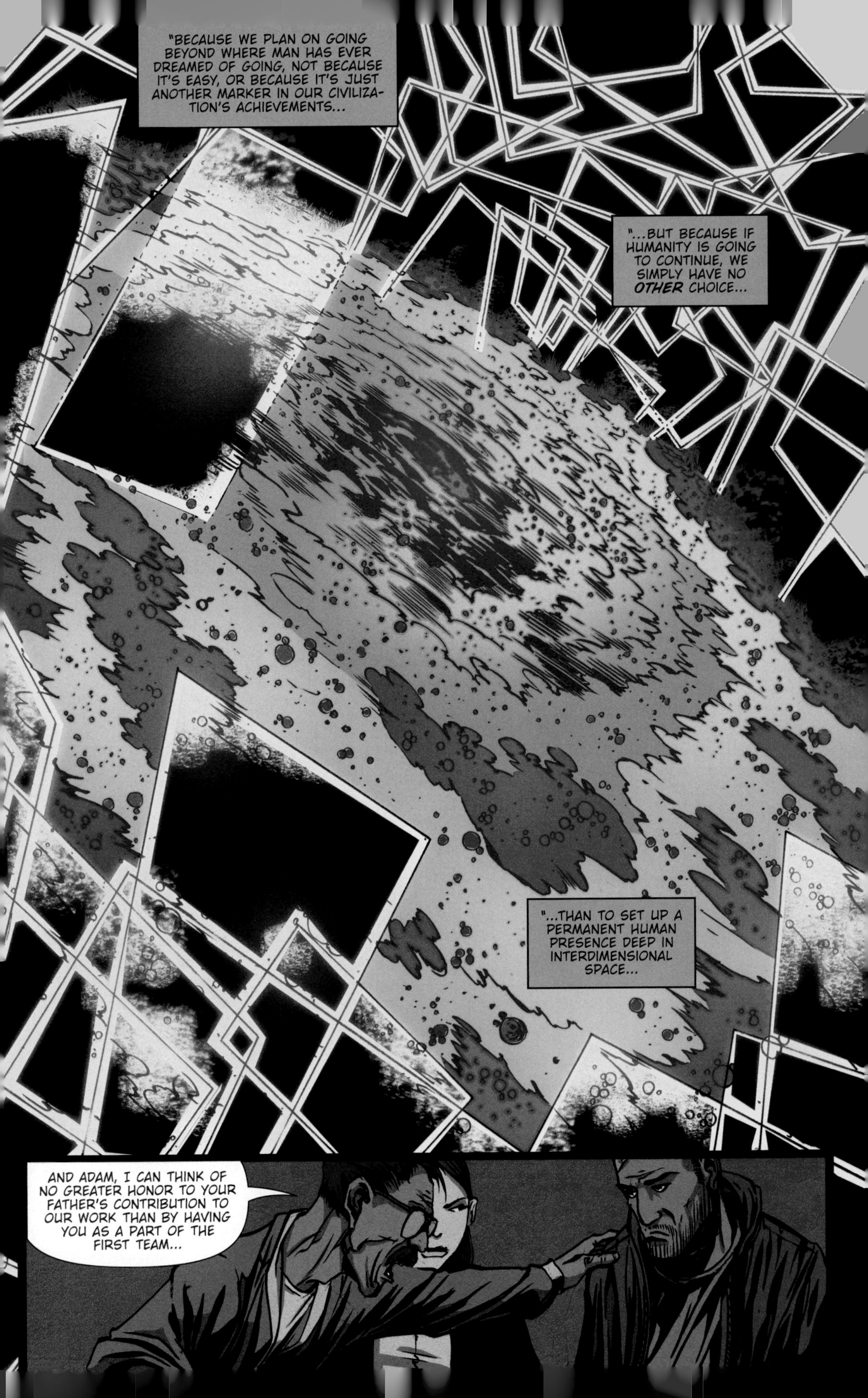
"BECAUSE WE PLAN ON GOING BEYOND WHERE MAN HAS EVER DREAMED OF GOING, NOT BECAUSE IT'S EASY, OR BECAUSE IT'S JUST ANOTHER MARKER IN OUR CIVILIZA-TION'S ACHIEVEMENTS...
"...BUT BECAUSE IF HUMANITY IS GOING TO CONTINUE, WE SIMPLY HAVE NO *OTHER* CHOICE...
"...THAN TO SET UP A PERMANENT HUMAN PRESENCE DEEP IN INTERDIMENSIONAL SPACE...
AND ADAM, I CAN THINK OF NO GREATER HONOR TO YOUR FATHER'S CONTRIBUTION TO OUR WORK THAN BY HAVING YOU AS A PART OF THE FIRST TEAM...

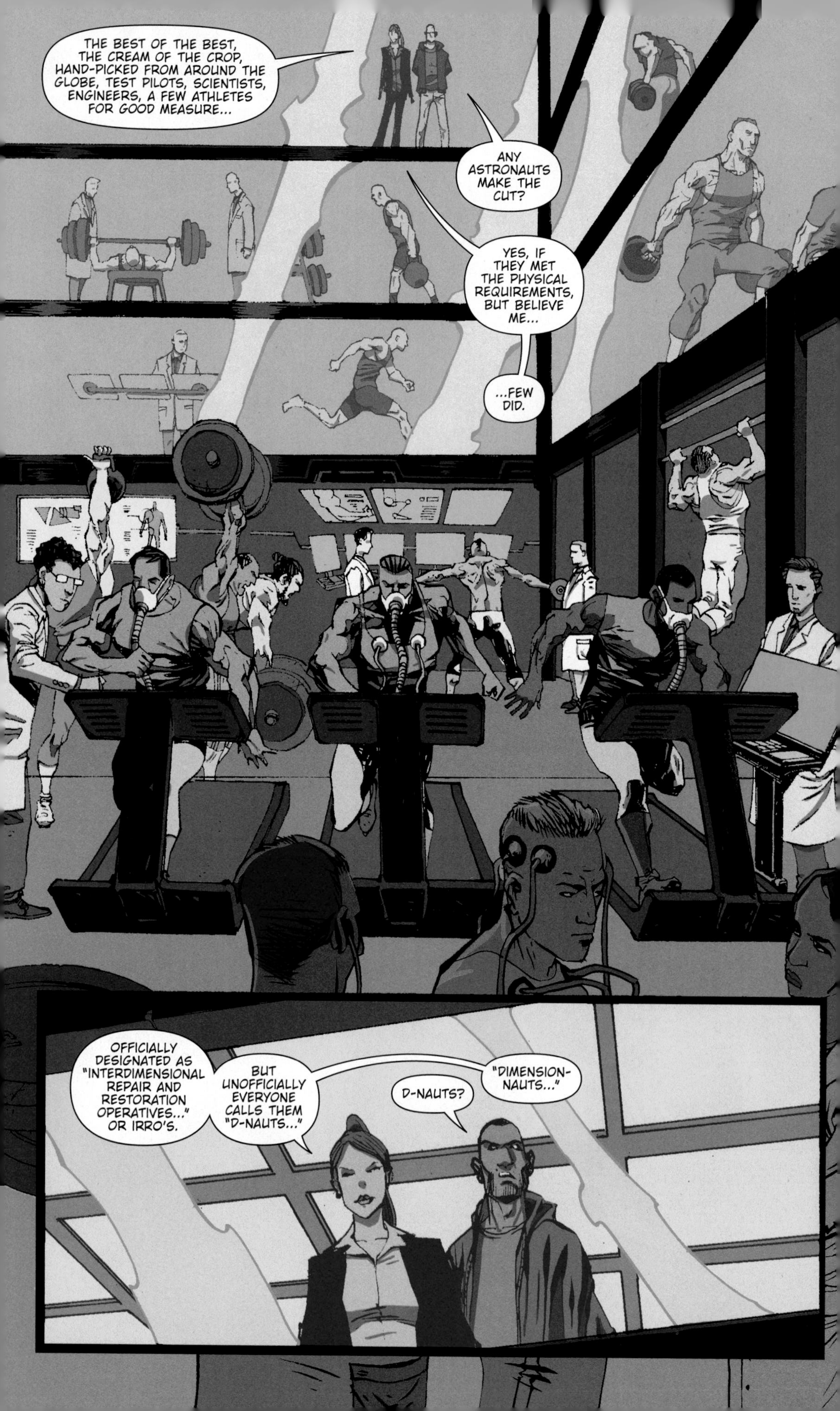
THE BEST OF THE BEST, THE CREAM OF THE CROP, HAND-PICKED FROM AROUND THE GLOBE, TEST PILOTS, SCIENTISTS, ENGINEERS, A FEW ATHLETES FOR GOOD MEASURE...
ANY ASTRONAUTS MAKE THE CUT?
YES, IF THEY MET THE PHYSICAL REQUIREMENTS, BUT BELIEVE ME...
...FEW DID.
OFFICIALLY DESIGNATED AS "INTERDIMENSIONAL REPAIR AND RESTORATION OPERATIVES..." OR IRRO'S.
BUT UNOFFICIALLY EVERYONE CALLS THEM "D-NAUTS..."
D-NAUTS?
"DIMENSION-NAUTS..."

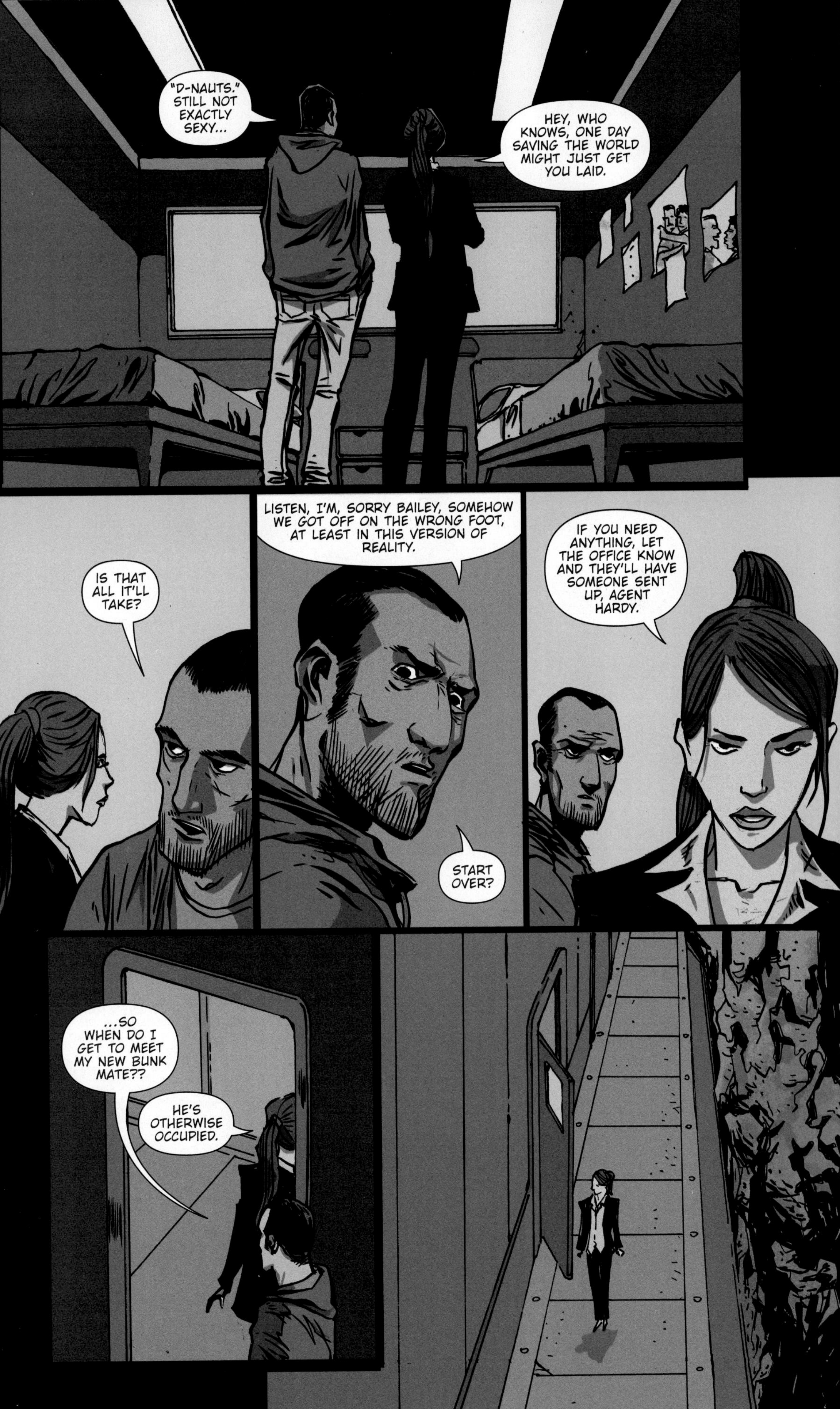
"D-NAUTS." STILL NOT EXACTLY SEXY...
HEY, WHO KNOWS, ONE DAY SAVING THE WORLD MIGHT JUST GET YOU LAID.
IS THAT ALL IT'LL TAKE?
LISTEN, I'M, SORRY BAILEY, SOMEHOW WE GOT OFF ON THE WRONG FOOT, AT LEAST IN THIS VERSION OF REALITY.
START OVER?
IF YOU NEED ANYTHING, LET THE OFFICE KNOW AND THEY'LL HAVE SOMEONE SENT UP, AGENT HARDY.
...SO WHEN DO I GET TO MEET MY NEW BUNK MATE??
HE'S OTHERWISE OCCUPIED.

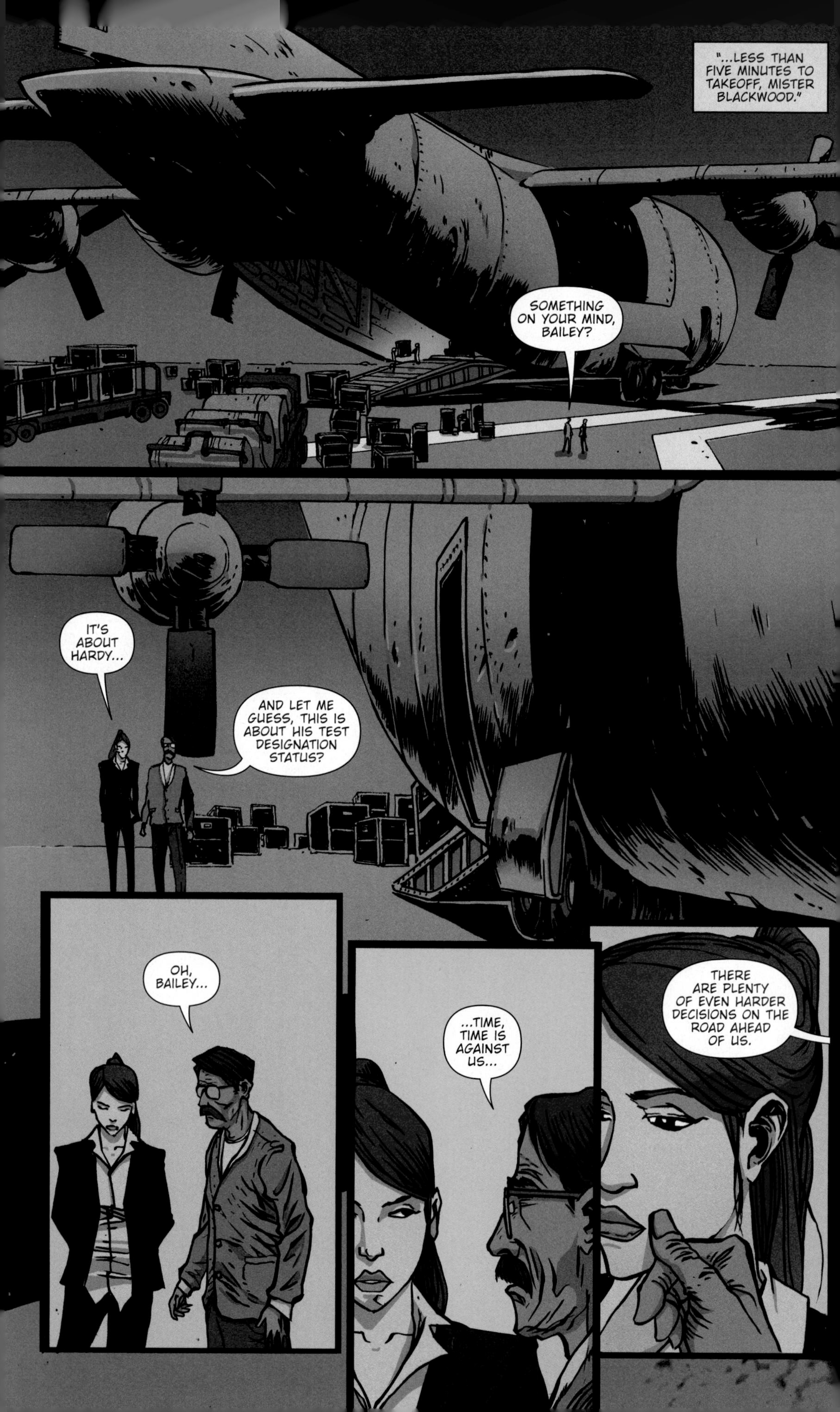
"...LESS THAN FIVE MINUTES TO TAKEOFF, MISTER BLACKWOOD."
SOMETHING ON YOUR MIND, BAILEY?
IT'S ABOUT HARDY...
AND LET ME GUESS, THIS IS ABOUT HIS TEST DESIGNATION STATUS?
OH, BAILEY...
...TIME, TIME IS AGAINST US...
THERE ARE PLENTY OF EVEN HARDER DECISIONS ON THE ROAD AHEAD OF US.

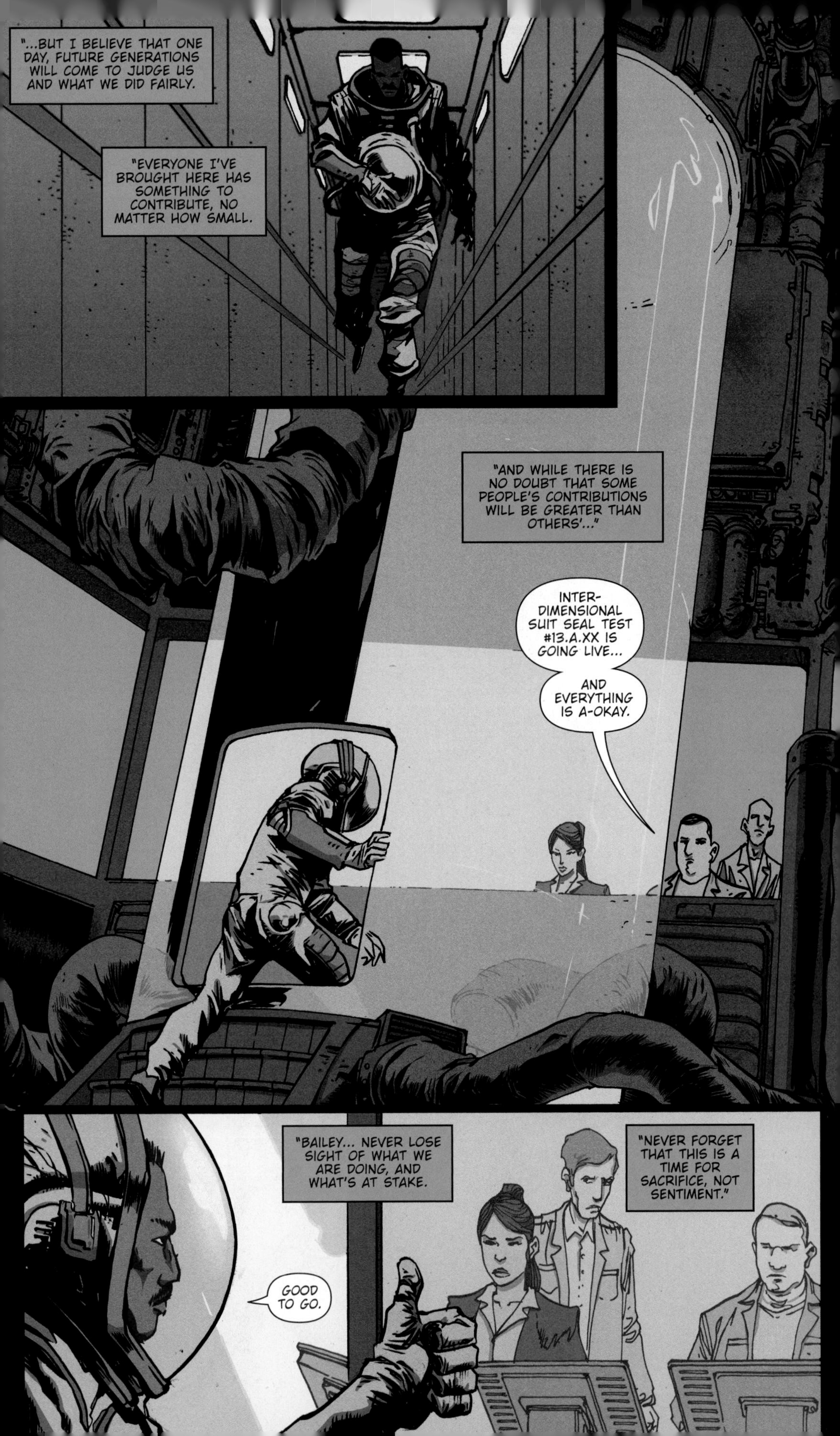
"...BUT I BELIEVE THAT ONE DAY, FUTURE GENERATIONS WILL COME TO JUDGE US AND WHAT WE DID FAIRLY.
"EVERYONE I'VE BROUGHT HERE HAS SOMETHING TO CONTRIBUTE, NO MATTER HOW SMALL.
"AND WHILE THERE IS NO DOUBT THAT SOME PEOPLE'S CONTRIBUTIONS WILL BE GREATER THAN OTHERS'..."
INTER-DIMENSIONAL SUIT SEAL TEST #13.A.XX IS GOING LIVE...
AND EVERYTHING IS A-OKAY.
"BAILEY... NEVER LOSE SIGHT OF WHAT WE ARE DOING, AND WHAT'S AT STAKE.
"NEVER FORGET THAT THIS IS A TIME FOR SACRIFICE, NOT SENTIMENT."
GOOD TO GO.

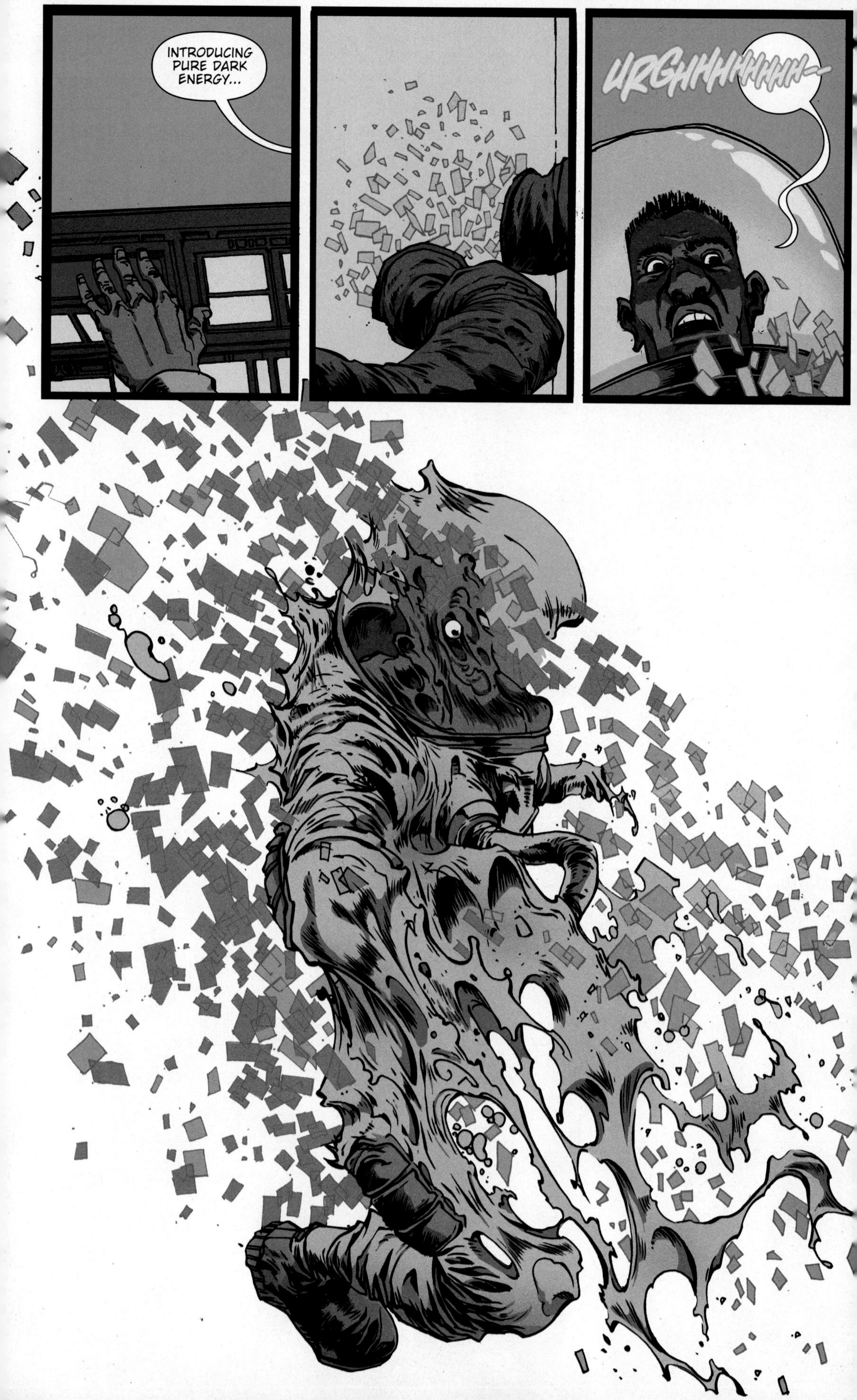
INTRODUCING PURE DARK ENERGY...
URGHHHHHHHHH--

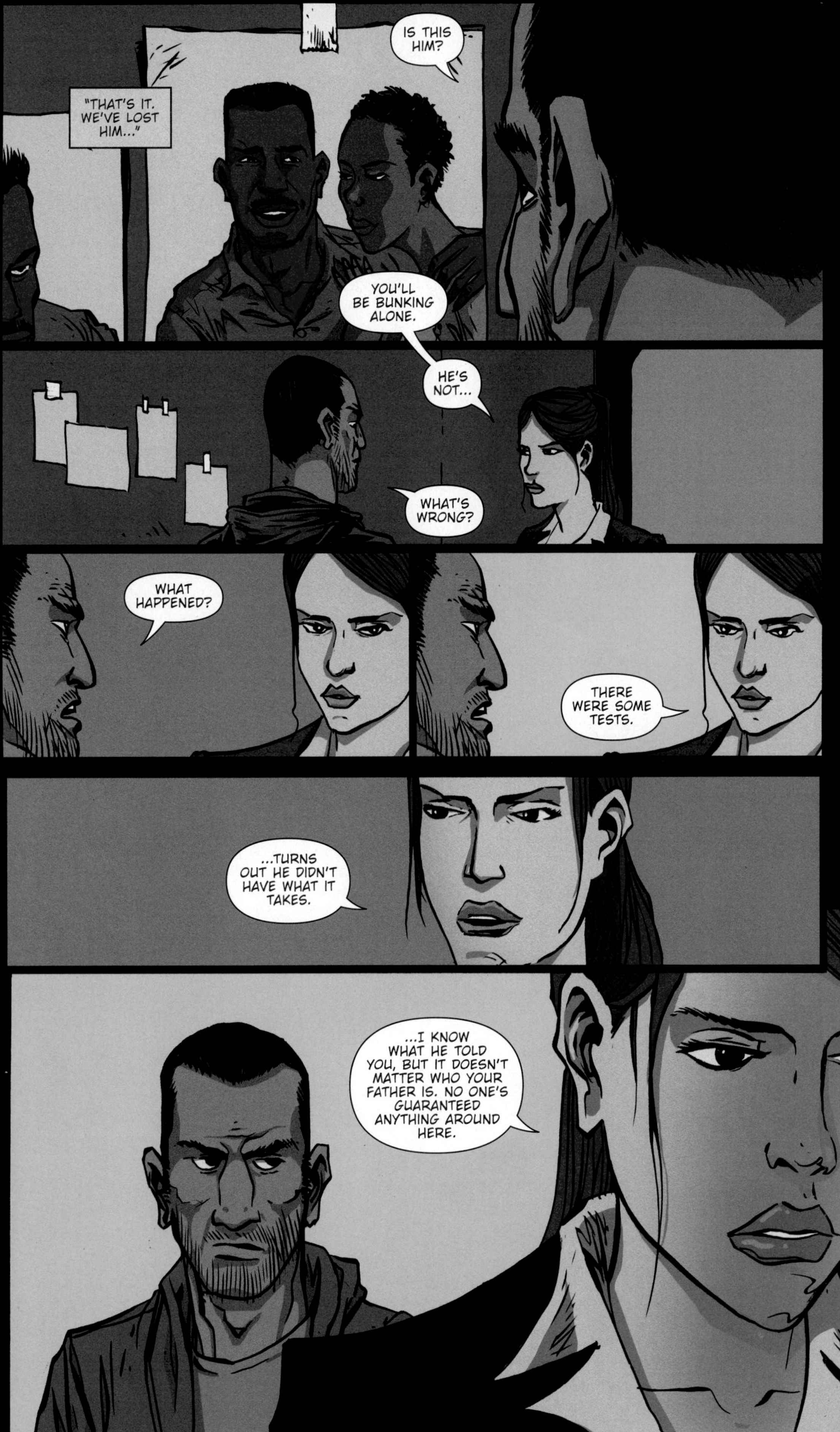
"THAT'S IT. WE'VE LOST HIM..."
IS THIS HIM?
YOU'LL BE BUNKING ALONE.
HE'S NOT...
WHAT'S WRONG?
WHAT HAPPENED?
THERE WERE SOME TESTS.
...TURNS OUT HE DIDN'T HAVE WHAT IT TAKES.
...I KNOW WHAT HE TOLD YOU, BUT IT DOESN'T MATTER WHO YOUR FATHER IS. NO ONE'S GUARANTEED ANYTHING AROUND HERE.

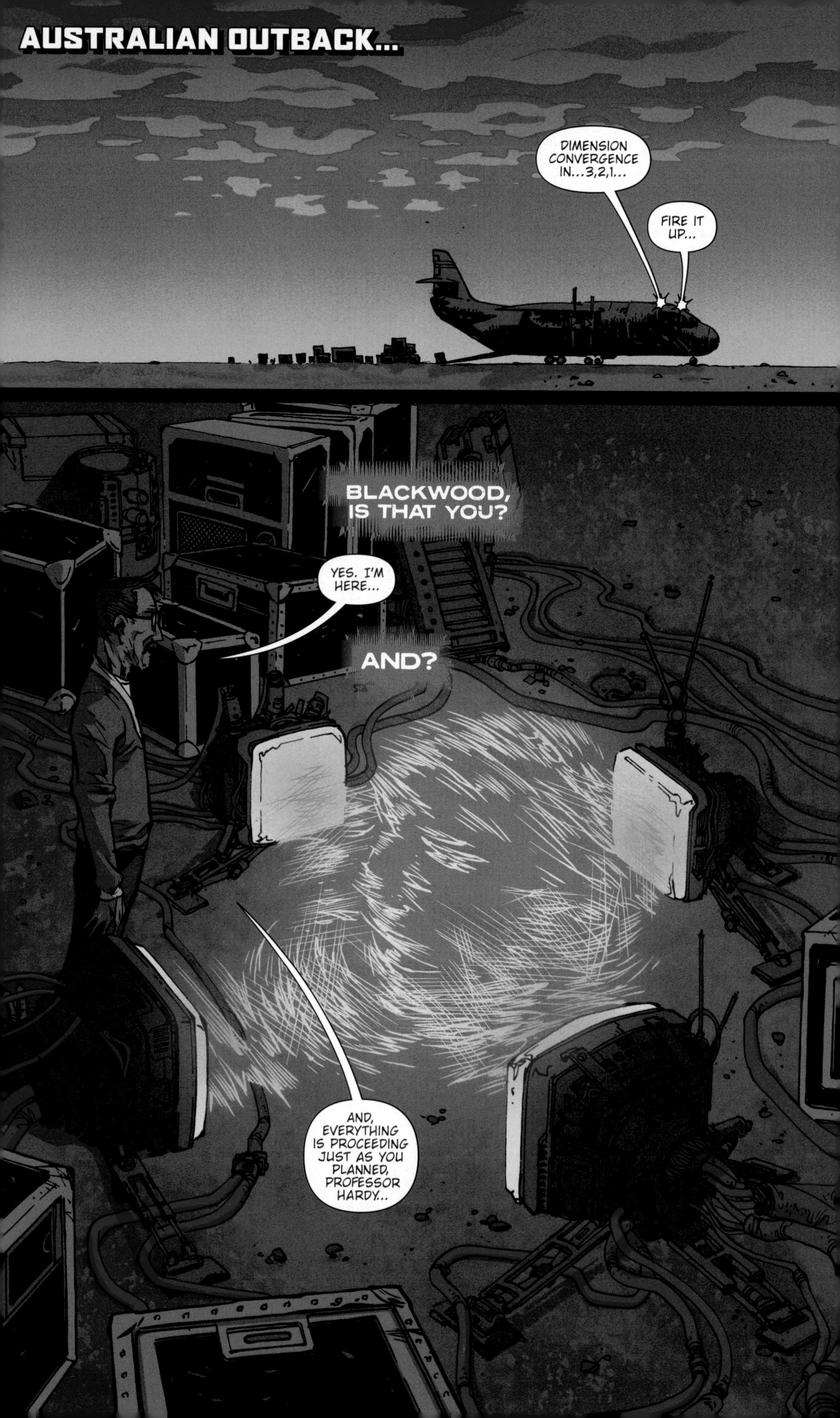
AUSTRALIAN OUTBACK...
DIMENSION CONVERGENCE IN...3,2,1...
FIRE IT UP...
BLACKWOOD, IS THAT YOU?
YES. I'M HERE...
AND?
AND, EVERYTHING IS PROCEEDING JUST AS YOU PLANNED, PROFESSOR HARDY...

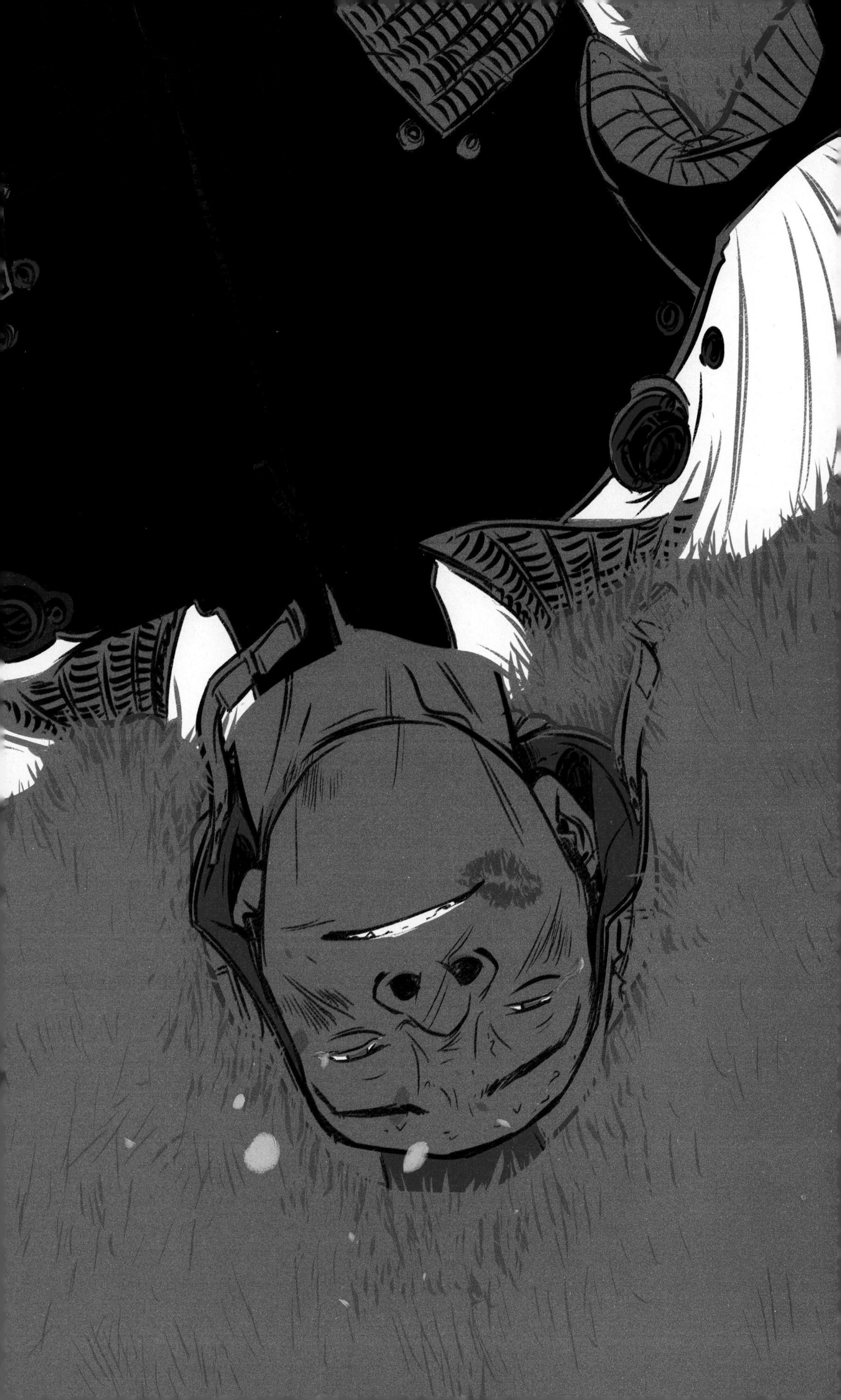

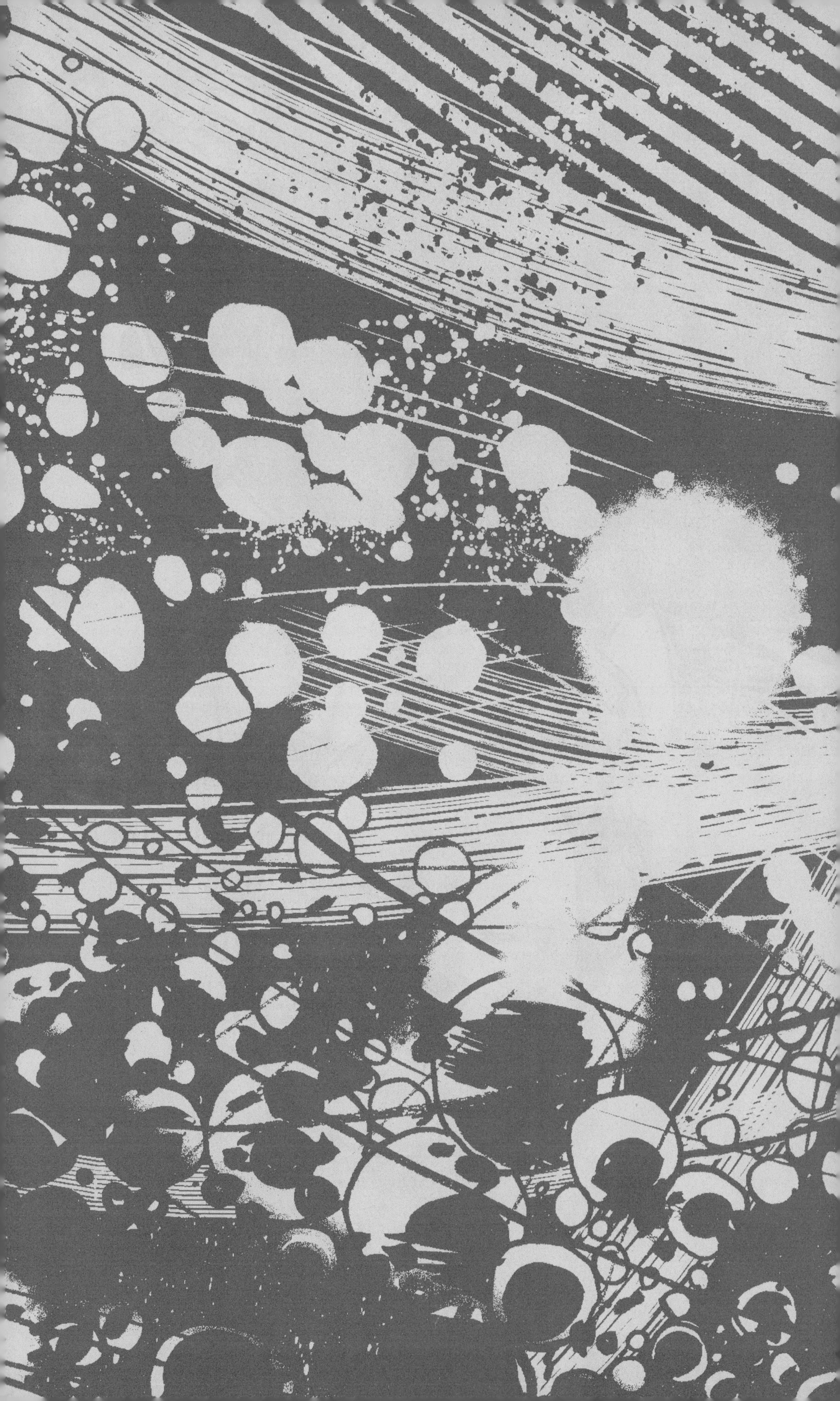

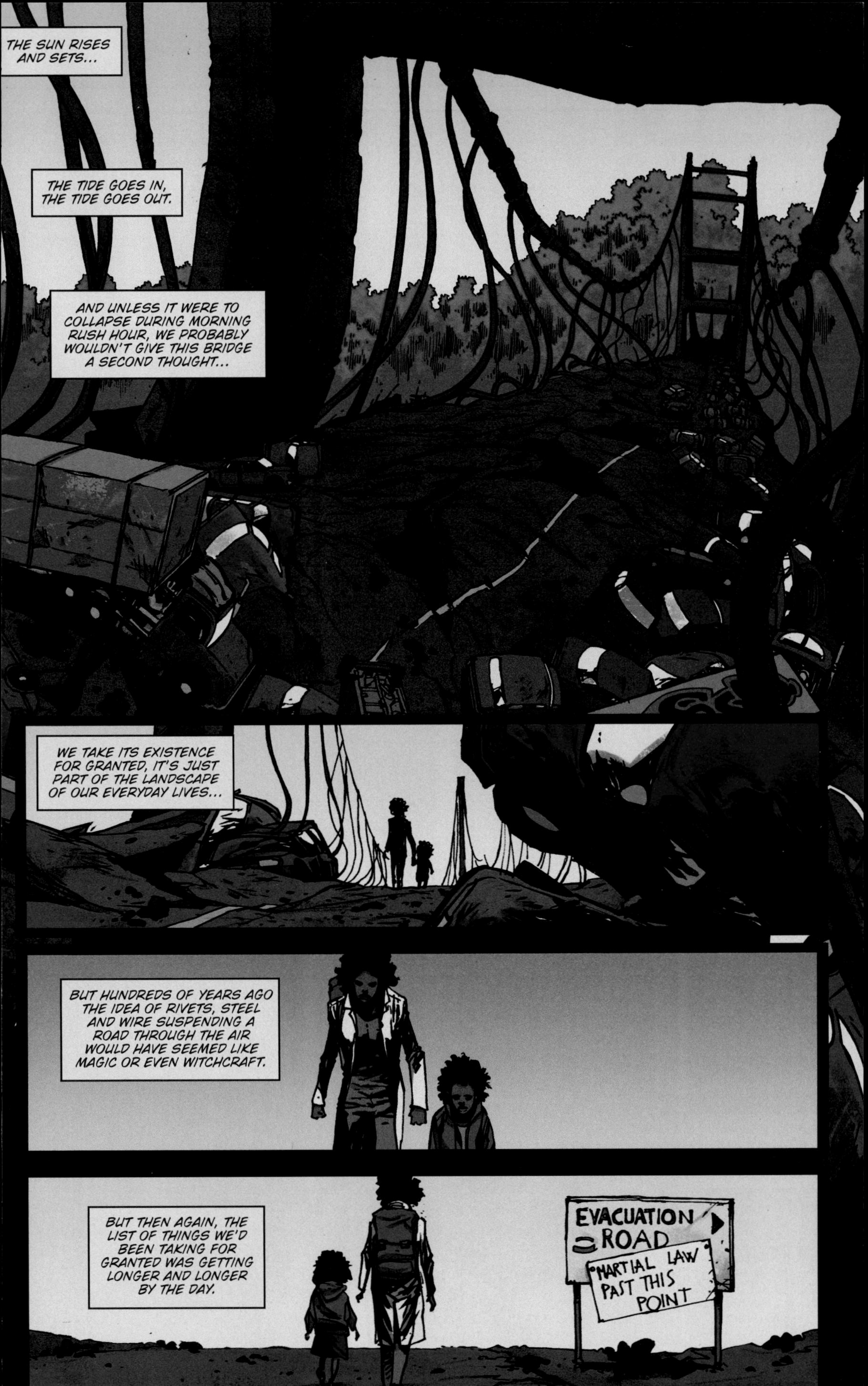
THE SUN RISES AND SETS...
THE TIDE GOES IN, THE TIDE GOES OUT.
AND UNLESS IT WERE TO COLLAPSE DURING MORNING RUSH HOUR, WE PROBABLY WOULDN'T GIVE THIS BRIDGE A SECOND THOUGHT...
WE TAKE ITS EXISTENCE FOR GRANTED, IT'S JUST PART OF THE LANDSCAPE OF OUR EVERYDAY LIVES...
BUT HUNDREDS OF YEARS AGO THE IDEA OF RIVETS, STEEL AND WIRE SUSPENDING A ROAD THROUGH THE AIR WOULD HAVE SEEMED LIKE MAGIC OR EVEN WITCHCRAFT.
BUT THEN AGAIN, THE LIST OF THINGS WE'D BEEN TAKING FOR GRANTED WAS GETTING LONGER AND LONGER BY THE DAY.
EVACUATION ROAD
MARTIAL LAW PAST THIS POINT

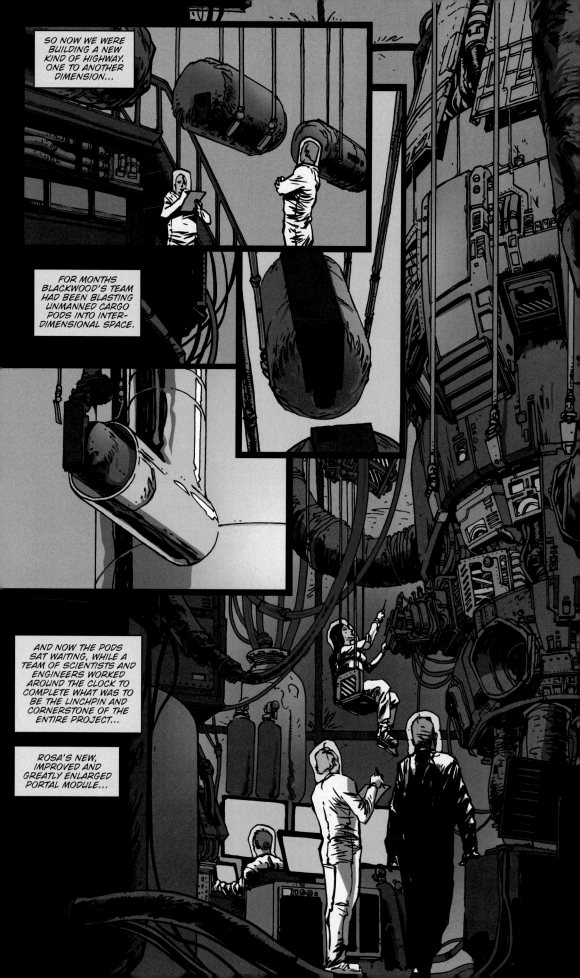

SO NOW WE WERE BUILDING A NEW KIND OF HIGHWAY. ONE TO ANOTHER DIMENSION...

FOR MONTHS BLACKWOOD'S TEAM HAD BEEN BLASTING UNMANNED CARGO PODS INTO INTER-DIMENSIONAL SPACE.

AND NOW THE PODS SAT WAITING, WHILE A TEAM OF SCIENTISTS AND ENGINEERS WORKED AROUND THE CLOCK TO COMPLETE WHAT WAS TO BE THE LINCHPIN AND CORNERSTONE OF THE ENTIRE PROJECT...

ROSA'S NEW, IMPROVED AND GREATLY ENLARGED PORTAL MODULE...

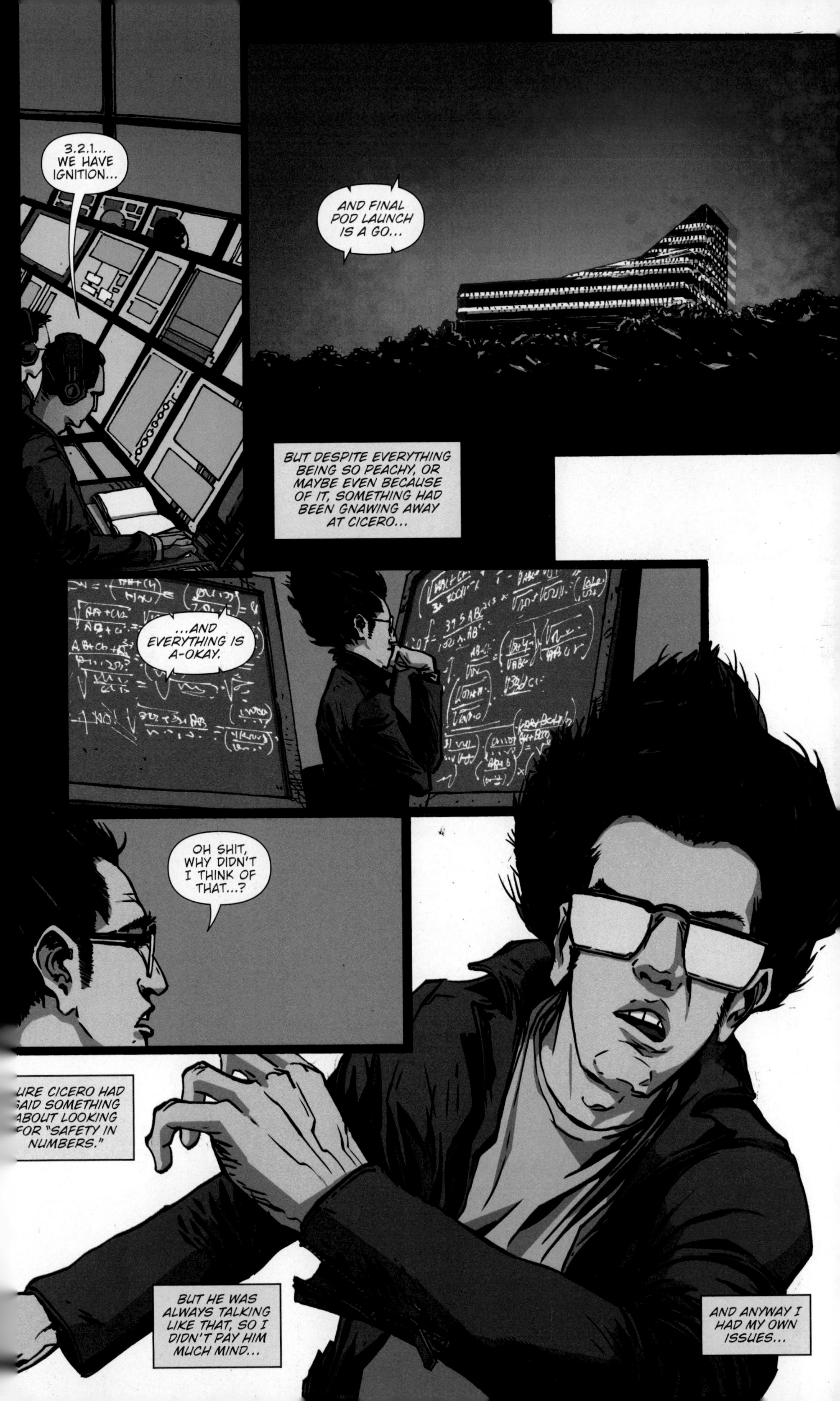
3.2.1... WE HAVE IGNITION...
AND FINAL POD LAUNCH IS A GO...
BUT DESPITE EVERYTHING BEING SO PEACHY, OR MAYBE EVEN BECAUSE OF IT, SOMETHING HAD BEEN GNAWING AWAY AT CICERO...
...AND EVERYTHING IS A-OKAY.
OH SHIT, WHY DIDN'T I THINK OF THAT...?
URE CICERO HAD AID SOMETHING ABOUT LOOKING FOR "SAFETY IN NUMBERS."
BUT HE WAS ALWAYS TALKING LIKE THAT, SO I DIDN'T PAY HIM MUCH MIND...
AND ANYWAY I HAD MY OWN ISSUES...

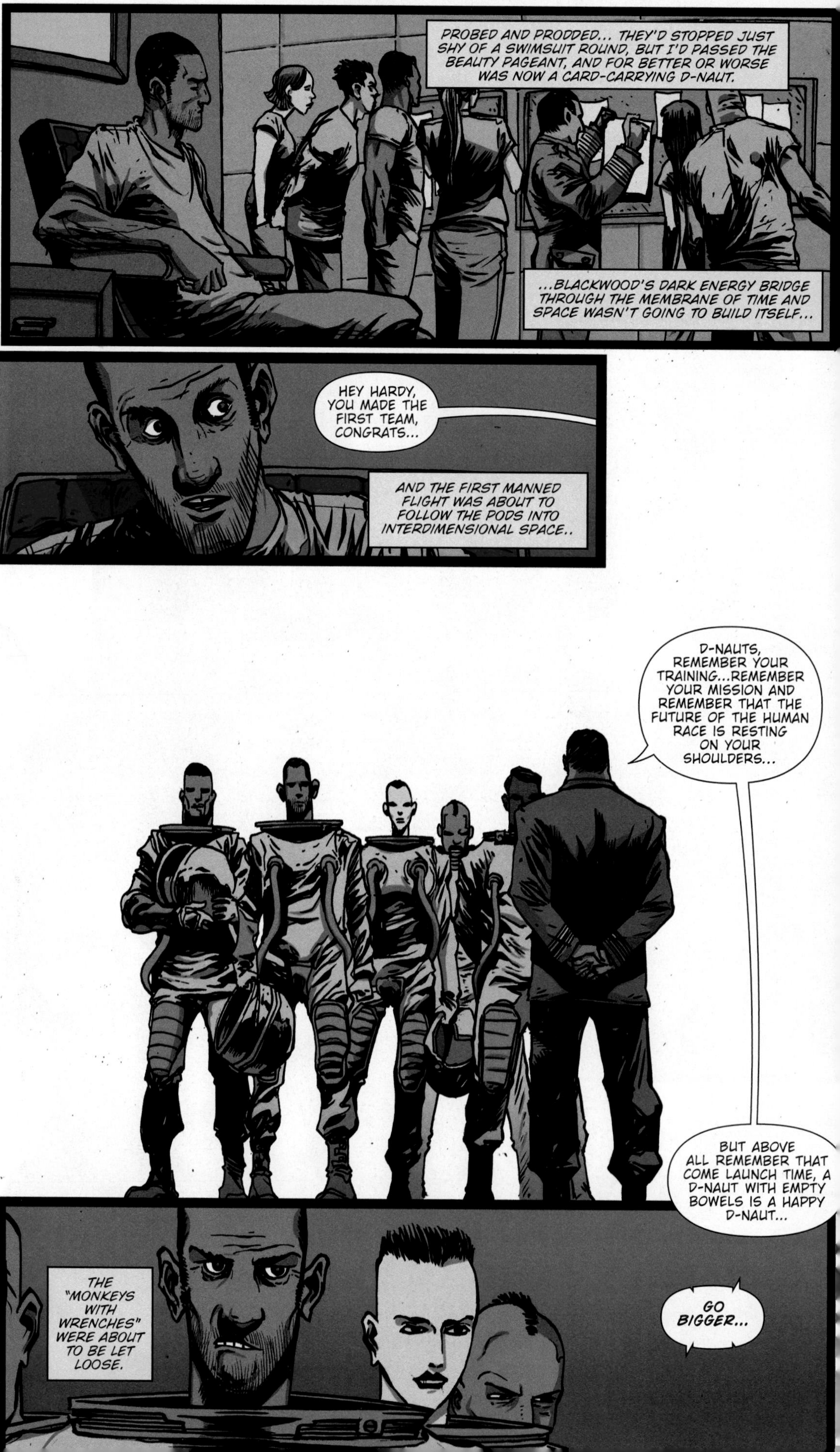
PROBED AND PRODDED... THEY'D STOPPED JUST SHY OF A SWIMSUIT ROUND, BUT I'D PASSED THE BEAUTY PAGEANT, AND FOR BETTER OR WORSE WAS NOW A CARD-CARRYING D-NAUT.
...BLACKWOOD'S DARK ENERGY BRIDGE THROUGH THE MEMBRANE OF TIME AND SPACE WASN'T GOING TO BUILD ITSELF...
HEY HARDY, YOU MADE THE FIRST TEAM, CONGRATS...
AND THE FIRST MANNED FLIGHT WAS ABOUT TO FOLLOW THE PODS INTO INTERDIMENSIONAL SPACE..
D-NAUTS, REMEMBER YOUR TRAINING...REMEMBER YOUR MISSION AND REMEMBER THAT THE FUTURE OF THE HUMAN RACE IS RESTING ON YOUR SHOULDERS...
BUT ABOVE ALL REMEMBER THAT COME LAUNCH TIME, A D-NAUT WITH EMPTY BOWELS IS A HAPPY D-NAUT...
THE "MONKEYS WITH WRENCHES" WERE ABOUT TO BE LET LOOSE.
GO BIGGER...

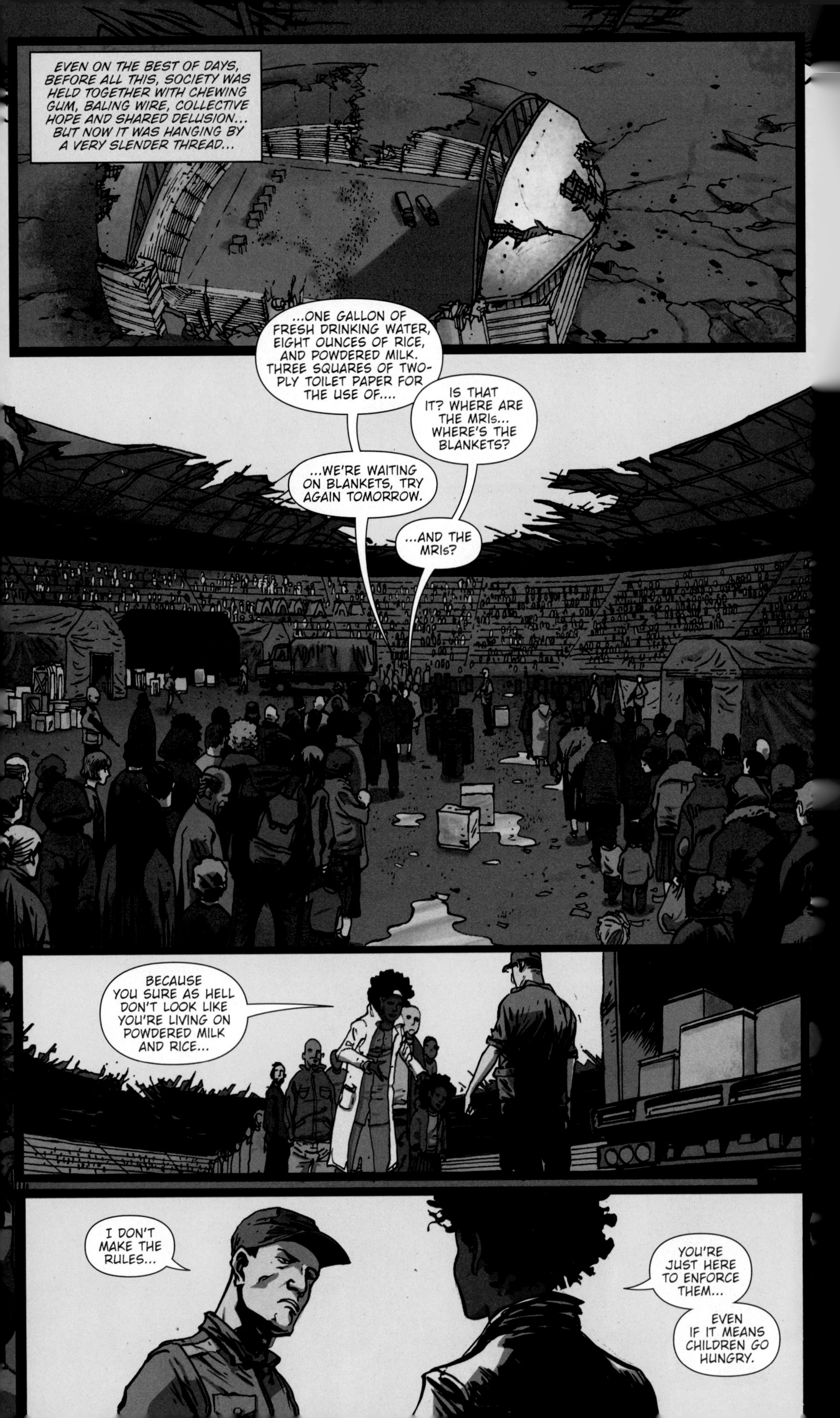

EVEN ON THE BEST OF DAYS, BEFORE ALL THIS, SOCIETY WAS HELD TOGETHER WITH CHEWING GUM, BALING WIRE, COLLECTIVE HOPE AND SHARED DELUSION... BUT NOW IT WAS HANGING BY A VERY SLENDER THREAD...
...ONE GALLON OF FRESH DRINKING WATER, EIGHT OUNCES OF RICE, AND POWDERED MILK. THREE SQUARES OF TWO-PLY TOILET PAPER FOR THE USE OF....
IS THAT IT? WHERE ARE THE MRIs... WHERE'S THE BLANKETS?
...WE'RE WAITING ON BLANKETS, TRY AGAIN TOMORROW.
...AND THE MRIs?
BECAUSE YOU SURE AS HELL DON'T LOOK LIKE YOU'RE LIVING ON POWDERED MILK AND RICE...
I DON'T MAKE THE RULES...
YOU'RE JUST HERE TO ENFORCE THEM...
EVEN IF IT MEANS CHILDREN GO HUNGRY.

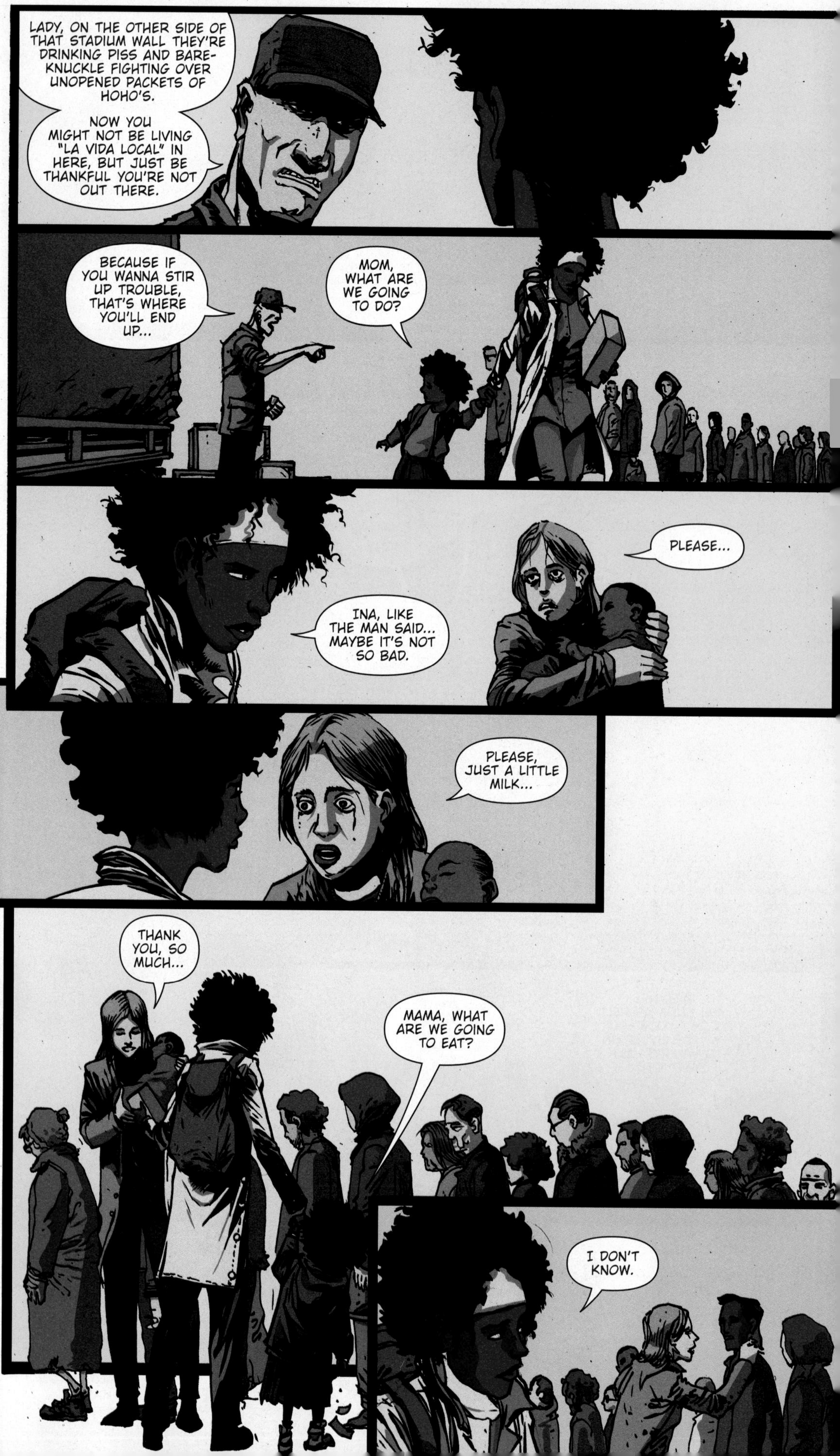
LADY, ON THE OTHER SIDE OF THAT STADIUM WALL THEY'RE DRINKING PISS AND BARE-KNUCKLE FIGHTING OVER UNOPENED PACKETS OF HOHO'S.
NOW YOU MIGHT NOT BE LIVING "LA VIDA LOCAL" IN HERE, BUT JUST BE THANKFUL YOU'RE NOT OUT THERE.
BECAUSE IF YOU WANNA STIR UP TROUBLE, THAT'S WHERE YOU'LL END UP...
MOM, WHAT ARE WE GOING TO DO?
PLEASE...
INA, LIKE THE MAN SAID... MAYBE IT'S NOT SO BAD.
PLEASE, JUST A LITTLE MILK...
THANK YOU, SO MUCH...
MAMA, WHAT ARE WE GOING TO EAT?
I DON'T KNOW.

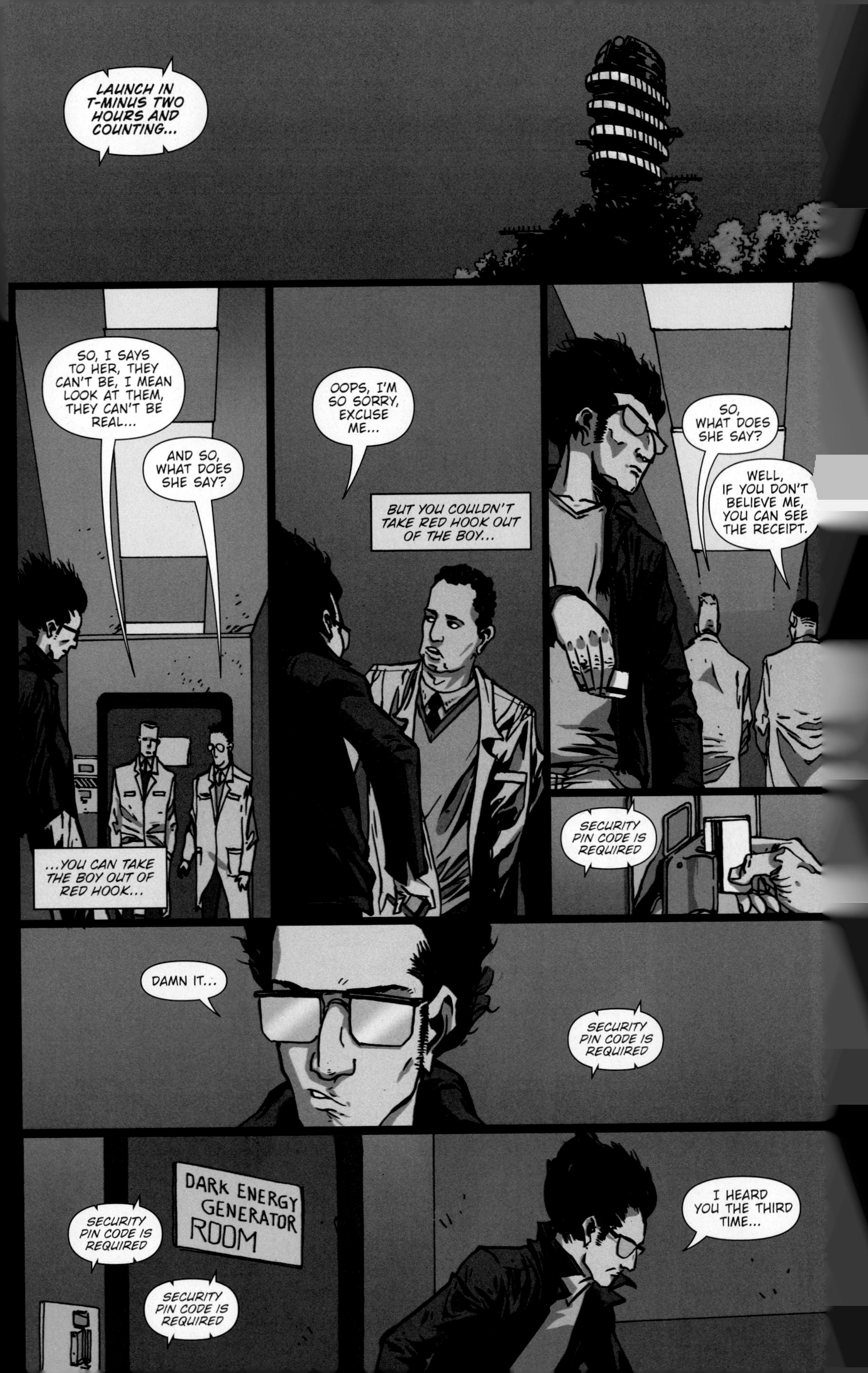
LAUNCH IN T-MINUS TWO HOURS AND COUNTING...
SO, I SAYS TO HER, THEY CAN'T BE, I MEAN LOOK AT THEM, THEY CAN'T BE REAL...
AND SO, WHAT DOES SHE SAY?
...YOU CAN TAKE THE BOY OUT OF RED HOOK...
OOPS, I'M SO SORRY, EXCUSE ME...
BUT YOU COULDN'T TAKE RED HOOK OUT OF THE BOY...
SO, WHAT DOES SHE SAY?
WELL, IF YOU DON'T BELIEVE ME, YOU CAN SEE THE RECEIPT.
SECURITY PIN CODE IS REQUIRED
DAMN IT...
SECURITY PIN CODE IS REQUIRED
DARK ENERGY GENERATOR ROOM
SECURITY PIN CODE IS REQUIRED
SECURITY PIN CODE IS REQUIRED
I HEARD YOU THE THIRD TIME...

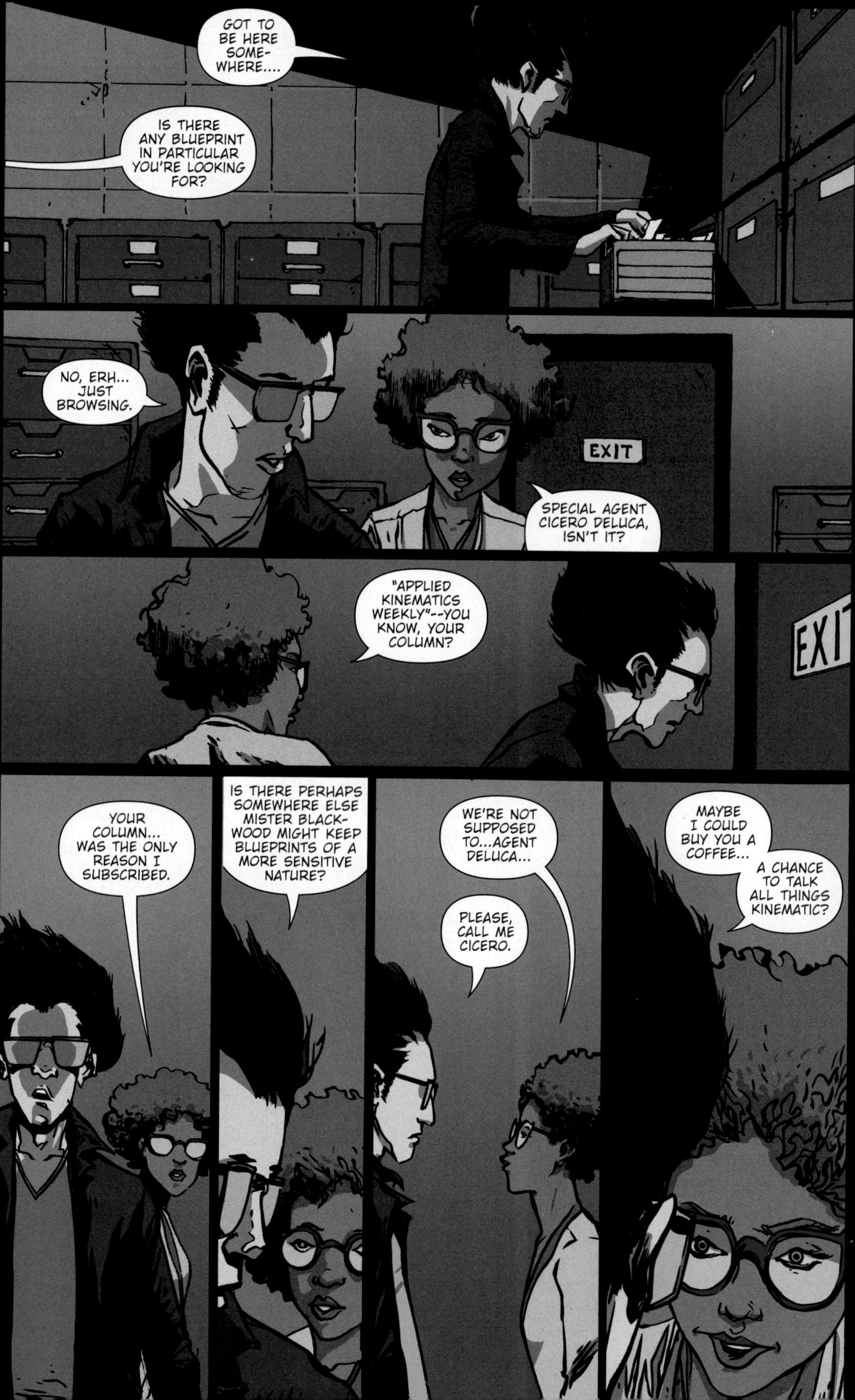
GOT TO BE HERE SOME-WHERE....
IS THERE ANY BLUEPRINT IN PARTICULAR YOU'RE LOOKING FOR?
NO, ERH... JUST BROWSING.
EXIT
SPECIAL AGENT CICERO DELUCA, ISN'T IT?
"APPLIED KINEMATICS WEEKLY"--YOU KNOW, YOUR COLUMN?
EXIT
YOUR COLUMN... WAS THE ONLY REASON I SUBSCRIBED.
IS THERE PERHAPS SOMEWHERE ELSE MISTER BLACK-WOOD MIGHT KEEP BLUEPRINTS OF A MORE SENSITIVE NATURE?
WE'RE NOT SUPPOSED TO...AGENT DELUCA...
PLEASE, CALL ME CICERO.
MAYBE I COULD BUY YOU A COFFEE...
A CHANCE TO TALK ALL THINGS KINEMATIC?

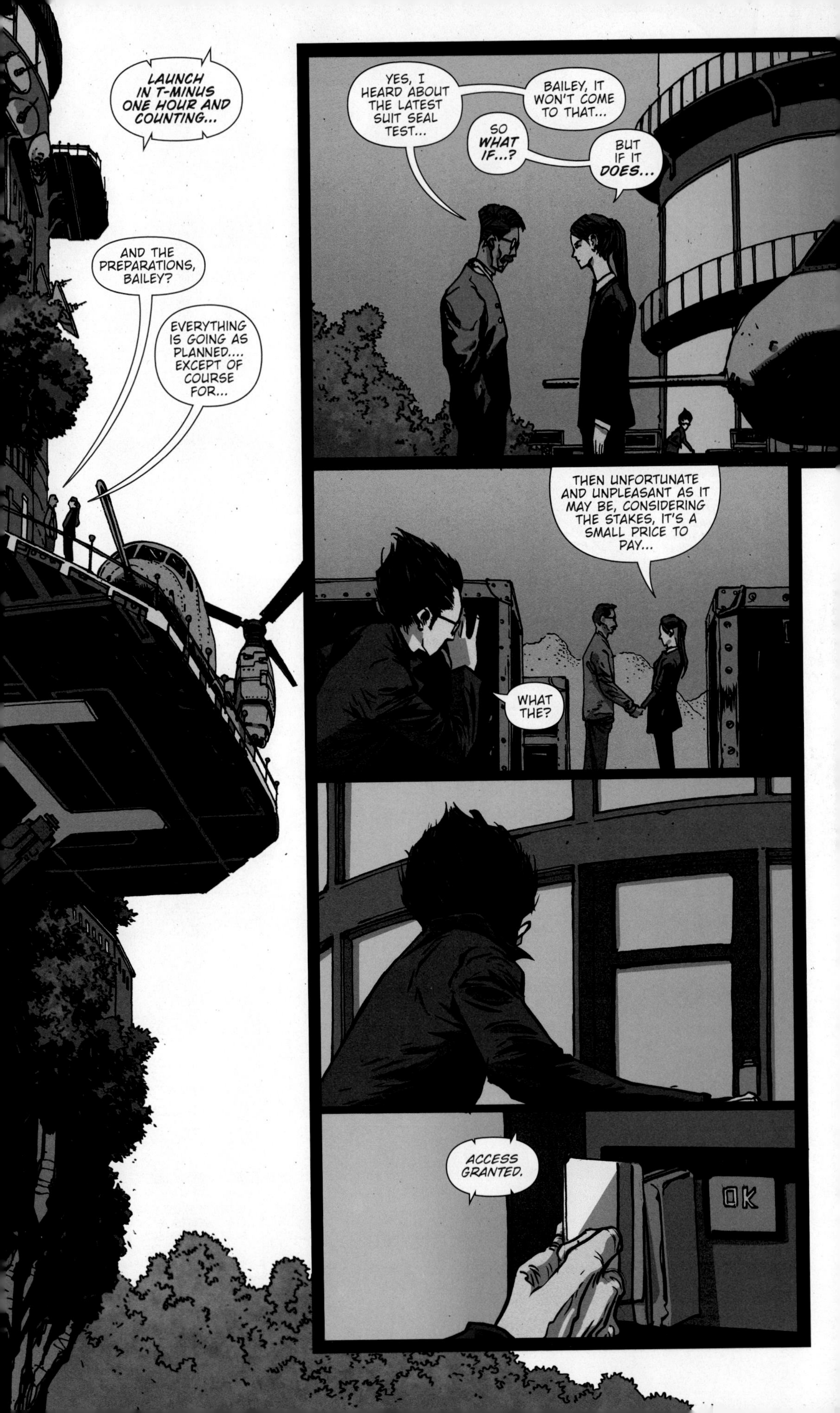
LAUNCH IN T-MINUS ONE HOUR AND COUNTING...
AND THE PREPARATIONS, BAILEY?
EVERYTHING IS GOING AS PLANNED.... EXCEPT OF COURSE FOR...
YES, I HEARD ABOUT THE LATEST SUIT SEAL TEST...
BAILEY, IT WON'T COME TO THAT...
SO WHAT IF...?
BUT IF IT DOES...
THEN UNFORTUNATE AND UNPLEASANT AS IT MAY BE, CONSIDERING THE STAKES, IT'S A SMALL PRICE TO PAY...
WHAT THE?
ACCESS GRANTED.
OK

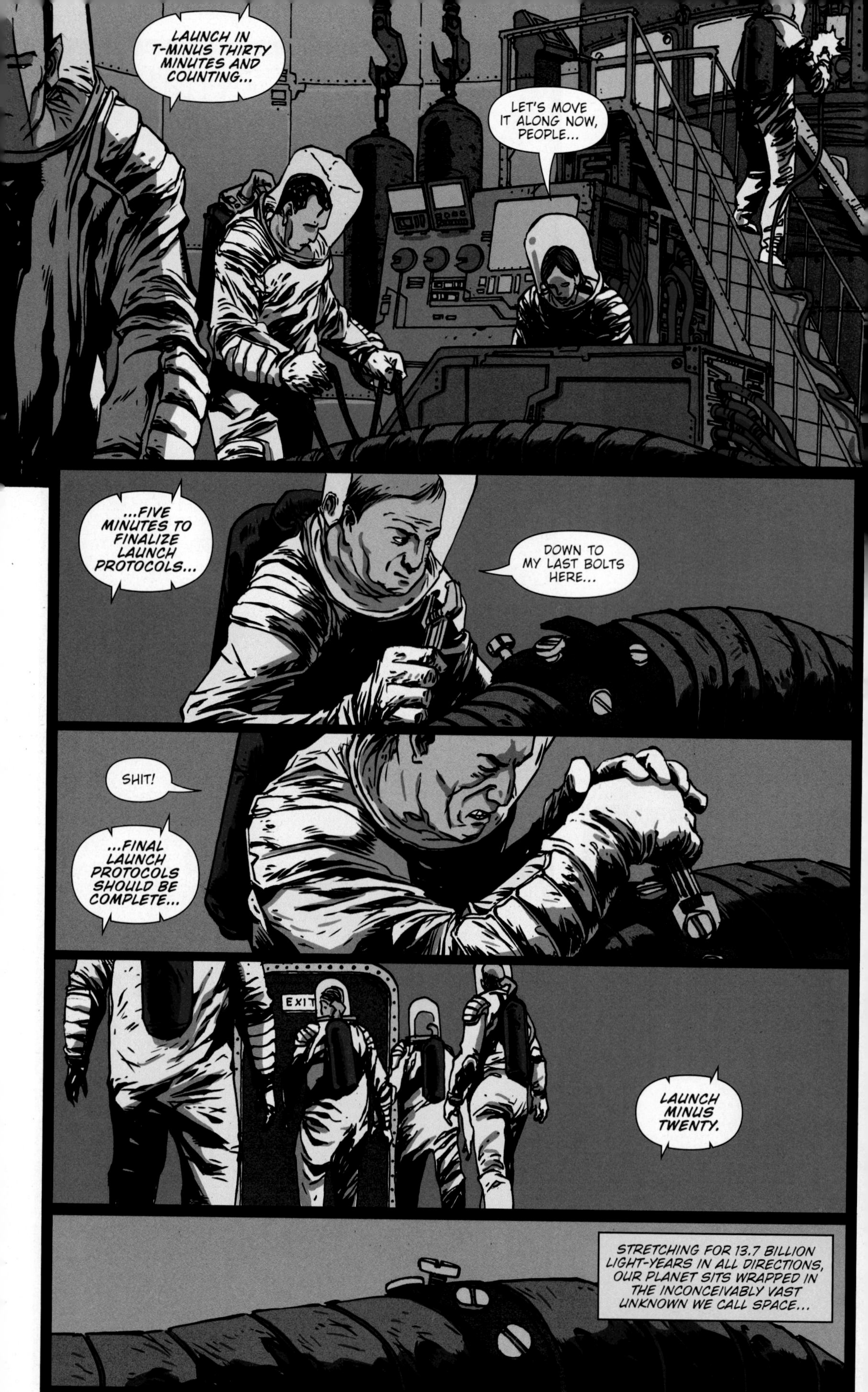
LAUNCH IN T-MINUS THIRTY MINUTES AND COUNTING...
LET'S MOVE IT ALONG NOW, PEOPLE...
...FIVE MINUTES TO FINALIZE LAUNCH PROTOCOLS...
DOWN TO MY LAST BOLTS HERE...
SHIT!
...FINAL LAUNCH PROTOCOLS SHOULD BE COMPLETE...
EXIT
LAUNCH MINUS TWENTY.
STRETCHING FOR 13.7 BILLION LIGHT-YEARS IN ALL DIRECTIONS, OUR PLANET SITS WRAPPED IN THE INCONCEIVABLY VAST UNKNOWN WE CALL SPACE...

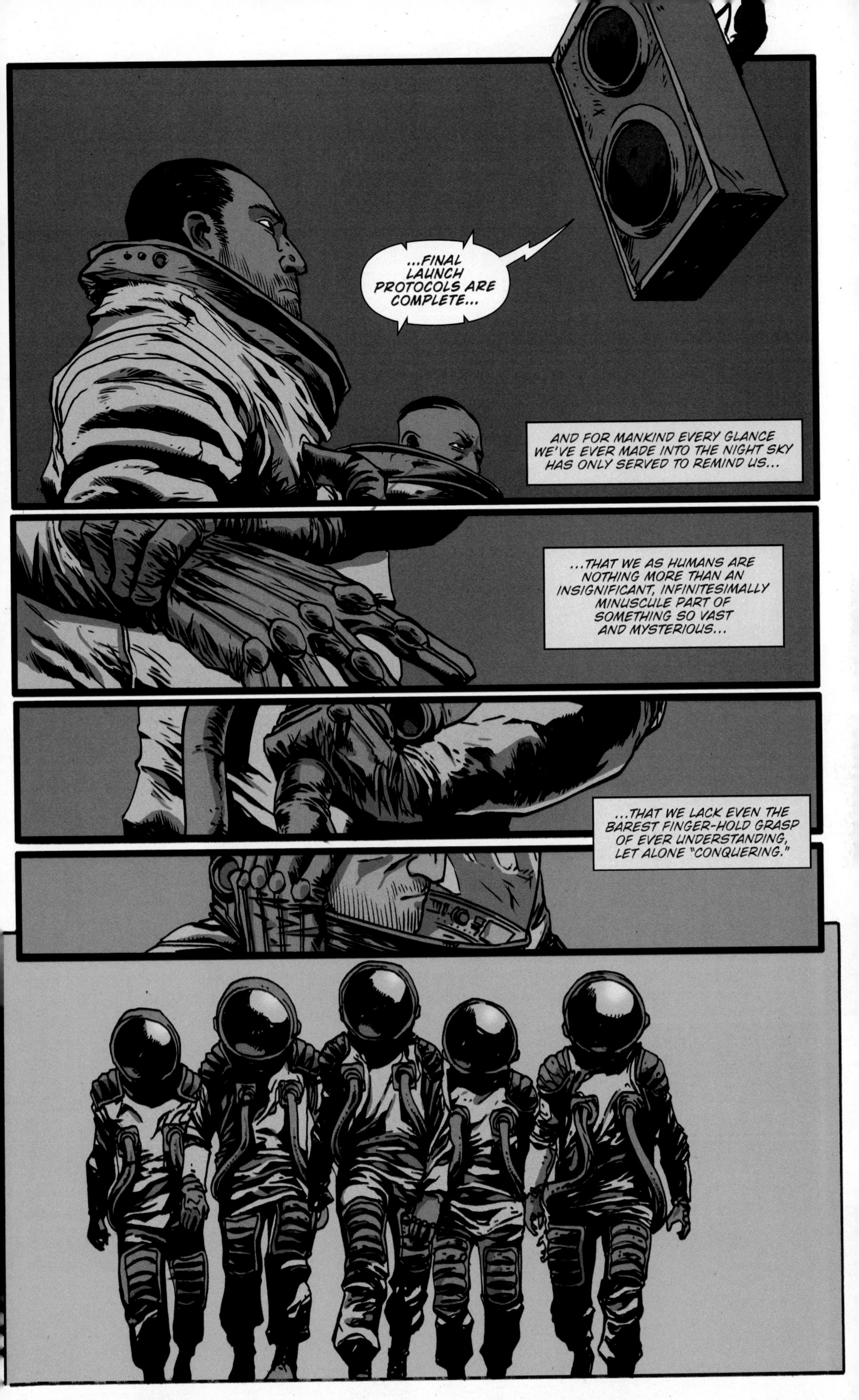
...FINAL LAUNCH PROTOCOLS ARE COMPLETE...
AND FOR MANKIND EVERY GLANCE WE'VE EVER MADE INTO THE NIGHT SKY HAS ONLY SERVED TO REMIND US...
...THAT WE AS HUMANS ARE NOTHING MORE THAN AN INSIGNIFICANT, INFINITESIMALLY MINUSCULE PART OF SOMETHING SO VAST AND MYSTERIOUS...
...THAT WE LACK EVEN THE BAREST FINGER-HOLD GRASP OF EVER UNDERSTANDING, LET ALONE "CONQUERING."

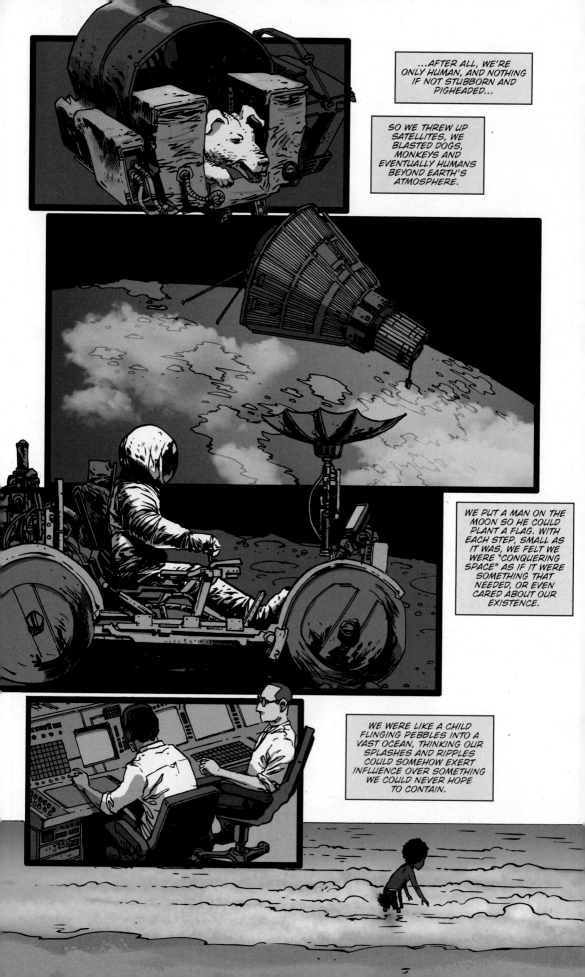

...AFTER ALL, WE'RE ONLY HUMAN, AND NOTHING IF NOT STUBBORN AND PIGHEADED...

SO WE THREW UP SATELLITES, WE BLASTED DOGS, MONKEYS AND EVENTUALLY HUMANS BEYOND EARTH'S ATMOSPHERE.

WE PUT A MAN ON THE MOON SO HE COULD PLANT A FLAG. WITH EACH STEP, SMALL AS IT WAS, WE FELT WE WERE "CONQUERING SPACE" AS IF IT WERE SOMETHING THAT NEEDED, OR EVEN CARED ABOUT OUR EXISTENCE.

WE WERE LIKE A CHILD FLINGING PEBBLES INTO A VAST OCEAN, THINKING OUR SPLASHES AND RIPPLES COULD SOMEHOW EXERT INFLUENCE OVER SOMETHING WE COULD NEVER HOPE TO CONTAIN.

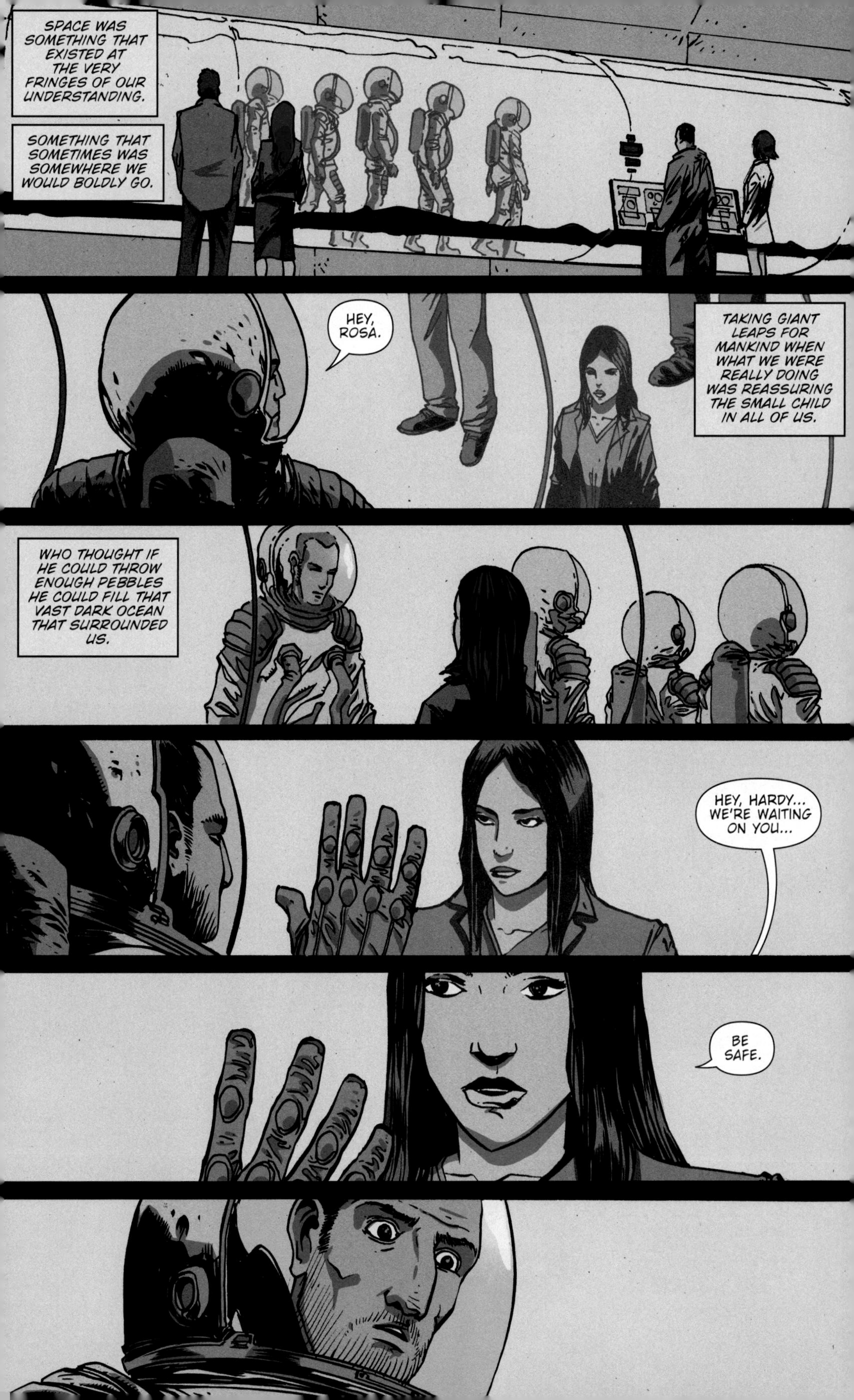
SPACE WAS SOMETHING THAT EXISTED AT THE VERY FRINGES OF OUR UNDERSTANDING.
SOMETHING THAT SOMETIMES WAS SOMEWHERE WE WOULD BOLDLY GO.
HEY, ROSA.
TAKING GIANT LEAPS FOR MANKIND WHEN WHAT WE WERE REALLY DOING WAS REASSURING THE SMALL CHILD IN ALL OF US.
WHO THOUGHT IF HE COULD THROW ENOUGH PEBBLES HE COULD FILL THAT VAST DARK OCEAN THAT SURROUNDED US.
HEY, HARDY... WE'RE WAITING ON YOU...
BE SAFE.

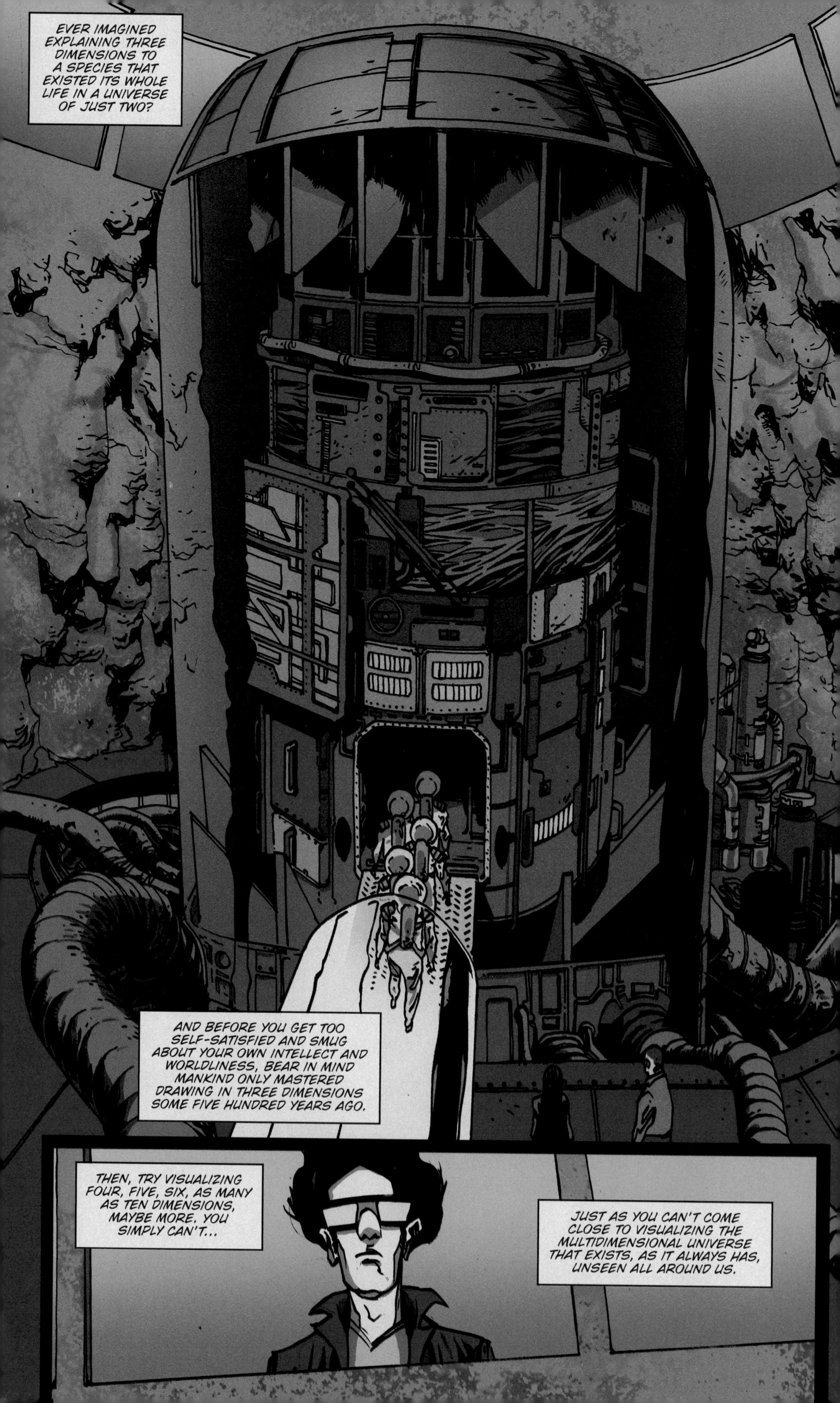
EVER IMAGINED EXPLAINING THREE DIMENSIONS TO A SPECIES THAT EXISTED ITS WHOLE LIFE IN A UNIVERSE OF JUST TWO?
AND BEFORE YOU GET TOO SELF-SATISFIED AND SMUG ABOUT YOUR OWN INTELLECT AND WORLDLINESS, BEAR IN MIND MANKIND ONLY MASTERED DRAWING IN THREE DIMENSIONS SOME FIVE HUNDRED YEARS AGO.
THEN, TRY VISUALIZING FOUR, FIVE, SIX, AS MANY AS TEN DIMENSIONS, MAYBE MORE. YOU SIMPLY CAN'T...
JUST AS YOU CAN'T COME CLOSE TO VISUALIZING THE MULTIDIMENSIONAL UNIVERSE THAT EXISTS, AS IT ALWAYS HAS, UNSEEN ALL AROUND US.

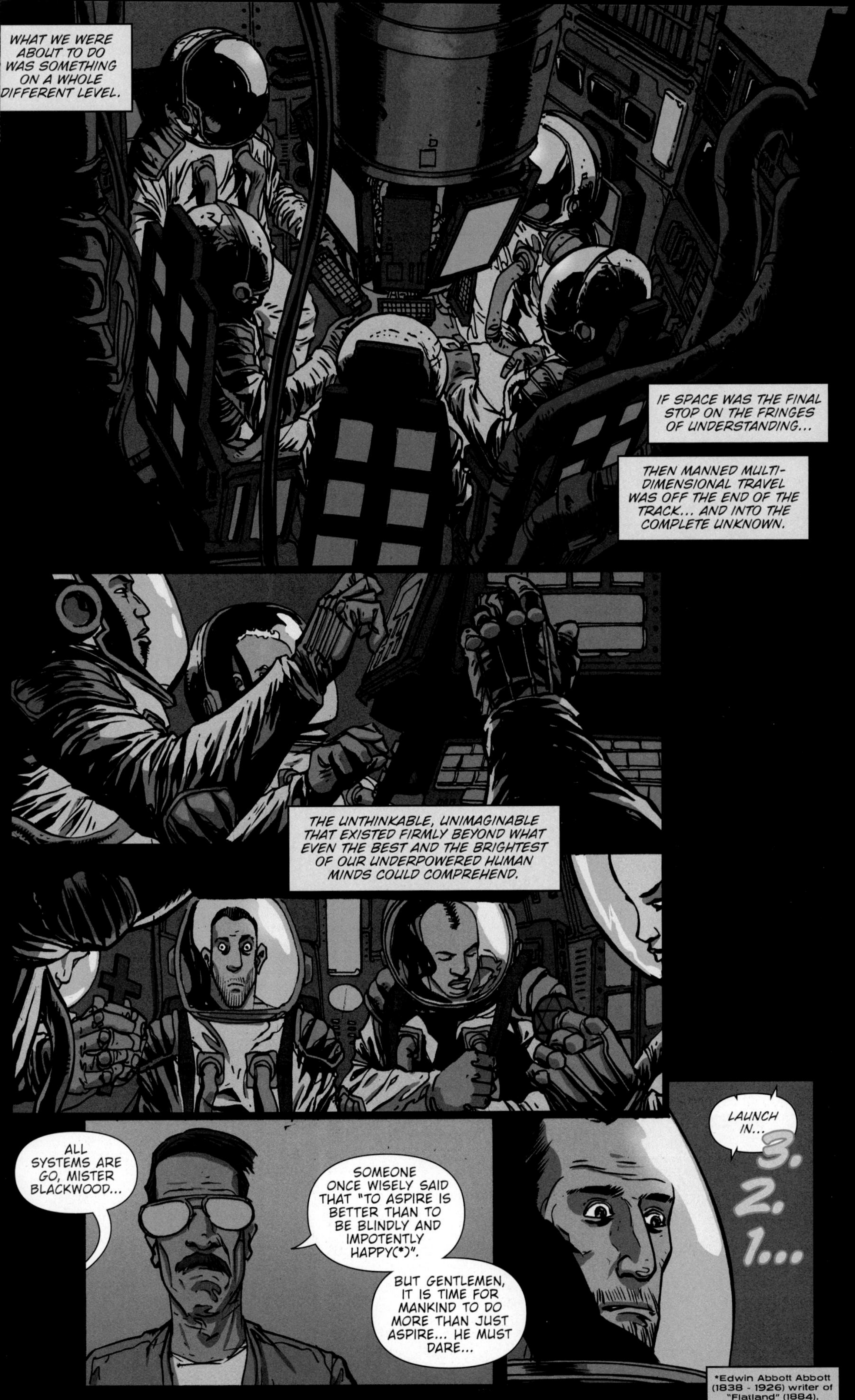
WHAT WE WERE ABOUT TO DO WAS SOMETHING ON A WHOLE DIFFERENT LEVEL.
IF SPACE WAS THE FINAL STOP ON THE FRINGES OF UNDERSTANDING...
THEN MANNED MULTI-DIMENSIONAL TRAVEL WAS OFF THE END OF THE TRACK... AND INTO THE COMPLETE UNKNOWN.
THE UNTHINKABLE, UNIMAGINABLE THAT EXISTED FIRMLY BEYOND WHAT EVEN THE BEST AND THE BRIGHTEST OF OUR UNDERPOWERED HUMAN MINDS COULD COMPREHEND.
ALL SYSTEMS ARE GO, MISTER BLACKWOOD...
SOMEONE ONCE WISELY SAID THAT "TO ASPIRE IS BETTER THAN TO BE BLINDLY AND IMPOTENTLY HAPPY(*)".
BUT GENTLEMEN, IT IS TIME FOR MANKIND TO DO MORE THAN JUST ASPIRE... HE MUST DARE...
LAUNCH IN...
3.
2.
1...

*Edwin Abbott Abbott (1838 - 1926) writer of "Flatland" (1884).

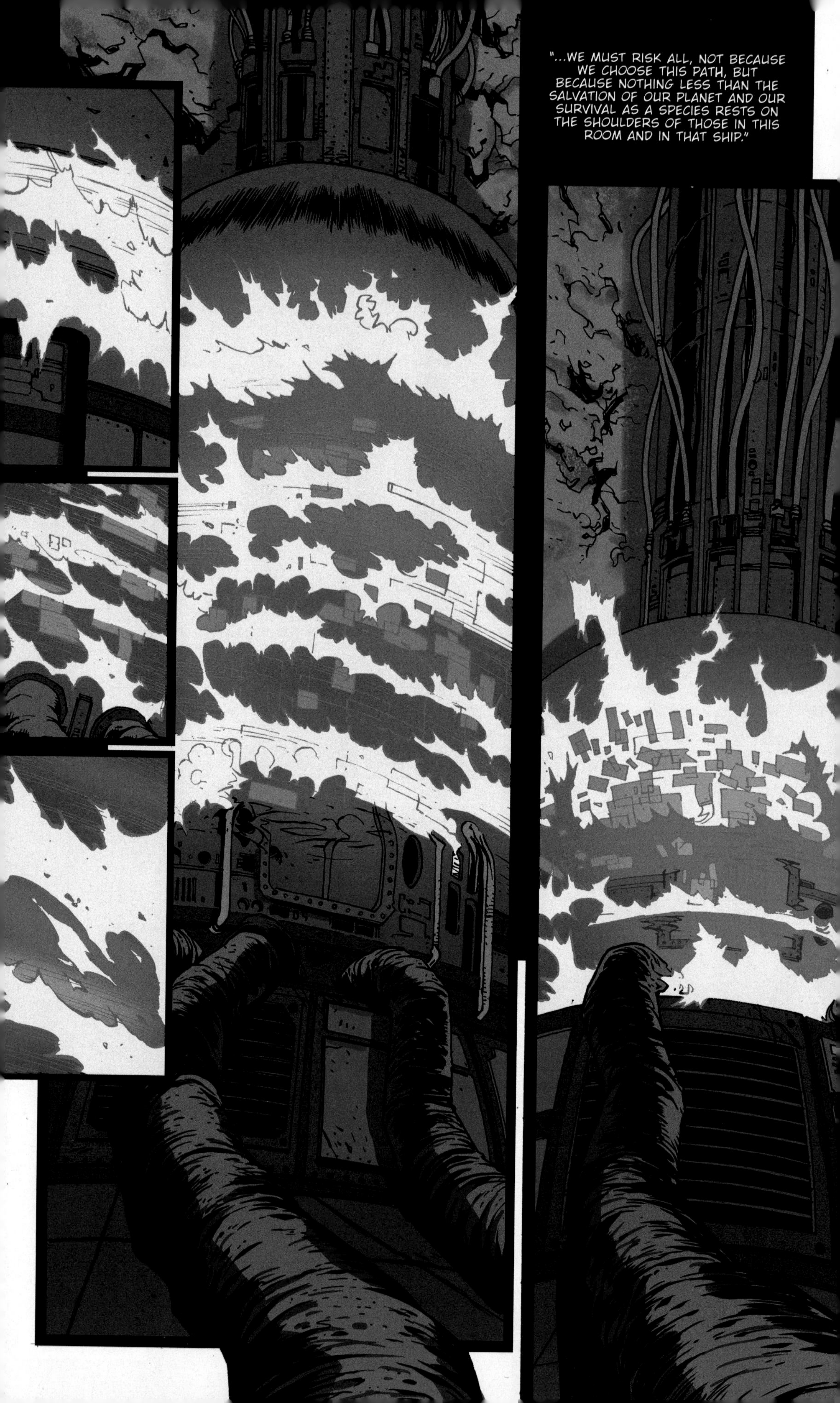
"...WE MUST RISK ALL, NOT BECAUSE WE CHOOSE THIS PATH, BUT BECAUSE NOTHING LESS THAN THE SALVATION OF OUR PLANET AND OUR SURVIVAL AS A SPECIES RESTS ON THE SHOULDERS OF THOSE IN THIS ROOM AND IN THAT SHIP."

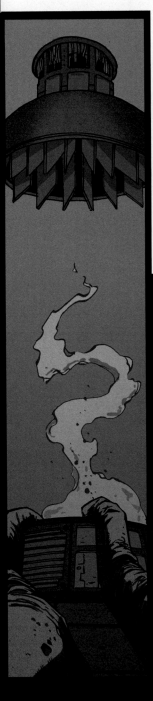

IT'S IN GOD'S HANDS NOW.

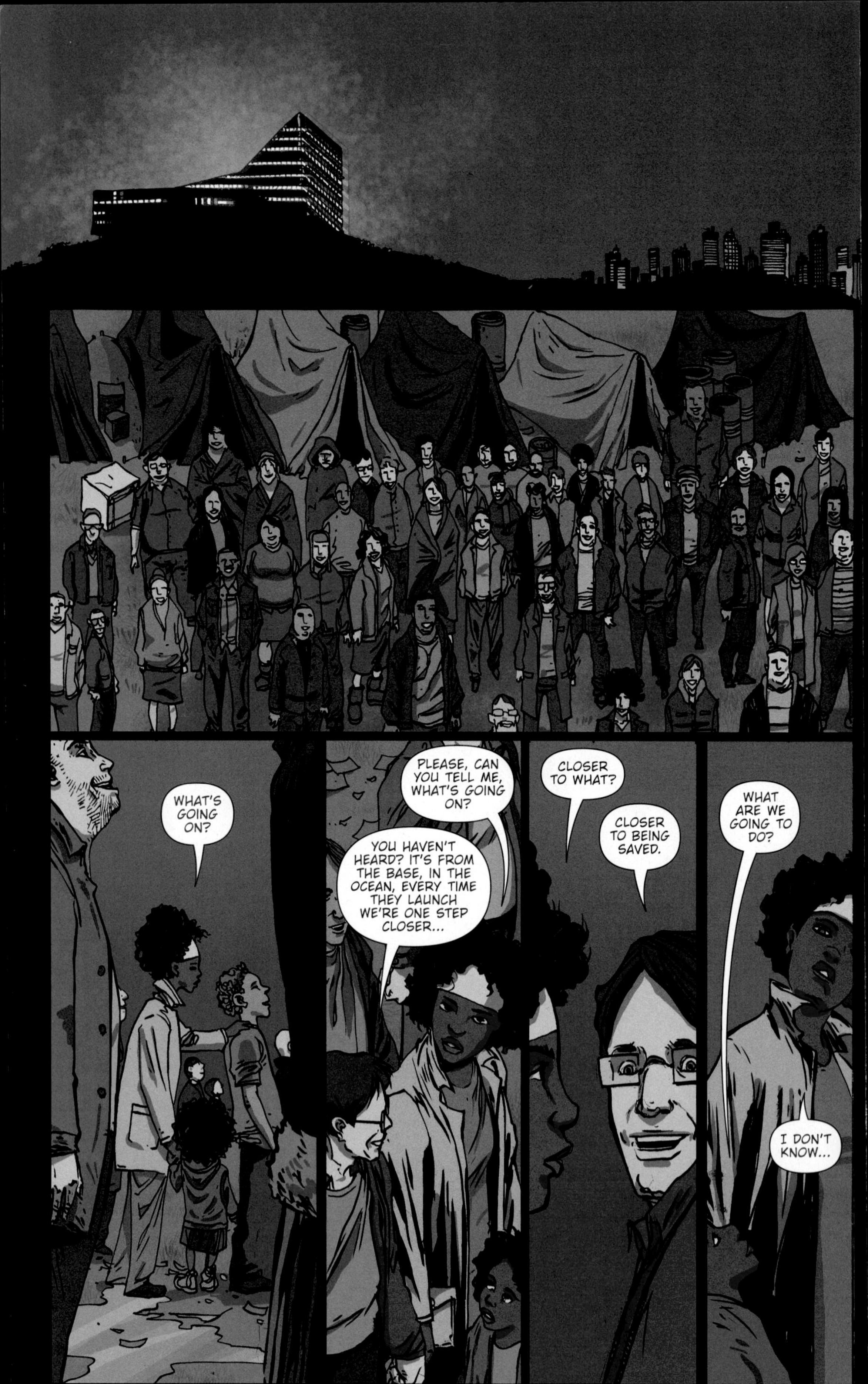
WHAT'S GOING ON?
PLEASE, CAN YOU TELL ME, WHAT'S GOING ON?
YOU HAVEN'T HEARD? IT'S FROM THE BASE, IN THE OCEAN, EVERY TIME THEY LAUNCH WE'RE ONE STEP CLOSER...
CLOSER TO WHAT?
CLOSER TO BEING SAVED.
WHAT ARE WE GOING TO DO?
I DON'T KNOW...

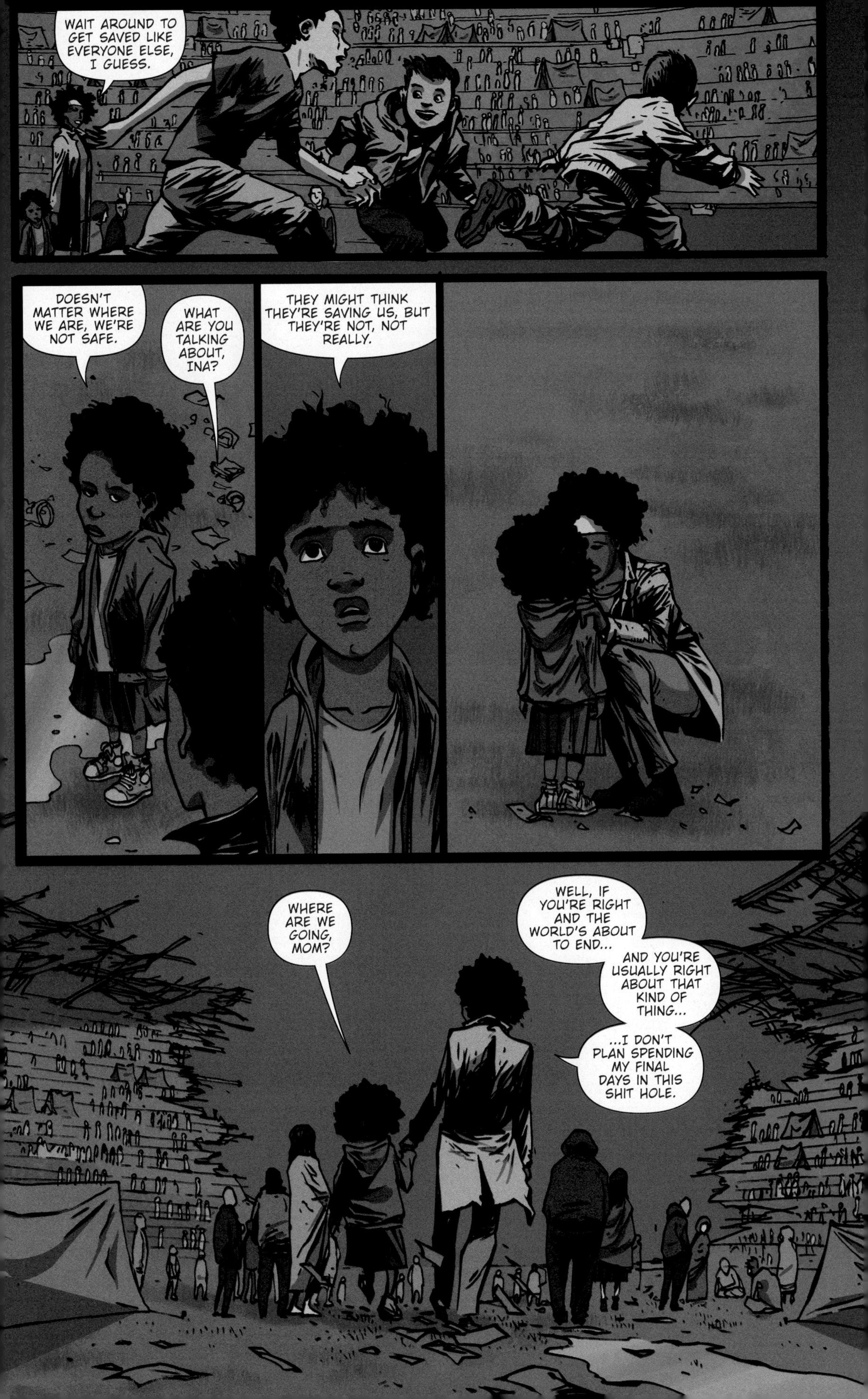
WAIT AROUND TO GET SAVED LIKE EVERYONE ELSE, I GUESS.
DOESN'T MATTER WHERE WE ARE, WE'RE NOT SAFE.
WHAT ARE YOU TALKING ABOUT, INA?
THEY MIGHT THINK THEY'RE SAVING US, BUT THEY'RE NOT, NOT REALLY.
WHERE ARE WE GOING, MOM?
WELL, IF YOU'RE RIGHT AND THE WORLD'S ABOUT TO END...
AND YOU'RE USUALLY RIGHT ABOUT THAT KIND OF THING...
...I DON'T PLAN SPENDING MY FINAL DAYS IN THIS SHIT HOLE.

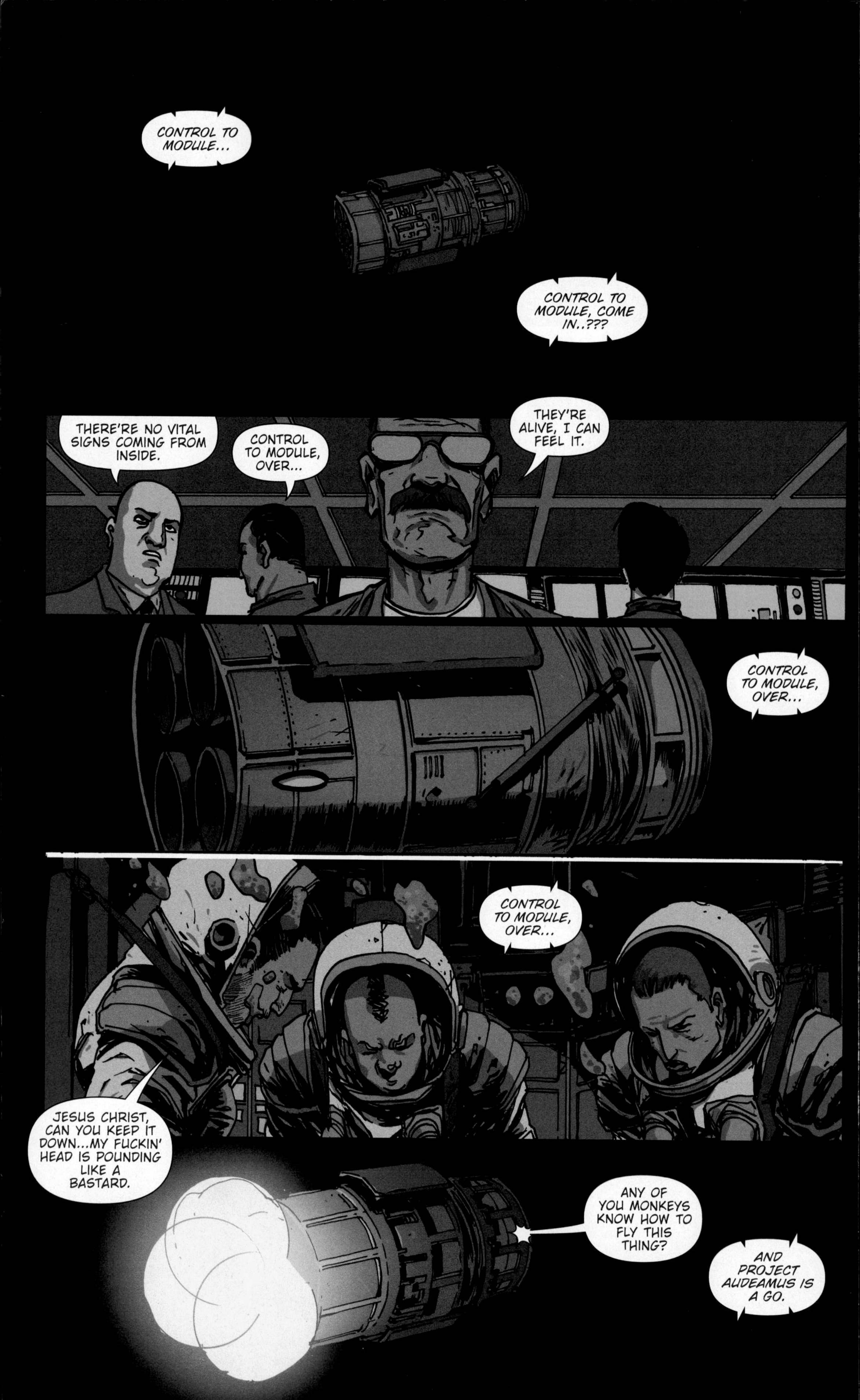
CONTROL TO MODULE...
CONTROL TO MODULE, COME IN..???
THERE'RE NO VITAL SIGNS COMING FROM INSIDE.
CONTROL TO MODULE, OVER...
THEY'RE ALIVE, I CAN FEEL IT.
CONTROL TO MODULE, OVER...
CONTROL TO MODULE, OVER...
JESUS CHRIST, CAN YOU KEEP IT DOWN...MY FUCKIN' HEAD IS POUNDING LIKE A BASTARD.
ANY OF YOU MONKEYS KNOW HOW TO FLY THIS THING?
AND PROJECT AUDEAMUS IS A GO.

Character sketches by
Alberto Ponticelli

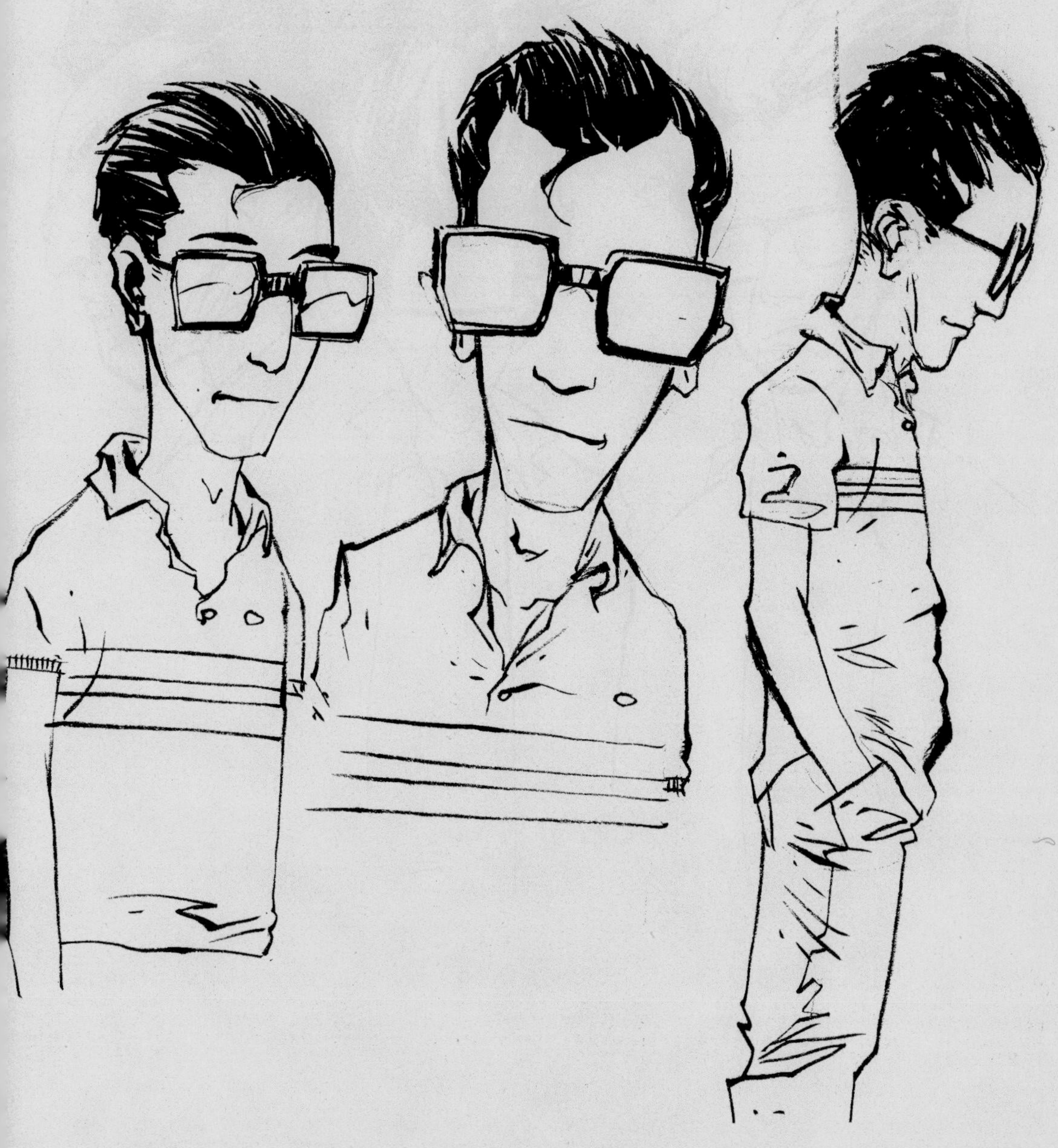

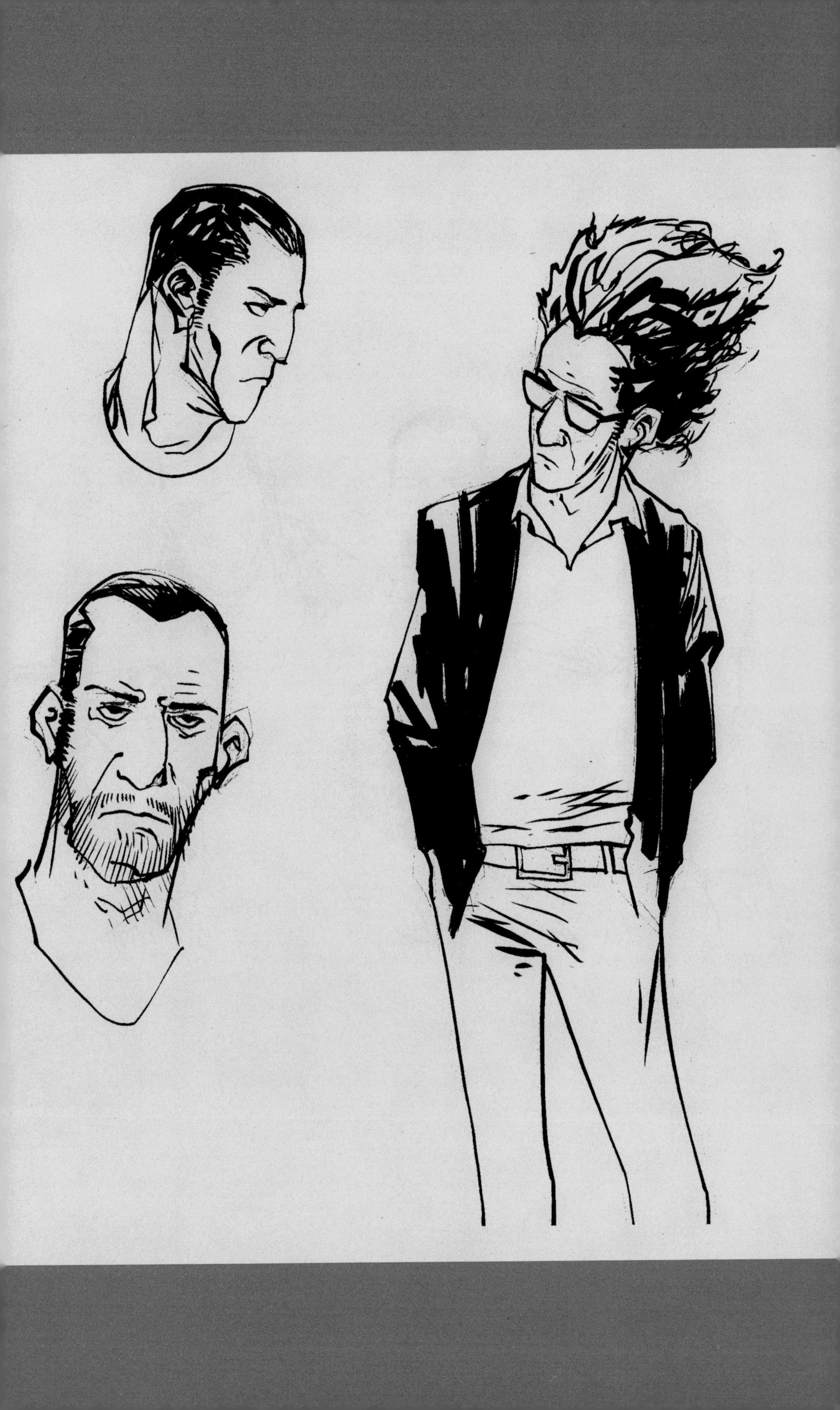

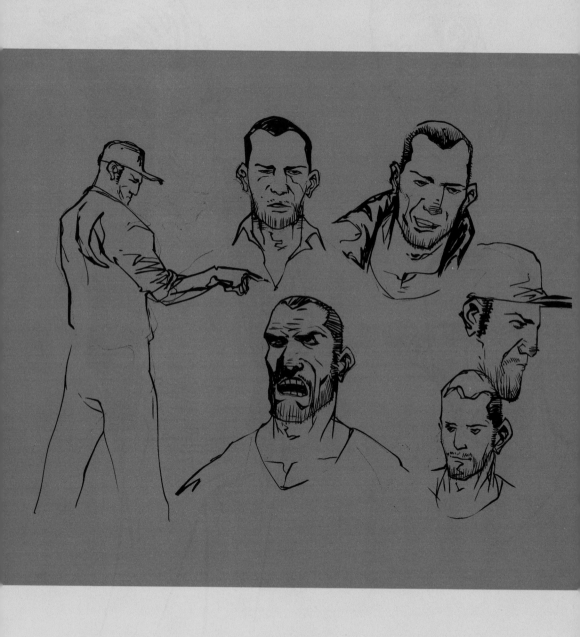

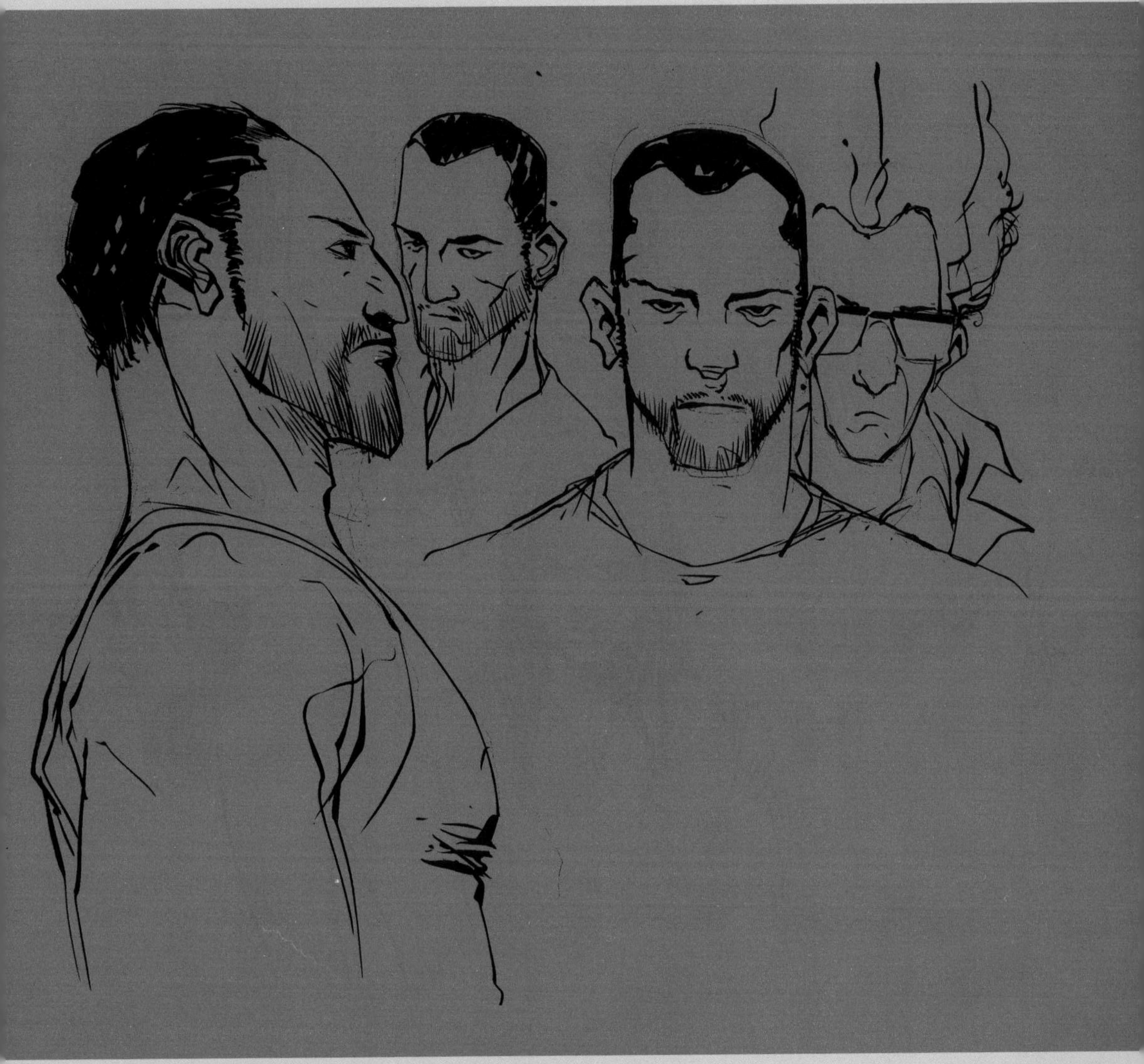

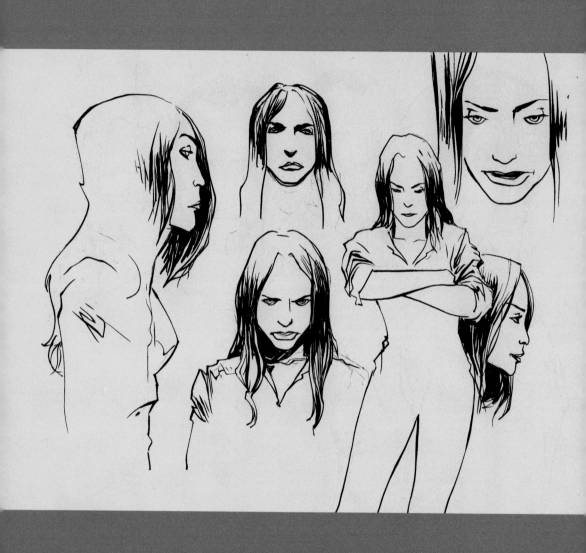

ISSUE #14
Pencils by Alberto Ponticelli

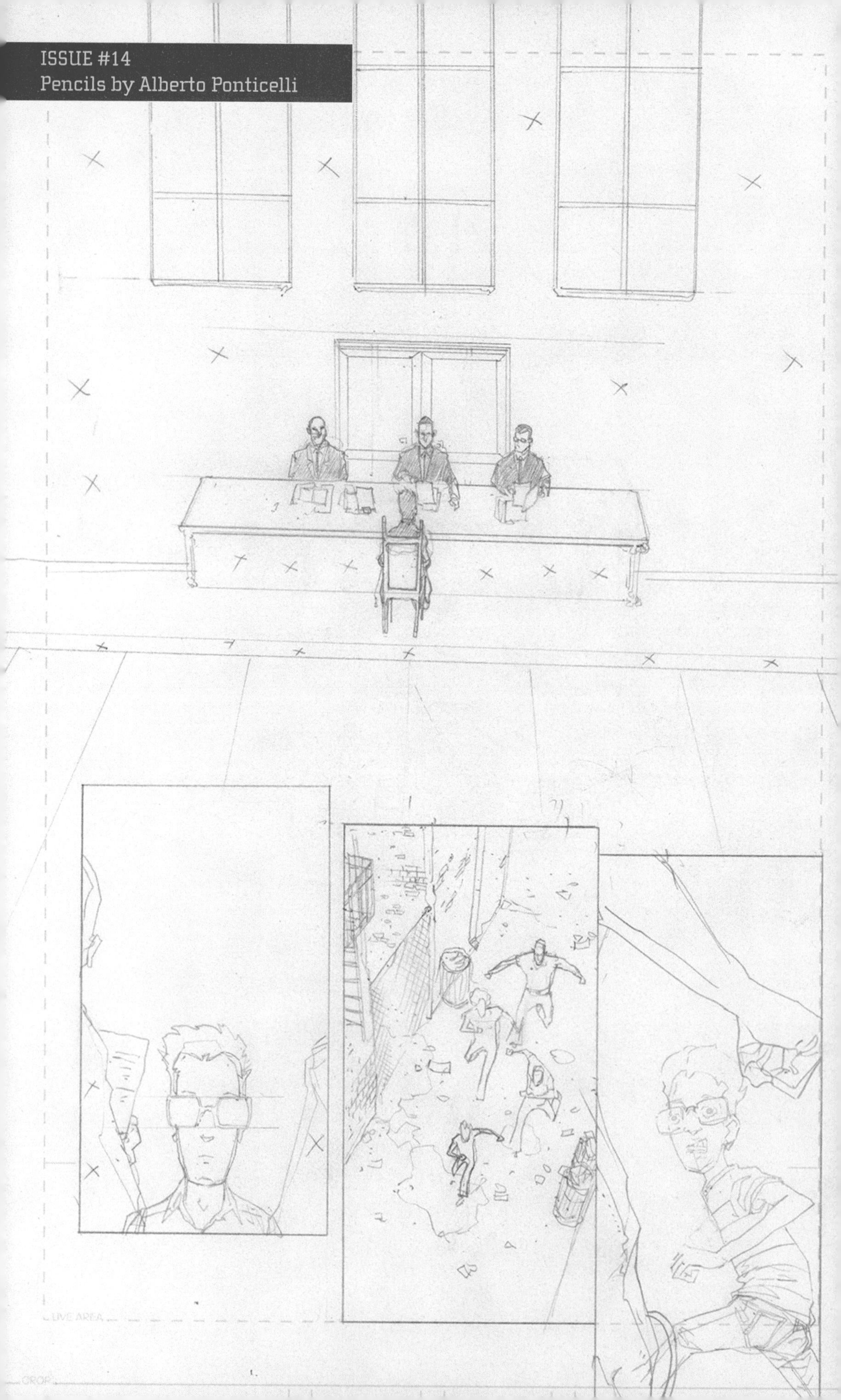

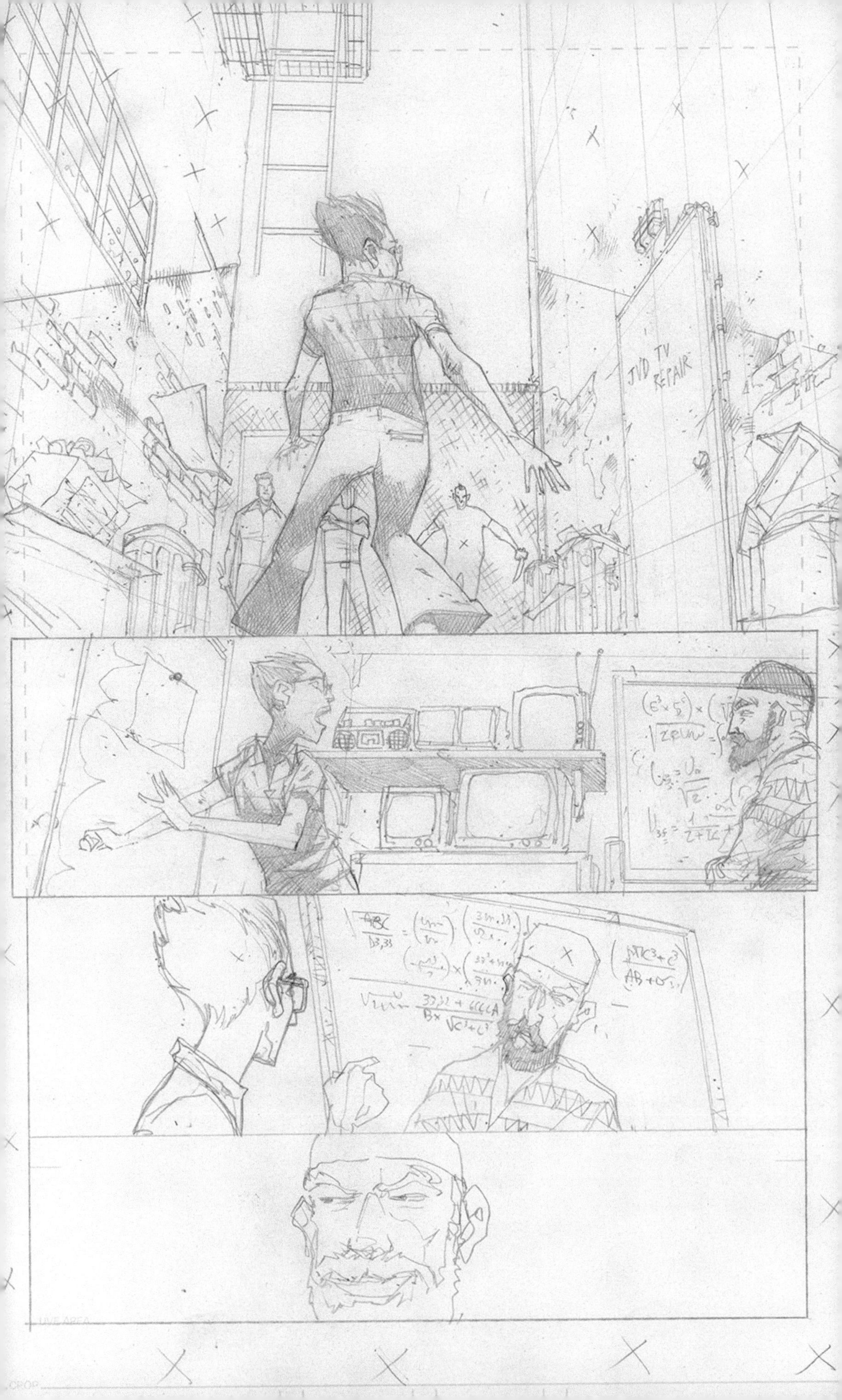
JVD TV REPAIR

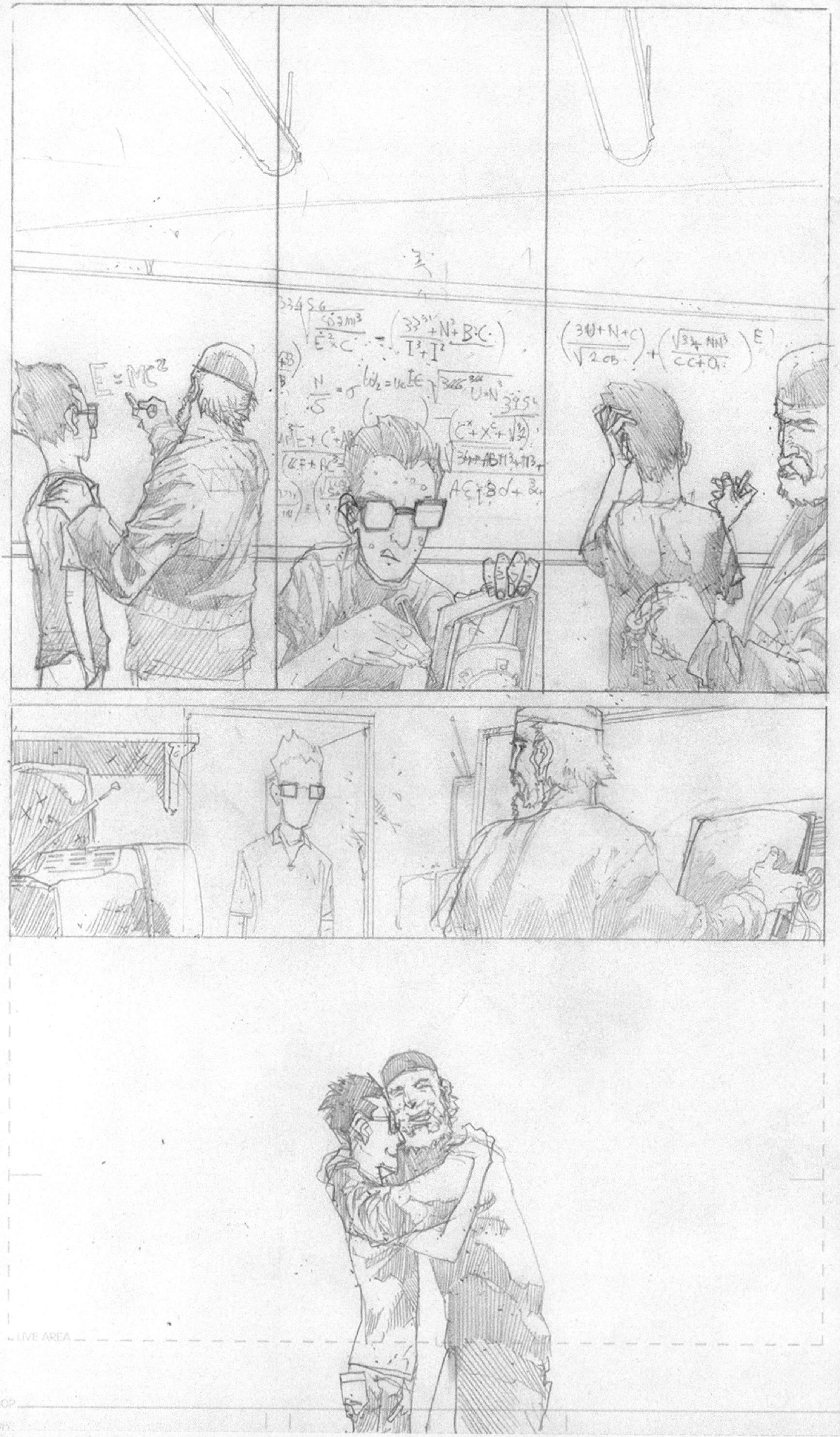
E = MC²

VERTIGO

"*THE INVISIBLES is that rare thing, a smart, spooky, exciting comic. Grant Morrison is a master of smart comics.*"
—TIME OUT

THE INVISIBLES VOL. 4:
BLOODY HELL IN
AMERICA

THE INVISIBLES VOL. 7:
THE INVISIBLE KINGDOM

READ THE ENTIRE
SERIES!

THE INVISIBLES
VOL. 1: SAY YOU WANT
A REVOLUTION

THE INVISIBLES
VOL. 2:
APOCALIPSTICK

THE INVISIBLES
VOL. 3: ENTROPY IN
THE U.K.

THE INVISIBLES
VOL. 4: BLOODY HELL
IN AMERICA

THE INVISIBLES
VOL. 5: COUNTING
TO NONE

THE INVISIBLES
VOL. 6: KISSING
MISTER QUIMPER

THE INVISIBLES
VOL. 7: THE INVISIBLE
KINGDOM

FROM THE WRITER OF *WE3* AND *ANIMAL MAN*
GRANT MORRISON
with STEVE YEOWELL & JILL THOMPSON

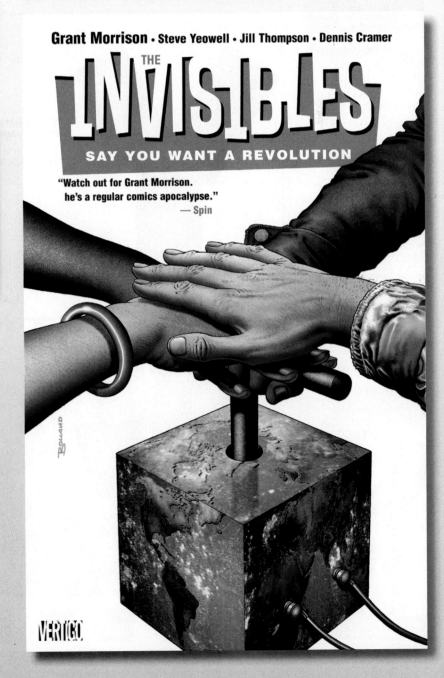

Grant Morrison • Steve Yeowell • Jill Thompson • Dennis Cramer

THE
INVISIBLES
SAY YOU WANT A REVOLUTION

"Watch out for Grant Morrison.
he's a regular comics apocalypse."
— Spin

VERTIGO

VERTIGO

"A seriously funny, nuanced fable. Grade A."
—ENTERTAINMENT WEEKLY

"Complete and utter comic gold."
—PUBLISHERS WEEKLY (STARRED REVIEW)

"Funny and scary. An utterly believable critique of society. A+."
—WASHINGTON POST

Y: THE LAST MAN
VOL. 10: WHYS AND
WHEREFORES

READ THE COMPLETE
SERIES!

Y: THE LAST MAN VOL. 1:
UNMANNED

Y: THE LAST MAN VOL. 2:
CYCLES

Y: THE LAST MAN VOL. 3:
ONE SMALL STEP

Y: THE LAST MAN VOL. 4:
SAFEWORD

Y: THE LAST MAN VOL. 5:
RING OF TRUTH

Y: THE LAST MAN VOL. 6:
GIRL ON GIRL

Y: THE LAST MAN VOL. 7:
PAPER DOLLS

Y: THE LAST MAN VOL. 8:
KIMONO DRAGONS

Y: THE LAST MAN VOL. 9:
MOTHERLAND

Y: THE LAST MAN VOL. 10:
WHYS AND
WHEREFORES

Y: THE LAST MAN:
THE DELUXE EDITION
BOOK ONE

ALSO AVAILABLE AS
DELUXE HARDCOVER IN
A 5-VOLUME SERIES

FROM THE *NEW YORK TIMES* #1 BEST-SELLING AUTHOR
BRIAN K. VAUGHAN
with PIA GUERRA

VERTIGO
BOOK 1

*"This is why God created
comic books."*
— RevolutionSF.com

"This book blew us away."
— WIZARD

Winner of the Eisner Award for Best Writer
Brian K. Vaughan
Pia Guerra
José Marzán, Jr.

THE LAST MAN

Unmanned